Romani Politics in Contemporary Europe

Also by Nando Sigona

REFUGEE COMMUNITY ORGANISATIONS AND DISPERSAL: Networks, Resources and Social Capital (co-authored)

Romani Politics in Contemporary Europe

Poverty, Ethnic Mobilization, and the Neoliberal Order

Edited by

Nando Sigona and Nidhi Trehan

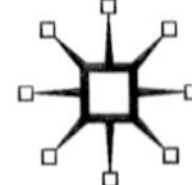

First published 2009 by
PALGRAVE MACMILLAN

Palgrave Macmillan in the UK is an imprint of Macmillan Publishers Limited,
registered in England, company number 785998, of Houndmills, Basingstoke,
Hampshire RG21 6XS.

Palgrave Macmillan in the US is a division of St Martin's Press LLC,
175 Fifth Avenue, New York, NY 10010.

Palgrave Macmillan is the global academic imprint of the above companies
and has companies and representatives throughout the world.

Palgrave® and Macmillan® are registered trademarks in the United States,
the United Kingdom, Europe and other countries.

ISBN: 978–0–230–51662–5 hardback

This book is printed on paper suitable for recycling and made from fully
managed and sustained forest sources. Logging, pulping and manufacturing
processes are expected to conform to the environmental regulations of the
country of origin.

A catalogue record for this book is available from the British Library.

A catalog record for this book is available from the Library of Congress.

10 9 8 7 6 5 4 3 2 1
18 17 16 15 14 13 12 11 10 09

Printed and bound in Great Britain by
CPI Antony Rowe, Chippenham and Eastbourne

Contents

Figures and Tables

Figures

Map

Tables

Foreword

*Etienne Balibar, University of Paris X (Nanterre) and
University of California (Irvine)*

In their excellent collection of essays, Nidhi Trehan, Nando Sigona, and their collaborators have told a story that is sad, but also fascinating, and vital for the future of the European continent. It is sad because it describes what is probably the oldest, but also one of the most brutal and vicious patterns of exclusion in Europe today, with its consequences of prejudice, stigmatization, discrimination, and overt or covert violence. For the first time, it proposes a comparative and cumulative account at the level of Europe, drawing upon the consequences of the recent reunification of the continent, and the incorporation of "Eastern" nations into the framework of the European Union. This comparison shows that – from the point of view of the Romani people – the European process of unification certainly has opened some hitherto nonexistent possibilities of communicating among themselves and claiming their rights in a more efficient, more legitimate manner. But it has not altered the basic pattern of persecution, or perhaps it has added new dimensions to it. It is also, for the same reasons, a fascinating story: what was largely invisible becomes visible, and a whole side of European history becomes understandable. Finally, it is vital for the future of Europe: it cannot be built on exclusions, it is not an Empire. Officially, it presents itself as a space for the realization of democratic rights, and the common happiness of its peoples. Practically, it will win legitimacy in the minds and hearts of its citizens (something more difficult than initially imagined) only if it amounts to an *advance* towards more democratic institutions, and a culture with more solidarity, not less. In this respect, the persecution of Roma in Europe, shifting over time from one country to another, in a process of negative emulation as it were, is not a problem for each country separately, it is a "common" and a "communitarian" problem. By addressing it as such – most of the time having to work against the grain – Europeans will not only eliminate a source of internal conflicts and violence that could become unbearable, they will construct their common citizenship. And, by claiming their rights, raising their voice from the cultural to the civic level, finding the institutional interlocutors and popular allies they need, Roma from all over Europe will win an integration that concerns us collectively.

Being no expert on Romani history and sociology myself, but a European citizen and a philosopher who has worked on other aspects of exclusion and their impact on the development of democracy, I do not want to evaluate the scholarship of this research, but to react to what I perceived in it to form three major questions at stake. The first concerns exclusion and citizenship, and their transformations at the pan-European level. As the contributions show in great detail, Romani people (also called Gypsies, Sinti, etc.) are deprived of certain basic rights in many European countries and in Europe as such, in spite of the fact that they are European citizens, since they are full citizens of the Member States. These basic rights include circulation, residence, employment, education, health, and cultural rights. Romani people are forced to stay in certain areas, from which they can also become arbitrarily expelled. They are targeted either as "nomads" or as nationals coming from certain countries. They are *a priori* labelled a delinquent or a dangerous population. They are never admitted or and are grossly underrepresented in most manual and intellectual professions (with rates of unemployment that reach absolute maxima). Needless to say, these include within public offices. These phenomena are either illegal or legal, under the cover of rules and interstate agreements which concern hygiene, social security, employment policies, and cultural norms. They take place within a background of persistent "popular" extreme violence which is also carried on by neo-fascist groups and criminal gangs, only verbally condemned by many European Member States. Only the most outrageous *pogroms* are reported nationally or internationally in the press. The construction of the EU has had very contradictory effects, which are one of the primary objects of investigation of this book. It has produced a *categorization* of the Romani people as such at the European level, since they have come to be treated as a "problem" in their own right by the EU. This is a preliminary step in the new *racialization* of the Roma. It puts them in the same category as the "migrants" of extra-communitarian origin, in the general framework of what I have labelled the emerging *European apartheid*, the dark side of the emergence of a 'European citizenship' (Balibar 2003). The difference comes from the fact that "migrants" (and descendants of migrants) are seen as an *external other*, whereas "Gypsies" are seen as an *internal other*. This indeed reinforces the old stereotype of the *enemy from within*, which has murderous effects.

In spite of dramatic historical and social changes, especially after World War II and the end of the Cold War which have led Europe very far away from its past, these phenomena testify to a lasting trace of persecutions in European history.[1] The comparison is inevitable with the much more publicized case of the persecution of a 'racial group' in European history, namely the Jews. The two 'pariah groups' have been jointly targeted by the Nazi genocide (as were also several "deviant" populations). They represent entirely different cases of religious and economic trajectory, but – it is important to note – they both played a central role in establishing connections between the different cultures of Europe (especially in the artistic realm, in the case of "Gypsies"), incarnating the "cosmopolitan" element without which "national" cultures remain isolated and sterile.[2]

This leads me to considering a second question, which more specifically concerns trends of racialization in Europe. Some years ago, I had asked whether one should admit that there is something like a "European" racism or neo-racism, which would have the same relationship of complementarity and excess to the 'supra-national' construction as traditional racisms (anti-Semitism, colonial racism, etc.) had to the nation-state and the classical imperialist constructions (Balibar 2002). One has to be very careful in proposing such formulations. Nevertheless, disturbing phenomena can be observed, which give credit to the hypothesis, placing Roma in the unfortunate position of a test case. At the very least, it could be said that the unification of Europe has made the racialization of the 'Gypsy-problem' more *visible*, because it shows such a blatant contradiction with the general *official* trend towards the overcoming of ethnic and national prejudices, on which the 'new Europe' is built. From this point of view, there are at least three phenomena that I find particularly relevant:

One of them concerns the tendency of European nations to *project* onto Roma their own racial prejudices *vis-à-vis other nations*. Clearly, it is the case that the French press, for example, is eager to report on pogroms taking place in Italy or Hungary, or discrimination in Romania, but remains almost silent on the way in which local councils in France reject "nomads" from their territory, or the way in which the French border police expels Romanian and Bulgarian citizens to maximize their official records, knowing full well that, as EU citizens, they will soon be returning.

We are thus led to the phenomena of scapegoating, and more precisely, the way in which European "nations", officially considering each other as members of the same community, having surmounted their age-old hostilities, are in fact still full of mutual resentment and distrust – which to some extent comes from the fact that the European construction, has remained suspended half way. They tend to be projected onto "deviant" groups. The Roma are like a *nation in excess* in Europe, which is singled out for hate not only because it is spread across borders, but because it incarnates the archetype of a *stateless people*, resisting the norms of territorialization and cultural normalization (all the more ironic given that, in many respects, this singularity is itself the result of persecutions).

This problem, as we know, is exceptionally acute when considering the relationship of "western" and "eastern" Europe. It is a fact that the Soviet-type regimes in Eastern Europe during the Cold War, in countries which also had important Romani populations, combined coercive and normative policy agendas with programmes of economic integration, helping to label Roma as "protégés of socialism" in countries where today the majority populations see admission to the EU (but for how long?) as the quickest way towards full economic and social liberalization. Within the other half of the continent, "Western" countries and public opinions perceive them as perfect illustrations of the poverty and deregulation with which the enlargement of the EU threatens its old members. In both cases, they are rejected and seen as "Oriental" rather than properly European.[3] This is where the choice of the book to closely associate the situation of Romani people with neoliberal economic and social policies, and more generally a neoliberal conception of European governance, becomes particularly relevant.

With this remark, we reach the third aspect of these contributions that I find important for the European constituency as such. A protracted assignment of the Romani to the negative condition of 'stateless' community (*de facto* rather than *de jure*: they certainly live under the jurisdiction of states, but are seen as both unable and hostile to entering the institutional fabric of the modern state), which lies at the roots of their discrimination, also reveals the limits of the construction of the public sphere in Europe. It could be compared with a 'statism without a state'. Such a dubious situation, combined with other factors, tends to exacerbate various forms of 'popular racism', especially in the form of an obsession with security. On the other hand, it has led to the creation of a rather dense network of institutions and organizations dealing with the 'Roma question' at the European level. As the book finely explains, some of these organizations and governmental initiatives can enhance the development of an autonomous consciousness and civic practice in the Roma community, while others tends to reduce them to the status of a group which is monitored, protected and placed under surveillance. This dilemma seems to me to refer to another crucial problem, concerning the *roads to emancipation* offered to the Romani people in Europe. Abstractly speaking, there are two roads, as in other similar cases: one could be called 'majoritarian', and it relies on claiming the end of the 'exception', the actual recognition of basic rights which, in their principle, belong to every citizen. The other one could be called 'minoritarian', and it relies on a growing sense of identity and solidarity amongst Romani people, across national borders, leading to a greater cultural autonomy, and therefore a greater visibility as a 'quasi-national' group struggling against exclusion within the multi-national Europe. Clearly, the first road heavily depends on general advances in human rights and a return to inclusive social policies against the 'neoliberal' current, whereas the second is premised on a capacity to use the discourse and institutions of the European Union in order to establish an autonomous voice of their own. Neither is easy, nor probably sufficient. This book very powerfully shows that it will be the responsibility of the Romani people themselves to forge the most effective combination. But it is also our responsibility, and our interest, *qua* European democrats, to support them in this process, fighting the resurgence of racism in our midst and inventing a 'more perfect Union'.

Notes

1. Although R.I. Moore does not explicitly refer to 'Gypsies' in his classical book *The Formation of a Persecuting Society, Authority and Deviance in Western Europe 950–1250* (Moore 2007), many of the institutional and ideological

structures he describes would apply to them: possibly because the persecution in their case mainly crystallized in the early modern era (17th to 18th century), when 'strong' territorial nation-states were built, targeting 'nomadism' as a public danger, and to some extent, even needed 'nomads' to enforce security policies. They are mentioned prominently in a passage of Hobbes' *Leviathan*, Chapter 22, concerning unlawful associations.

2. I rely in particular on the work of the great French expert on the history of Gypsies/Roma in Europe, Henriette Asseo (see Asseo 2006).

3. As documented in the book, Socialist Yugoslavia was the only country in Europe, whether socialist or capitalist, where the Romani people had been granted the rights of an autonomous nationality. The ethnic wars which plagued Yugoslavia after the break-up of the Federation, and especially the conflict in Kosovo, have dismantled this relatively privileged situation and transformed much of the Romani population into refugees. It would be important to discuss the extent to which this situation is replicated outside the 'borders of Europe', in the countries of the former Soviet Union, which are not part of the EU, but are also 'European' in a different sense.

References

Asseo, H. (2006, new edition) *Les Tsiganes, une destine européenne*, Paris: Gallimard Découvertes.

Balibar, E. (2002) *Politics and the other Scene*, London: Verso.

Balibar, E. (2003) *We, The People of Europe? Reflections on Transnational Citizenship*, Princeton: University Press.

Moore, R.I. (2007, 2nd ed.) *The Formation of a Persecuting Society, Authority and Deviance in Western Europe 950–1250*, Oxford: Blackwell.

Preface and Acknowledgements

We are now faced with the fact my friends, that tomorrow is today. We are confronted with the *fierce urgency of now*. In this unfolding conundrum of life and history, there is such a thing as being too late. Procrastination is still the thief of time. Life often leaves us standing bare, naked, and dejected with a lost opportunity [...]. There is an invisible book of life that faithfully records our vigilance or our neglect. Omar Khayyam is right, 'The moving finger writes, and having writ moves on.' We still have a choice today: non-violent coexistence or violent *co-annihilation*. We must move past indecision to action.

Dr. Martin Luther King Jr. ('Beyond Vietnam',
Riverside Baptist Church, New York City, 1967)

Over three years ago, this book began as a conversation between us about the glaring paradoxes of the contemporary neoliberal order in Europe, and in particular, its crucial impact – both ideological and material – on the emerging Romani social movement and political mobilization and the generation of policies vis-à-vis Romani Europeans. At front and centre of our minds were the contradictions we witnessed over the dramatic rise in unemployment and poverty levels amongst Romani communities in post-socialist countries which had experienced, to varying degrees, economic 'shock therapies' over the past two decades. This was coupled with the simultaneous upsurge in mobilization along ethnic lines, in many instances, the result of predominantly American philanthropic sponsorship of the minority rights agenda as mediated by civil society organizations such as OSI, PER, etc., who either implicitly or explicitly promoted a neoliberal agenda of reform in the post-socialist region. A growing sense of disbelief, coupled with resignation, at the deterioration of life chances (access to education, health care, and labour markets) for Roma in Europe today can be observed, as well as an awareness that the 'Europeanization' of the Romani issue, and the promise of human rights protections and institutional structures at the European level, may not be the panacea that many Romani and non-Romani activists and liberal human rights advocates had initially conceived it to be.

As this book goes in for publication in the spring of 2009, we are deeply concerned about the state of the social compact for *all* of Europe's citizens, which appears in peril, particularly for those groups deemed to be 'passive' participants within the European project – and with respect to Romani Europeans, it is questionable whether they were ever fully part of the social compact to begin with. A series of violent attacks on Romani migrants from Eastern Europe in Italy, which has one of the most advanced legislative and human rights frameworks in the region, the recent rise in violence targeting Hungarian and Czech citizens of Romani background (including murders and petrol bombings in 2008 and early 2009), as well as increasing tensions amongst Roma and non-Roma in Slovakia, Bulgaria, Romania, and other parts of Europe compel us to take notice as even wealthier EU countries (Germany, France, UK, Spain, the Netherlands, etc.) experience significant contractions in their economies, crisis in the financial sector, and growing recession. This will have profound consequences for labour migration in Europe and impact Romani migrant and indigenous communities alike.

It is within this climate of economic uncertainty, rising violent xenophobia, and the potential for increasing socio-political upheaval, that the deep-seated structural problems facing Europe's approximately eight million Romani citizens need to be urgently examined and addressed, and this book is but one small step in that direction. In 1967, Martin Luther King Jr. referred to the *fierce urgency of now* in reference to the need for a dramatic shift in America's policies of militarism abroad and racism at home – it was a plea for social change and justice – both for Black Americans in the face of segregation and injustice, and for the millions of Southeast Asians that America was continuing to wrong in Vietnam. We would like to invoke that same urgency today in calling for an understanding of the complex situation of Europe's Romani citizens.

This book has been the culmination of a collective effort on the part of our contributors, whom we now take this opportunity to thank for their enthusiasm and commitment to the project and their patience – the process of drafting (and re-drafting!) was quite long. We would like to give a special mention to Will Guy who kindly commented on several chapters on top of efficiently producing his own. We would also like to thank the editorial team at Palgrave, in particular Philippa Grand and Olivia Middleton, and the team at Newgen Imaging Systems for their support, encouragement and patience throughout the project.

Nidhi Trehan would like to thank in particular the London School of Economics and Political Science and the UCL School of Public Policy/Political Science for providing institutional homes during this process, as well as the ESRC for funding her post-doctoral research. She would also like to thank Ian Hancock, Angela Kóczé, Orhan Galjus, Florina Zoltan, Martin Kovats, Dufunia Gregory Kwiek, and Orhan Demirovski for their friendship and keen insights on the subject. Finally, I wish to thank my dear family and friends (in Europe and the United States) for their unwavering support and tolerance during the entire process of manuscript preparation.

Nando Sigona would like to thank in particular the Refugee Studies Centre (University of Oxford) and the Oxford Brookes Department of Planning for providing institutional homes during the long preparation of this collection, as well as the Oxford Department of International Development for having provided some funding for the finalization of the manuscript. I would also like to thank my family and friends, in particular Julia Bell for her love, support and encouragement (and editorial assistance) and OsservAzione, the collective which together with a group of friends and activists I founded in 2005 and which combats anti-Romani racism against Roma and Sinti in Italy – a very hard and demanding task in these troublesome times. Finally I would like to thank and remember Claudio Marta (1949–2008), who first introduced me to the Romani world and who was a wonderful and inspiring mentor and friend.

NANDO SIGONA AND NIDHI TREHAN

The publishers wish to state that they have made every effort to contact the copyright holders, but if any have been overlooked the publishers will be pleased to make the necessary arrangement at the first opportunity.

Contributors

Will Guy is a research fellow in the Department of Sociology and member of the Centre for the Study of Ethnicity and Citizenship at the University of Bristol. After living and working in Czechoslovakia during the latter half of the 1960s, he completed a PhD in the 1970s on the Communist regime's attempt to assimilate Czechoslovakia's Romani minority. In 2001, he edited a volume on the situation of Roma in East–Central Europe and the Balkans and in 2004, co-edited a study on Romani migration for the Ethnological Institute of the Czech Academy of Sciences. As well as academic research, he has carried out Roma-related studies for international NGOs and for the European Commission, evaluating EU-funded Roma programmes in the Czech Republic, Slovakia, Hungary, Bulgaria, Spain, and Croatia.

Angela Kóczé is a PhD researcher at the Central European University in Budapest. She is former director of the European Roma Information Office (ERIO) in Brussels, as well as former director of the human rights education programme at the European Roma Rights Centre (ERRC) in Budapest, Hungary. She is active in the movement for the emancipation of Roma in Europe, and has a particular interest in issues of women's political representation and social justice.

Miguel Laparra is Director in the Department of Social Work (Universidad Pública de Navarra) and Coordinator of the ALTER Research Group. His research focuses on social exclusion, social policy, employment, immigration, and Romani studies. He has published in journals such as the *Italian Journal of Social Policy, South European Society & Politics, European Journal of Social Quality, Zeitschrift für Sozialreform*, and *Revue Française des Affaires Sociales*, and has collaborated with the FOESSA foundation and the Spanish Ministry of Work and Social Affairs.

Almudena Macías holds a BA in Psychology and a PhD in Social Sciences from the Department of Social Work at the Public University of Navarre, Spain. Her research interests include the study of welfare policies and the migration of the Romani populations from Eastern

Europe within the context of EU enlargement. Her doctoral thesis was on the migration flows of the Romani population between Romania and Spain.

Martin Marušák graduated in computer science and works at the University of Prešov in Eastern Slovakia. He has been involved in anti-racist activism for many years.

Jud Nirenberg holds an MBA from the Ecole Superieure de Gestion in Paris and a BA in international affairs from The American University in Washington, D.C. A Romani activist, he was CEO of the European Roma and Travellers Forum. He has worked for several international Romani organizations and their donors. He directed, for example, the Open Society Institute's Roma Participation Program from 1998 to 2000.

Jo Richardson is a Principal Lecturer in the Centre for Comparative Housing Research at De Montfort University, Leicester. Her book on the impact of discourse on Gypsies and Travellers was published in 2006, and her report on site provision for the Joseph Rowntree Foundation (JRF) was published by the Chartered Institute of Housing in 2007. Jo's current work includes research on the impact of Circular 1/06 on site provision and she is co-writing a 'good practice toolkit' for local councillors on developing Gypsy and Traveller site provision.

Iulius Rostas is a researcher with the Institute for Studying National Minorities Issues in Romania. He is a former director of Roma programmes at the Open Society Institute. Previously, he worked for the European Roma Rights Centre and for the Government of Romania. He holds an MA in Human Rights from the Legal Department of Central European University.

Andrew Ryder is the National Policy Officer of the Irish Traveller Movement in Britain. He has done postgraduate research on Roma/ Travellers and education at Greenwich and Middlesex Universities. Prior to this, Andrew was the Policy Officer of the Gypsy and Traveller Law Reform Coalition (which won the Liberty Human Rights Award in 2004) and researcher for the All Party Parliamentary Group for Traveller Law Reform.

Nando Sigona is a researcher at the Refugee Studies Centre, University of Oxford, where he specializes in undocumented migration in the

UK and European Roma migration. He also teaches refugee studies at Oxford Brookes University. His research interests are forced migration and EU asylum policy and practice, claims-making and mobilization of migrant communities, and Romani politics and social exclusion. He has worked as researcher and consultant on a number of research projects funded by the UK Home Office, EU, OSCE (Organization for Security and Co-operation in Europe), Refugee Housing Association, Joseph Rowntree Foundation, and Paul Hamlyn Foundation. Nando is also a co-founder of OsservAzione, an independent action research group working on anti-racism and Roma rights in Italy.

Katrin Simhandl focuses her research on minority politics in Europe. As a researcher at the Institute for Peace Research and Security Policy in Hamburg, she analysed the discourse of EU institutions on Romani minorities as part of her PhD thesis. She has worked on the politics of the High Commissioner on National Minorities of the OSCE, and has examined the EU Eastern Enlargement process with regard to political, economic and monetary issues as an analyst with the Austrian Central Bank. She is currently a consultant on diversity issues.

Leo Singer holds an MA in Social Development at the Development School at London Metropolitan University. Since 2001, he has been working as a community worker in Slovakia, and involved in anti-racist activism and worker's movements.

Nidhi Trehan is an ESRC (Economic and Social Research Council) research fellow at the University College London's School of Public Policy and Political Science. She holds a PhD from the London School of Economics and Political Science, and works in the areas of human rights as a practitioner and academic. She has published in the areas of human rights, identity politics, NGOs, social movements and migration, with a focus on the Romani communities of Europe. She serves as an expert witness for the UK Home Office on asylum cases, and has worked with Romani NGOs. She previously worked for the ERRC, and has consulted for the OSCE and the UNHCR, as well as the Open Society Institute.

Abbreviations

ALDE	Alliance of Liberals and Democrats for Europe
ARU	Alliance for Roma Unity (Romania)
BNP	British National Party
CEDAW	Convention on the Elimination of All Forms of Discrimination against Women (UN)
CEE	Central and Eastern Europe
CERD	UN Committee on the Elimination of Racial Discrimination
CLGDCLG	(Department for) Communities and Local Government (UK)
CoE	Council of Europe
CRE	Commission on Racial Equality (now Equality and Human Rights Commission, UK)
CRER	Community of Roma Ethnicity from Romania
CSCE	Commission on Security and Co-operation in Europe (see OSCE)
EC	European Commission
ECOSOC	UN Economic and Social Council
ECRI	European Commission against Racism and Intolerance
EPP-ED	European Peoples' Party-European Democrats
ERIO	European Roma Information Office
ERPC	European Roma Policy Coalition
ERRC	European Roma Rights Centre
ERTF	European Roma and Travellers Forum (consultative status with CoE)
ESF	European Social Fund
EUMC	European Monitoring Centre on Racism and Xenophobia
Decade	Decade on Roma Inclusion
DG	Directorate-General (EU)
DURR	Democratic Union of Roma from Romania
FERYP	Federation of European Romani Young People

FIDESZ	Fiatal Demokraták Szövetsége/Magyar Polgári Szövetség (Alliance of Young Democrats/ Hungarian Civic Union coalition)
FRA	European Union Agency for Fundamental Rights (formerly EUMC)
FSG	Fundación Secretariado Gitano (Spain)
GTAA	Gypsy Traveller Accommodation Assessment (UK)
IDP	Internally Displaced Person
INGO	International Non-Governmental Organization
IRU	International Romani Union
JOBBIK	Movement for a Better Hungary
KLA	Kosovo Liberation Army
LGA	Local Government Authority (UK)
MEP	Member of European Parliament
NAPSI	National Plan for Social Inclusion
NATO	North Atlantic Treaty Organization
NDI	National Democratic Institute (USA)
NEKI	Legal Defence Bureau for National and Ethnic Minorities
ODIHR	Office of Democratic Institutions and Human Rights (part of OSCE)
ODPM	Office of the Deputy Prime Minister (UK)
OPRC	Office of the Plenipotentiary for Roma Communities (Slovakia)
OSCE	Organization for Security and Co-operation in Europe
OSI	Open Society Institute
PER	Project on Ethnic Relations (USA)
PHARE	Poland and Hungary: Assistance for Restructuring their Economies (EU)
PR	Partida Romilor (Romania)
RAE	Roma, Askhali and Egyptians
RBP	Regional Planning Body (UK)
RC	Rifondazione Communista (Italy)
RCAR	Roma Civic Alliance from Romania
RNC	Roma National Congress
Romani Criss	Roma Center for Social Intervention and Studies (Romania)

RPA	Roma Polgárjogi Alapítvány (Roma Civil Rights Foundation), Hungary
RPA	Roma Press Agency (Slovakia)
RNL	Romano Nevo Lil (Slovak periodical)
Social OMC	Open Method of Coordination on Social Protection and Social Inclusion
SPE (PSE)	Party of European Socialists
SZDSZ	Szabad Demokraták Szövetsége (Alliance of Free Democrats), Hungary
UNDP	United Nations Development Programme
UNFMI	United Nations Forum on Minority Issues
UNHCR	United Nations High Commissioner for Refugees
UNICEF	United Nations Children's Fund
UNIFEM	United Nations Development Fund for Women
UNMIK	United Nations Mission in Kosovo
USAID	United States Agency for International Development
WCAR	World Conference against Racism, Racial Discrimination, Xenophobia and Related Forms of Intolerance
WHO	World Health Organization

1
Introduction: Romani Politics in Neoliberal Europe

Nando Sigona and Nidhi Trehan

> Liberalism was never a doctrine of the Left; it was always the quintessential centrist doctrine. Its advocates were sure of their moderation, their wisdom, and their humanity. They arrayed themselves simultaneously against an archaic past of unjustified privilege (which they considered to be represented by conservative ideology) and a reckless levelling that took no account of either virtue or merit (which they considered to be represented by socialist/radical ideology). Liberals have always sought to define the rest of the political scene as made up of two extremes between which they fall.
>
> (Wallerstein 1995: 1–2)

> What was needed instead [...] was public action to provide decent housing and jobs, a clamp down on exploitation of migrant workers and support [for] economic development in Europe's neighbours. That opportunity has now been lost, as Italy is gripped by an ominous and retrograde spasm.
>
> (Milne, *The Guardian*, 10 July 2008 [comment on rising anti-Romani violence in Italy])

Europe in the last two decades has experienced unprecedented economic, political and social transformations – the collapse of the Soviet Union and its satellite states, the neoliberal restructuring of post-WWII welfare systems in Western (as well as Eastern) states, the violent disintegration of Yugoslavia in the 1990s, the enlargement of NATO (North Atlantic Treaty Organization) and the European

Union to include former socialist countries, and a growing economic crisis – all these pivotal events define this period.

The new geopolitical order has brought with it an affirmation and consolidation of neoliberal policies and polities throughout Europe (most markedly within many EU Member States), and the redefinition of the political and ideological boundaries of Europe (cf. Gowan 1995). Two visible by-products of this phenomenon have been the increasing marginalization and pauperization of groups, which do not, for various reasons, 'fit' the new socio-economic regime. Amongst these are millions of Romani citizens, for whom chronic unemployment and social exclusion have become the norm. This has been coupled with the emergence and spread of extreme-right political movements with a markedly anti-immigrant and anti-Gypsy agenda.

This introduction is divided into three parts. In the first part, we discuss two key issues: a) the impact of neoliberal policies on the socio-economic situation of Romani communities in Europe, and in particular, in former socialist countries; and b) the rise and spread of violent forms of anti-Gypsyism in the context of the collapse of the Soviet Union (and its satellite states) and the crisis of European socialism. We subsequently explore the relationship between these two phenomena. In the second part, we outline the institutional responses to these phenomena, their motivations and rationale (in particular, the fear of westward migration of Roma) and the emergence, salience and limitations of minority and human rights frameworks. In the final section of this introductory chapter, we look at the spaces of political participation for Romani communities and the issue of leadership in the context of the critique of the neoliberal racialization of political spaces occurring in Europe.

Neoliberalism, poverty and anti-Gypsyism

The profound shifts in economic policy towards neoliberal market principles in the 1990s in the former socialist countries of Europe (in some cases, a 'shock therapy') resulted in catastrophic unemployment for many Roma. Although some scholars have discussed the adverse implications of 'liberal democratic transitions' in former socialist states for Roma in particular (Bárány 2001; Pogány 2004; Kovats 1998; Guy 2001; Bancroft 2005; Klimová-Alexander 2005), few have analysed the impacts of neoliberal ideologies which have dominated Europe since the 1980s (cf. Templer 2006). Only recently have Western NGOs and European governments begun to discuss the scale of the challenges posed by the past two decades of neglect and poor policy interventions vis-à-vis Roma in Europe (Ringold et al. 2003; Cahn 2002; Kósáné Kovács 2009; Cretu 2009; Járóka 2009). It appears as if the European policy-making elite in post-socialist Europe was concentrated in one corner of the room focusing on an American-led 'democratization' and a civil and political rights enhancement agenda (via legislative and 'rule-of-law' reforms), while the social and economic (material) conditions of Romani communities went neglected in the opposite corner for many years.

The belated recognition of Europe's Roma as the 'biggest losers' of the transition from communism to neoliberal capitalism has been part of the mainstream political discourse only since 2003, when two key figures of the global neoliberal economy – the former president of the World Bank James Wolfensohn, and George Soros,[1] a billionaire philanthropist who played a crucial role in the collapse of the Soviet Empire and the 'Americanization' of Eastern Europe – declared:

> Roma have been among the biggest losers in the transition from communism since 1989. They were often the first to lose their jobs in the early 1990's, and they have been persistently blocked from re-entering the labor force due to their often inadequate skills and pervasive discrimination. (Wolfensohn and Soros 2003: 1)

However, this label of 'losers of the transition' does not in itself suggest possible ways forward, nor does it embody the actual crisis that Romani communities across Central and Eastern Europe have been mired in since their experience of relative upward mobility (in terms of labour market access, education, housing and, in some aspects, even political participation) of the 1960s, 1970s and 1980s came to an abrupt halt, resulting in increasing impoverishment and growing marginalization.

The promise of prosperity and wealth brought by Western capitalism never reached a large majority of the Romani population of Central and Eastern Europe who had, long before the current economic crisis, at the height of 'neoliberal' wealth creation in Europe during the 1990s, begun to experience *declining* household incomes. These were the results of large-scale factory closures and the shift from a command economy to laissez-faire capitalism which effectively squeezed out Roma from the labour market *en masse* (cf. Guy 2001; Barány 2001; Kovats 1998). For example, the employment statistics for Roma in Hungary (considered to be one of the most advanced socialist states practicing a 'mixed economy') speak for themselves: in 1985, the employment rate for Romani men was almost on par with that of the general male population, hovering around 85%; today in 2009, an estimated 70% (or more) of Hungarian Romani men are unemployed. Add to this the incidence of chronic poverty and malnutrition amongst European citizens of Romani origin across the EU, and the figures are sobering: for two recent Member States – Bulgaria and Romania – the figures for poverty rates of Romani citizens in 1997 were 84.3% and 78.8% respectively. Further, absolute deprivation can be seen in the rates of child under-nourishment of countries in the region:[2] Bulgaria is the most extreme example, where, across its society, over 50% of children are 'constantly starving', in Romania this figure is over 40%, in Hungary, just under 10%, followed by Czech Republic at 7% and Slovakia at 3% (Ringold et al. 2003; UNDP 2002). That is why it is not a coincidence that Romani communities comprise a 'Third World' in Europe today and that a majority of Roma living in Central Eastern Europe believe their living conditions were better in the past (in Romania and Slovakia a striking 80% of respondents for example, cf. UNDP 2002).

In parallel to structurally induced marginalization resulting from rapid economic transformations along neoliberal lines, the transition to the 'free market' in former socialist countries also occurred in the context of a major reconfiguration of the political map of Europe. The transition forced former nomenclatures and emerging political *élites* to engage in a battle for the definition of a new 'social contract' between the democratic state and its citizens, producing new narratives of belonging and redefining the boundaries of the 'nation' – in Brubaker's words 'reframing nationalism' (1996). This process was mirrored by similar processes evolving within Western European democracies that, with the collapse of the Soviet Union, had lost their 'nemesis'. The loss of the ideological, political and institutional backing of the USSR triggered a radical reshaping of progressive political and social forces in Western Europe and the disappearance or significant downsizing of Western Communist parties.

The massive reorganization of political spaces along national lines therefore defines the context of the (re)emergence of various nationalist movements (Barány 2001; Cordell and Wolff 2004; Muller 2008), and the appearance or singling out of new public enemies (or the rediscovery of old ones, cf. Sigona 2003, 2009). Creating the 'enemy' is a crucial factor in the making of a feeling of shared belonging, and national identity is many times defined in its relation to the Other (Bauman 1992). What we have witnessed since the early 1990s in the post-socialist region is not a novel phenomenon, as the following statement by Lord Acton confirms. Writing in 1862 at a time when the European political landscape was dominated by empires, he noted:

> By making the state and the nation commensurate with each other in theory, [nationalism] reduces practically to a subject condition all other nationalities that may be within the boundary [...] According, therefore, to the degree of humanity and civilization in that dominant body which claims all the rights of the community, the inferior races are exterminated, or reduced to servitude, or outlawed, or put in a condition of dependence. (cited in Muller 2008)

With respect to Romani citizens, it is crucial to understand how the concept of 'Socialist citizen' or 'comrade' underwent a swift transformation at this juncture, and was subsumed by a relatively reductionist concept of 'nation' (the majority ethnic group in power), and thus Roma began to be viewed as no longer part of the broader citizenry (now increasingly equated with the majority 'nation') within former Socialist countries (cf. Guy 2001; Trehan 2009). In Western Europe, due to their perceived 'alienness' and 'Otherness' (cf. Heuss 2000; Lee 2005), Roma were never fully part of the body politic in the first place, indeed, there had never been a conscious attempt in post-WWII Western Europe to engineer this. Attempts, therefore, at integrating Roma within the Socialist bloc countries were rendered stillborn by the early 1990s, after nearly 40 years of upward mobility of many formerly disenfranchised Roma (many of whom had become 'proletarians') came to a standstill.[3] Commenting on the 'bitter experiences' of Roma during the transition, Will Guy wrote:

> The initial promise of democratic freedoms and the satisfaction at the long-awaited recognition of their ethnic identity soon turned sour. Instead, they were left exposed – to the ruthless logic of a

> fledgling market economy in which they were made redundant, to the moral vacuum of a legal interregnum in which they were left defenceless against an upsurge of murderous racism and to democratically-elected governments which were uninterested in a constituency without electoral power. (2001: xv)

Today, in 2009, it is clear that these phenomena are becoming amplified, and moreover, are no longer the preserve of former socialist countries, but are being witnessed in Western Europe as well. Long-standing unresolved tensions and the current climate of economic recession appear to be generating a resurgence of violence (for example, in Hungary, Italy, Czech Republic, Slovakia and Russia). And the re-emergence of anti-Romani racism, hate speech and violence is not a *niche* phenomena limited to a few extreme right groups and parties. Quite the opposite, it is part of a broader political process of ideological readjustment after the collapse of socialist regimes that involves the majority of citizens within European societies. The results of two polls by Eurobarometer (2007, 2008) confirm this point: 24% of EU citizens would not like to have Roma as neighbours (amongst them, fully 47% of Czech and Italian citizens).[4] Some suggest these latest results underestimate the actual level of rejection and hostility towards Roma.[5] According to Michael Guet, a senior civil servant at the Council of Europe who specializes on Romani issues:

> While the social and political debate on all forms of anti-Semitism and xenophobia relies on a variety of instruments, beginning with education up to advocacy with political and social representatives as well as legal restrictions, anti-Gypsyism remains almost a normal thing to which no attention needs to be drawn. (2008: 5)

This lack of interest in the forms of persecution and discrimination against Roma is also illustrated in the paucity of historiography on the persecution of Roma and Sinti (including the Holocaust), suggesting a deep and pervasive denial within European societies (cf. Bernadac 1996; Hancock 1987; Heuss 2000). Moreover, as Nicolae (2008: 1) emphasizes, '[D]espite the fact that anti-Gypsyism fits academic descriptions of racism [...] analyses of racism have by and large ignored or simply paid cursory attention to the plight of the Roma.' Nonetheless, a wave of scholarship is emerging which builds upon earlier works by Romani and non-Romani scholars in this arena, attempting to offer a more nuanced analysis of both state practices vis-à-vis Roma, and the response of, and impact on the Romani communities themselves (cf. Kapralski 1997; Oprea 2004; van Baar 2008; Trehan and Kóczé 2009; Sigona 2003, 2005, 2009).

Increasing anti-Romani racism and socio-economic segregation of Romani communities are two separate, though connected phenomena that adversely impact on the life chances of millions of Roma throughout Europe. Neither is contemporary racism the sole cause of Romani socio-economic segregation, which has deep historical, structural and policy roots; nor is poverty *per se* a reason for the resurgence of violent racism against Roma, though it does render Romani communities and individuals ever more vulnerable to scapegoating. Racism is one of the main obstacles Roma encounter in gaining access to the job market; and poverty can also become a trigger for anti-Romani racism if Roma are perceived as squandering limited welfare resources.

Both phenomena are crucial push factors behind Romani migration in contemporary Europe. We will come back to migration later; for the moment suffice to say that the attempts to control and deter this mainly westward migration by western European Member States has had a significant impact not only on the public opinion in the respective states fostering a 'tidal wave' syndrome, but affected also indigenous Romani populations who had to cope with growing anti-Romani hostility.

How policy makers, human rights entrepreneurs and Romani activists and politicians frame the nature of the relationship between poverty and racism has important consequences for the policies and programmes developed to address the 'Roma issue'.

Responses to the status quo and the emergence of EU discourse on Roma

In the 1990s, as a response to the deteriorating socio-economic conditions of millions of Roma and to growing anti-Gypsy violence, human rights and minority rights discourses and regimes emerged, consolidating alongside an embryonic Romani political movement (Guy 2001; Kovats 2003; Pogány 2004; Trehan 2001, 2009; Vermeersch 2001, 2005, 2006). In line with the practices of primarily

American human rights INGOs (International Non-Governmental Organizations) and foundations which played a major role in this process, these rights discourses tended to emphasize the primacy of civil and political rights, at the expense of economic and social rights (which only emerged after 2000 vis-à-vis Roma). The imprint of neoliberalism on the generation of human rights discourses and discursive practices surrounding the rights agenda remains particularly strong in Eastern Europe (cf. Trehan in this volume) and has gained more ground in the West following the enlargement of the EU. These discourses were mostly a by-product of the 'rule of law', 'democratization' and human rights priorities championed by American and Euro-Atlantic liberal and neoliberal political elites (Ali 2007; Bourdieu 1998; Guilhot 2005; Harvey 2005).

Unsurprisingly, the neoliberal gaze on Roma privileges spaces and forms of political mobilization which are ultimately 'safe' because they do not pose a threat to the assumptions on which the neoliberal order rests, and hence do not confront nor address the structural causes of the socio-economic marginality that affects the vast majority of Romani communities. Mainstream human and minority rights discourses operate within the neoliberal order providing an 'acceptable', although inadequate, we argue, framework for understanding and addressing Romani marginalization and anti-Gypsyism (cf. Balibar and Wallerstein 1991).

From an institutional point of view, the EU's direct involvement with European Roma dates back to the early 1990s and was at first mediated via the Organization for Security and Cooperation in Europe (OSCE) and Council of Europe (CoE). The preoccupation with the westward mobility of Roma was at this point the main, if not only, concern of Western countries who initially responded to this perceived 'threat' by adopting mainly repressive and deterrence measures (i.e. bilateral agreements for fast track repatriation; lists of 'safe countries'; corrosion of the right of asylum; introduction of severe visa restrictions and enhanced police border cooperation) (Matras 2000; Sobotka 2003). Gradually, we witnessed a shift in policy towards a 'mixed approach' that tried to anchor Romani people to their countries of origin (and citizenship) by improving their living conditions there.

An important step in this direction was the decision taken at the Copenhagen EU Council summit in 1993 to include the protection of minorities among the criteria accession states had to fulfil in order to join the EU. However, minority protection was initially a matter of concern exclusively for CEE (Central and Eastern Europe) countries, as Western EU Member States did not want to be held accountable for the condition of their indigenous Romani communities (Sasse 2006; Tesser 2003; Guglielmo and Waters 2005). Safeguarding the separation between the condition of Western Romani communities and Eastern ones was essential for preserving the legitimacy of the EU's discourse on minority protection. This is also recorded in the shift of the EU discourse on Roma as discussed in Simhandl's chapter in this collection.

Crucially, the EU enlargement process, along with the concomitant increase in Romani migration resulting from precarious circumstances in home countries, is transforming the demography of Romani populations in Western states (cf. Cahn and Guild 2008).[6] This demographic shift has also forced a change of approach within EU Member States and institutions, triggering a chain of reactions which this volume attempts to capture in the making. According to one Socialist MEP (Member of European Parliament) from Romania, Gabriella Cretu (2009):

> A European solution to the problems the Roma people are currently dealing with needs to observe several essential principles. Roma are citizens like any of us, although many of the Roma people are currently found in a more vulnerable position, due to discrimination and poverty.

It is the arrival of Romani migrants in Western Europe – initially as asylum seekers escaping the wars which partitioned Yugoslavia and the threat of violent persecution resulting from resurgent nationalism in other post-socialist states; later, primarily as economic migrants following the lifting of the visa regimes on EU accession countries, and eventually as full EU citizens – that calls into question the separation between the Eastern and Western halves of Europe (cf. Balibar 2004). It also reveals the fiction of a Romani population intrinsically *alien* to the EU, despite the fact that many countries have long established and numerically significant indigenous Romani communities. Importantly, the enlargement has also made the mobility of Romani EU citizens an 'internal affair' (Gugliemo and Waters 2005).

This, of course, does not mean that Romani migration westwards is no longer perceived as a 'problem' by European policy-makers, but migration occurs now within an entirely different legal framework. Respectively, the chapters on Spain (Laparra and Macías, chapter 11) and Italy (Sigona, chapter 13) offer insights into the encounter between indigenous Gitanos and Romanian Roma migrants, and the process of the denial of Italian Romani and Sinti political subjectivities through their conflation with foreign Roma.

These demographic and policy changes have produced a domino effect: producing a shift in the public perception of the 'Gypsy issue', hence placing the issue back on the political agenda (for example, Michael Howard's 2005 electoral campaign in Britain, see also Richardson and Ryder, chapter 12). This in turn has driven the development of new representative bodies and organizations both at the national (for example, the *Federazione Rom e Sinti Insieme* in Italy) and international levels, pushing existing Romani organizations to open up to newcomers and raise important questions on the making of a common European Romani identity and its limits.

More recently, we witnessed another important change. The episodes of violence and racism which emerged in Italy during November 2007 played a crucial role in pushing the EU to acknowledge that the 'Roma issue' is relevant to the whole EU and not only to new Member States (cf. Guy, chapter 2, and Mohácsi, chapter 6).

Ethnopolitics and socio-economic segregation: challenges to Romani politics

> There is no question that the Roma of the end of the twentieth century and the beginning of the twenty-first are in the most uncertain period of their European history. In which direction their newly born ethnonationalism will evolve, which paths the elites will choose to guide their people into the next century, and what strategies they will employ to reach their political goals – all of these are still open questions.
>
> (Mirga and Gheorghe 1997)

Twelve years after Mirga and Gheorghe's seminal paper on 'The Roma in the Twenty-First Century', the contentious issues of direction, leadership and goals continue to remain 'open questions" in the Romani movement (cf. Acton 1974; Kawczynski 1997; Vermeersch 2001). Nonetheless, this statement also reflects a relatively unproblematic perspective on the relationship between Romani communities and the Romani political elite, thereby reproducing the 'classic' hierarchical model of elite/mass relations based on nineteenth century nationalist frameworks and nation-building discourses in Europe. Indeed, despite the fact that the roots of post-socialist nationalism clearly emanate from the nineteenth century European nationalist tradition (a tradition that the socialist regimes disavowed and attempted to suppress), after 1989, 'new' political elites in post-socialist Europe (including some Romani political elites) drew heavily upon the very same legacy to shape and frame new nationalist projects. The exclusion of Roma and other minorities is partly the result of this process.

However, unlike the ethnonationalisms exhibited by nation-states with modern armies and extensive bureaucratic infrastructures, the case of Romani ethnonationalism is more of *a reaction to* the broader resurgent ethnonationalist (post-socialist) power struggles of Europe (in some cases, a strategic response by communities under siege, even though it may bear little fruit). Romani ethnonationalism therefore must be differentiated from those of actually existing nation-states (cf. Trehan, chapter 3, for an analysis on the potential role of organic intellectuals in the development of alternative policy priorities in Romani communities).

The enlargement of the EU to include Central and Eastern European states is the defining event of this period and has profoundly affected the trajectory of Romani politics. As Kovats (2003) exhorts, 'neither Roma politics itself, nor the Roma issue in general, should be considered in isolation from the wider political environment in Europe'. Furthermore, he identifies two essential characteristics of this political environment in particular: growing inequality and societal fragmentation along ethnic lines. The use of ethnic identity as a signifier in political struggle is therefore instrumental in key ways to the utilization of existing political and institutional opportunity structures (Koopmans and Statham 2000; McGarry 2008).

As some of the contributions in this volume demonstrate, the political environments, both at the EU and the national levels in which select Romani representatives operate, are not only defined by policies driven by neoliberalism, but are also immersed in broader neoliberal discourses and institutional frameworks which mark the spaces and possibilities of political mobilization by defining both 'the problem' and its solution. Moreover, as analysed in detail in Trehan's chapter, INGOs have played a decisive role in setting the agenda for the Romani movement.[7] To what extent this has been done in collaboration with Romani communities and in response to their actual needs, or by indoctrinating a young Romani leadership sympathetic to the priority of donors, is open to discussion (see the interview with Mustafa and Salijevic, chapter 10). Certainly Dušan Ristic, a Serbian Romani artist and activist invited by the European Roma Rights Center (ERRC) to contribute to a round-table discussion on 'The Romani movement: what shape, what direction?', sees 'the Romani movement' as something of a misnomer:

> On a larger level, the Romani movement does not exist. [...] To be honest, in reality, to me it looks more as if non-Romani people are presently making the Romani movement, with the participation of some Roma. (ERRC 2001)

Nonetheless, the dominant discourse is beginning to be contested and, as the chapters by Nirenberg, Kóczé and Rostas illustrate, there is space for resistance and contestation by Romani intellectuals and interlocutors. Moreover, through direct street action against neoliberal cuts to the welfare state (as in the case of Slovakia), and through state policies and institutional practices (as in Spain, where socio-economic indicators suggest that the overall material condition of Spanish Gitanos has improved in past decades), the diversity of political engagement vis-à-vis Roma is demonstrated.

In this collection, contributors provide several original and multidisciplinary perspectives on how European enlargement has affected the direction of Romani politics and the challenges which lie ahead, some of which are particular to the history of political mobilization of Roma in Eastern and Western Europe (for example, on the concept of 'democratic deficit', see Acton and Klimová 2001), whilst others are inherent to ethnopolitical mobilization itself.

Romani politics is a product of its times and it is an expression of the multiplicity of interests and political orientations which exist amongst the Romani communities of Europe. Some of these voices are included in this collection. Such a variety of interests and agendas often clash with the process of 'Europeanization of the Roma issue' as well as the pressure from international Romani leadership and non-Romani advocates to generate one Romani voice at the European level (see Nirenberg, chapter 5).

In 2001, Dimitrina Petrova, founder and former executive director of the ERRC, confidently proclaimed, 'it would seem that the human rights agenda is a unifying factor in a movement otherwise fragmented and conflictual' (Petrova in ERRC 2001). Today, after 20 years of failed promises of progress and wealth for all, it would seem that this consensus around the human rights and minority rights agenda is being called into question. Dissonant voices can be heard nowadays not only at the fringes of the neoliberal power structure, but also at its very core. MEP Livia Járóka, a Romani Hungarian politician for the centre-right party FIDESZ (Fiatal Demokraták Szövetsége/Magyar Polgári Szövetség), has made it clear in recent public statements that there is a need to move beyond the anti-discrimination paradigm which has failed to provide answers to the socio-economic marginalization of a large section of the European Romani population. She argues:

> The Roma in Europe are at a similar level as people of sub-Saharan Africa. But in this they don't differ from other underprivileged social groups. Therefore, I do not want a special Commissioner for Roma affairs in Brussels. This is a cross-cutting issue, which should be located with the commissioners who are concerned about health, education, working conditions and social welfare issues. [...] Instead of wasting its time on mini projects for small charities, the state should itself become more involved. [...] Why can't the state operate factories in regions with high unemployment? (Járóka 2009)

Summary of the book

The book is divided into two main parts, and is a collection of contributions from a variety of disciplinary fields bringing together Romani and non-Romani scholars, activists and politicians alike. Part One – The Romani Political Space in Europe – explores the making of the 'Romani issue' at the European level, tracing the key trajectories of Romani political development from the 1970s to the contemporary scene. Part Two – Domestic Perspectives – examines the national and local levels of political engagement. As a whole, the book places emphasis on the multiple dimensions and levels within the sphere of Romani politics (EU, state, regional, local and self-organization).

Taking as a starting point the fact that two decades after the collapse of Communist rule, and a full decade after the intensification of EU assistance to prepare former Socialist countries for EU membership, the situation of Europe's largest ethnic minority remains desperate, *Will Guy* reflects on EU initiatives for Romani communities as overseen by the Commission, and identifies limitations which prompt questions about how to continue.

Nidhi Trehan explores the position of the Romani subaltern within post-socialist European civil society, examining the confluence of neoliberalism and the 'NGO-ization' of the Romani movement. She explores the impact of these phenomena on broader questions of autonomy within the movement and the struggle for social justice, suggesting that the emergence of organic intellectuals working to strengthen community-level activity is one way forward.

Katrin Simhandl analyses the discourse on 'Gypsies', 'Travellers' and 'Roma' within the sphere of the institutions of the EU since the 1970s. She argues that the conceptualization of 'Gypsies'/'Roma' as an essentialist category forms the overall basis of the discourse. Building upon the most general, essentialist foundation of the EU discursive framework, she identifies three phases of the discourse, each guided by different interpretative patterns.

But how have Roma themselves mobilized in such a context? In his chapter, *Jud Nirenberg* investigates how the history of Romani political culture shapes the largest umbrella groups in Romani civil society today and their interaction with European policy-makers. In an interview with Nidhi Trehan, *Viktória Mohácsi*, Romani Hungarian MEP, reflects on her experiences working in the Hungarian NGO sector, as well as being a government minister responsible for the integration of Romani children in the school system. She then draws connections between these experiences and her work within the European Parliament and the battle for a comprehensive EU Roma strategy.

In the last chapter of Part One, *Angéla Kóczé* analyses various manifestations of 'Romani women's issues' in European public discourse, in particular the issue of forced sterilization which has primarily affected Romani women. She reflects on how such egregious practices by the State indirectly support the construction of a pan-European Romani political identity, wherein Romani leaders (mostly men) portray Romani women as the symbolic repository of collective identity. She also interrogates the intervention of Western liberal feminist discourse on those issues identified as 'Romani women's issues', in particular, early marriage.

In Part Two, *Iulius Rostas* explores the ways in which Roma participate in public life in Romania, providing an assessment of the degree of institutionalization of Romani organizations, the way they operate and the causes of the weak mobilization of the Roma.

Martin Marušak and *Leo Singer* focus on the remarkable events of the winter of 2003/2004 in Slovakia when a wave of social unrest and organized street protests circulated in the Romani communities as a direct reaction to the cuts in social benefits provision by the then prevailingly neoliberal government.

Avdula (Dai) Mustafa and *Gazmen Salijevic*, Romani activists in Kosovo, discuss with Nando Sigona the reasons for the failure of so many EU- and internationally-financed projects and initiatives to improve the socio-economic conditions of Roma, Askhali and Egyptians in post-war Kosovo. The chapter also provides some critical insights on the impact of the international community on local political dynamics and inter-ethnic relations, and on the relationship between Kosovo's Romani diaspora and those who remained or were returned to Kosovo.

Miguel Laparra and *Almudena Macías* describe the situation of the Spanish Gypsy community (*Gitanos*) and reveal how it has experienced growing integration since the 1950s, with improvements in education, housing and employment. They also investigate the recent arrival of Romani people from Eastern Europe to Spain, examining the relationship between indigenous *Gitanos* and foreign Romani migrants, thereby problematizing the idea of a common, shared Romani identity.

Jo Richardson and *Andrew Ryder* explore the effectiveness of new accommodation policies for Gypsies and Travellers in England that were introduced from 1997 onwards by the New Labour government, in an attempt to increase social inclusion for these minority groups.

Finally, *Nando Sigona* discusses experiences, possibilities and obstacles to the political participation of Roma and Sinti in Italy at the local level. He investigates the role of the 'Gypsy issue' in the political manifestos and electoral campaigns of the main political parties and coalitions, the media coverage of Roma and Sinti issues during the electoral campaign for local elections, and Romani and Sinti views on and experiences of political participation within local politics.

Notes

1. For a critical assessment of the role of George Soros and his interpretations of Karl Popper's concept of 'Open Society', see Clark (2003).
2. These are general country-wide statistics and not specific to Romani communities.
3. Indeed, large numbers of Roma who previously practised traditional occupations were integrated into the Socialist labour markets across the region (cf. Guy 2001; Stewart 1997).
4. It is noteworthy that even in countries without sizeable Romani communities (i.e. Denmark and Malta) we encounter similar results to countries with far larger populations. The notion of the 'mythical Gypsy' continues to be anchored in the collective European imagination and is perpetuated in literature, academic works and perhaps most critically, the media, serving as a receptacle of all things negative: child kidnapping, thievery, criminality, etc. to which the majority society then counterpoints with itself (cf. Trehan and Kóczé 2009).
5. The result of a poll carried out in 2007 in Italy seems to confirm this. According to the Institute for the Study of the Public Opinion (ISPO 2008), the large majority of Italians (72%) have a negative image of Roma, with 47% viewing Roma and Sinti as thieves, delinquents and criminals and 35% associating them with marginalization, degradation, poverty and homelessness (ISPO 2008; Arrigoni and Vitale 2008). See also Dral (2006) on the end of 'our Roma' sympathies by the majority in Slovakia. This is crucial as it is important to understand that across Eastern Europe, many Romani communities were sheltered by the local power structures (mayors, etc.) in defiance of fascist regimes during the Second World War. The broader point is that Roma have been seen as 'contributors' to European societies in the past (cf. Csalog 1994).
6. In Italy, for example, the arrival of Romani war refugees and economic migrants from the successor republics of former Yugoslavia and, more recently, from Romania has changed the balance between Italian Roma and Sinti and foreign Roma (Sigona 2009).
7. It is not a coincidence that Mirga and Gheorghe's paper was funded and nurtured by the Project on Ethnic Relations (PER), a US-based NGO whose board of directors include several former US ambassadors. According to its website, one of PER's key aims is 'to identify and to prepare a modern Romani elite to be an independent force in the interethnic dialogue about the Romani communities of Central and Southeastern Europe' (www.per-usa.org).

References

Acton, T. (1974) *Gypsy Politics and Social Change: The Development of Ethnic Ideology and Pressure Politics among British Gypsies from Victorian Reformism to Romani Nationalism*, London: Routledge and Kegan Paul.

Acton, T. and Klimová, I. (2001) 'The International Romani Union. An East-European answer to West European questions?' in Guy, W. (ed.) *Between Past and Future: the Roma of Central and Eastern Europe*.

Ali, T. (2007) 'Rights & needs: neo-liberalism, democracy, and military humanism', keynote paper at the conference on *Human Rights and Neoliberalism*, University of California, 2–3 March 2007, http://www.uctv.tv/search-details.asp?showID=12622.

Arrigoni, P. and Vitale, T. (2008) 'Quale legalità? Rom e gagi a confronto', *Aggiornamenti Sociali*, 3: 183–194.

Balibar, E. (2004) *We, the People of Europe? Reflections on Transnational Citizenship*, Princeton: Princeton University Press.

Balibar, E. and Wallerstein, I. (1991) *Race, Nation, Class: Ambiguous Identities*, London and New: Verso.

Bancroft, A. (2005) *Roma and Gypsy-Travellers in Europe: Modernity, Race, Space and Exclusion*, London: Ashgate.

Bárány, Z. (2001) *The East European Gypsies: Regime Change, Marginality, and Ethnopolitics*, Cambridge University Press.

Bauman, Z. (1992) 'Soil, blood and identity'. *The Sociological Review*, 40(4): 675–701.

Bernadac, C. (1996) *Sterminateli! Adolf Hitler Contro i Nomadi d'Europa*, Rome: Libritalia.

Bourdieu, P. (1998) 'The essence of neoliberalism', *Le Monde Diplomatique*, December, http://mondediplo.com/1998/12/08bourdieu.

Brubaker, R. (1996) *Nationalism Reframed: Nationhood and the National Question in the New Europe*, Cambridge: Cambridge University Press.

Cahn, C. (2002) 'Extreme poverty, human rights and Roma', *Roma Rights*, issue on 'Extreme Poverty', 1/2002, http://www.errc.org/cikk.php?cikk=712.

Cahn, C. and Guild, E. (2008) *Recent Migration of Roma in Europe*, Wien and Strasbourg: OSCE High Commissioner on National Minorities and Council of Europe Commissioner for Human Rights.

Clark, N. (2003) 'George Soros, a profile', *New Statesman*, 2 June 2003.

Cordell, K. and Wolff, S. (2004) (eds) *The Ethnopolitical Encyclopaedia of Europe*, London: Palgrave/Macmillan.

Cretu, G. (2009) 'Romania: MEP Cretu supports active role of Roma organisations', ERIO e-news, 16 March: 5.

Csalog, Zs. (1994) 'Gypsies in the Hungarian labour market', *Szociológiai Szemle*, 2: 75–78.

Dral, P. (2006) *Ethnicized Laziness: Roma in the Slovak Social Policy Discourse*, Budapest: Central European University MA Thesis.

ERRC (2001) 'The Romani movement: what shape, what direction?', *Roma Rights*, October 2001: 18–28, http://www.errc.org/cikk.php?cikk=1292.

Eurobarometer (2007) *Discrimination in the European Union*, 263/2007, Eurobarometer: Brussels.

Eurobarometer (2008) *Discrimination in the European Union*, 296/2008, Eurobarometer: Brussels.

Gowan, P. (1996) 'Eastern Europe, Western power and neoliberalism', *New Left Review*, I/216.

Guet, M. (2008) *What is Anti-Gypsyism/Anti-Tsiganism/Romaphobia?* Paper presented at the Anti-Discrimination Workshop under the Hungarian Presidency of the Decade for Roma Inclusion, Budapest, 16 April 2008.

Guglielmo, R. and Waters, T.W. (2005) 'Migrating towards minority status: shifting European policy towards Roma', *Journal of Common Market Studies*, 43/2005 (4): 763–86.

Guilhot, N. (2005) *The Democracy Makers: Human Rights and International Order*, New York City: Columbia University Press.

Guy, W. (2001) *Between Past and Future: The Roma of Eastern Europe*, Hatfield: University of Hertfordshire Press.

Hancock, I. (1987) *The Pariah Syndrome: An Account of Gypsy Slavery and Persecution*, Ann Arbor: Karoma Publishers.

Harvey, D. (2005) *A Brief History of Neoliberalism*, Oxford: Oxford University Press.

Heuss, H. (2000) 'Anti-Gypsyism' is not a new phenomenon. Anti-Gypsyism research: the creation of a new field of study' in Acton, T. (ed.) *Scholarship and the Gypsy Struggle*, Hatfield: University of Hertfordshire Press.

ISPO (2008) 'Italiani, rom e sinti a confronto. Una ricerca quali-quantitativa'. Paper presented at the *European Conference on Romani Population*, Rome, 22–23 January 2008, Rome: Ministero degli Interni.

Járóka, L. (2009) 'The politician Járóka on the situation of the Roma', *Die Tageszeitung*, 28 March 2009.

Kapralski, S. (1997) 'Identity building and the Holocaust: Roma political nationalism' *Nationalities Papers*, 25 (2: 269–284.

Klimová-Alexander, I. (2005) *The Romani Voice in World Politics* London: Ashgate.

Koopmans, R. and P. Statham (2000) *Challenging Immigration and Ethnic Relations Politics: Comparative European Perspectives*, Oxford: Oxford University Press.

Kósáné Kovács, M. (2009) 'Europe's Roma – stuck in a "vicious circle" of despair', http://www.europarl.europa.eu/news/public/story_page/016–51268-068–03-11–902-20090309STO51242–2009-09–03-2009/default_en.htm.

Kovats, M. (1998) *The Development of Roma Politics in Hungary 1989–1995*, PhD thesis, University of Portsmouth.

Kovats, M. (2003) 'The politics of Roma identity: between nationalism and destitution', OpenDemocracy.Net, http://www.opendemocracy.net/people-migrationeurope/article_1399.jsp.

Lee, K. (2005) 'Belated travelling theory, contemporary wild praxis: a Romani perspective on the practical politics of the open end', *Role of Romanies: Images and Counter-Images of 'Gypsies'/Romanies in European Cultures*, Liverpool: Liverpool University Press.

Matras, Y. (2000) 'Romani migrations in the post-Communist era: their historical and political significance', *Cambridge Review of International Affairs*, 13(2): 32–50.
McGarry, A. (2008) 'Ethnic group identity and the Roma social movement: transnational organizing structures of representation', *Nationalities Papers*, 36(3): 449–470.
Mirga, A. and Gheorghe, N. (1997) *The Roma in the Twenty-First Century*, Princeton: PER, http://www.per-usa.org/21st_c.htm.
Muller, J.Z. (2008) 'Us and them: the enduring power of ethnic nationalism', *Foreign Affairs*, March/April.
Nicolae V. (2008) 'Anti-Gypsyism – a definition', *European Roma Grassroots Organisation*, Bucharest: ERGO, http://www.ergonetwork.org/antigypsyism.htm.
Oprea, A. (2004) 'Re-envisioning social justice from the ground up: including the experiences of Romani women', *Essex Human Rights Review*, 1(1): 29–39.
Pogány, I. (2004) *The Roma Cafe: Human Rights and the Plight of the Romani People*, London: Pluto Press.
Ringold, D., Orenstein, M.A. and Wilkens, E. (2003) *Roma in an Expanding Europe: Breaking the Poverty Cycle*, Washington, D.C.: World Bank.
Sasse, G. (2006) 'Minority rights in Central and Eastern Europe before and after EU enlargement', paper presented at the conference *Ethnic Mobilization in the New Europe*, Brussels, 21–22 April 2006.
Sigona, N. (2003) 'How can a "nomad" be a "refugee"? Kosovo Roma and Labelling Policy in Italy', *Sociology*, 37(1): 69–79.
Sigona, N. (2005) 'Locating the "Gypsy problem": the Roma in Italy: stereotyping, labelling and nomad camps', *Journal of Ethnic and Migration Studies*, 31(4): 741–756.
Sigona, N. (2009) ' "Via gli zingari dall'Italia!" ("Gypsies out of Italy!"): social exclusion and racial discrimination of Roma and Sinti in Italy' in Mammone, A. and Veltri, G. (eds), *Contemporary Italy: The Sick Man of Europe*, London and New York: Routledge.
Sobotka, E. (2003) 'Romani migrations in the 1990s: perspectives on dynamic, interpretation and policy', *Romani Studies*, 13(2): 79–121.
Stewart, M. (1997) *The Time of Gypsies*, Boulder, CO: Westview.
Templer, B. (2006) 'Neoliberal strategies to defuse a power keg in Europe: the "Decade of Roma Inclusion" and its rationale', *New Politics* 10(4): http://www.wpunj.edu/~newpol/issue40/Templer40.htm.
Tesser, L. (2003) 'The geopolitics of tolerance: minority rights under EU expansion in East-Central Europe', *East European Politics and Societies*, 17(3): 483–532.
Trehan, N. (2001) 'In the name of the Roma? The role of private foundations and NGOs' in Guy, W. (ed.) *Between Past and Future: the Roma of Central and Eastern Europe*.
Trehan, N. (2009) *Human Rights Entrepreneurship in Post-Socialist Hungary: from 'Gypsy Problem' to 'Roma rights'*, PhD thesis, London School of Economics and Political Science, University of London.

Trehan, N. and Kóczé, A. (2009) 'Racism, (neo)colonialism, and social justice: the struggle for the soul of the Romani movement in post-socialist Europe', in Huggan, G. and Law, I. (eds) *Racism Postcolonialism Europe*, Liverpool: Liverpool UP.

UNDP (2002) *Avoiding the Dependency Trap: Roma in Central and Eastern Europe*, Bratislava: UNDP.

Van Baar, H. (2008) 'The way out of amnesia? Europeisation and the recognition of the Roma's past and present', *Third Text*, 22(3): 373–385.

Vermeersch, P. (2001) 'The Roma in domestic and international politics: an emerging voice?', *Roma rights*, October 2001: 5–13.

Vermeersch, P. (2005) 'Marginality, advocacy, and the ambiguities of multiculturalism: notes on Romani activism in Central Europe', *Identities: Global Studies in Culture and Power*, 12: 451–478.

Vermeersch, P. (2006) *The Romani Movement: Minority Politics and Ethnic Mobilization in Contemporary Central Europe*, London: Berghahn.

Wallerstein, I. (1995) *After Liberalism*, New York: New Press.

Wolfensohn, J.D. and Soros, G. (2003) 'Why the Roma matter in Europe', keynote paper at the conference on *Roma in an Expanding Europe: Challenges for the Future*, Budapest, 30 June–1 July 2003.

Part One

The Romani Political Space in Europe

2
EU Initiatives on Roma: Limitations and Ways Forward

Will Guy

Introduction: Roma policy at the crossroads

Two decades after the collapse of Communist rule in what was referred to as "Eastern Europe" and a full decade after intensification of EU assistance to prepare former Communist countries for Community membership, the situation of Europe's largest ethnic minority remains desperate. In spite of sustained EU financial aid to candidate countries throughout the accession process, targeted at the integration of Roma communities, the overwhelming majority of these citizens are even more marginalized than before. Furthermore, the recent wave of EU enlargement in 2007 led to violent attacks, emphatically confirming that discrimination and social exclusion suffered by Roma populations are unsolved problems throughout the continent. Consequently, in 2008, the European Commission – as the EU's executive arm – was confronted with a chorus of critical voices demanding concrete proposals for action.

This article reflects on EU initiatives for Roma communities, overseen by the Commission, identifying limitations which prompt questions about how to continue. In doing so, it draws upon the author's experience since the year 2000 of being involved in Commission evaluations of EU-supported Roma programmes in the Czech Republic, Slovakia, Hungary, Bulgaria and Croatia (EMS 2004b).[1]

Pressure mounts on the European Commission

The European Commission's 2008 Roma Summit was the first high-level EU conference on Roma issues and indicated the heightened significance of the social inclusion of Roma populations as a political issue. This Brussels conference, held on 16 September, brought together 350 representatives of EU institutions, member state governments and parliaments, and civil society as well as representatives of other European states participating in the Decade of Roma Inclusion.[2] However the growing importance on the EU agenda of the situation of the varied identities and diverse groupings gathered together under the umbrella term 'Roma' was demonstrated most clearly by the presence at the summit of the President and Vice-President of the European Commission and the Commissioners for Employment, Social Affairs, and Equal Opportunities and for Education, Training, Culture and Youth.

While procedures leading up to the Roma summit had an institutional momentum of their own, a rapidly deteriorating political situation in Italy with Europe-wide repercussions was the backdrop for the unprecedented action taken by EU bodies in late 2007 and 2008 to reconsider policy addressing the seemingly intractable problems of Roma marginality.

In November 2007, following intensive media coverage surrounding the murder of a naval officer's wife, the Italian authorities responded by tearing down a shantytown on the outskirts of Rome where the Romani suspect lived. At the same time, an emergency decree was issued, enabling prefects to expel EU citizens who were considered a threat to security. Disturbingly this last decision was taken not by any right-wing extremist, but by the respected, centre-left politician and former President of the European Commission, Romano Prodi. Meanwhile masked men beat up shantytown dwellers in revenge attacks (Hooper 2008; see also Sigona in this volume).

The crisis deepened in April 2008 with the election of the right-wing government of Silvio Berlusconi, duly followed in May by further police raids on shantytowns (Fraser 2008). Vigilante attacks were renewed but took a more sinister turn when mafia involvement was alleged in the burning of a Roma camp near Naples, sparked off by rumours that a young Romani woman had kidnapped a baby girl (Popham 2008). Northern League leader and government minister Umberto Bossi commented laconically: 'The people do what the political class isn't able to do'. Shortly after, in July, the government announced plans for the fingerprinting of all Roma, including children, while 'Italy's highest appeal court ruled that it was acceptable to discriminate against Roma on the grounds that "all Gypsies were thieves," rather than because of their "Gypsy nature"' (Milne 2008).

In this way, the consequences of both EU enlargement and Roma exclusion combined to threaten not only the relationship between two Member States but also the fundamental right to freedom of movement within the EU. These troubling events all emphasized the often overlooked fact that systemic discrimination and sporadic violence against Roma are prevalent in Western Europe and are not confined to former Communist-ruled countries. They also served as a sharp reminder that, in spite of over a decade of EU involvement and assistance, the problems of the vast majority of Roma inhabitants in new Member States remained unresolved, driving many to migrate westwards in search of a better life.

In December 2007 for the first time in its history the European Council, as the EU's highest political body directly addressed the issue of 'the very specific situation faced by the Roma across the Union' and called on Member States 'to use all means to improve their inclusion', it also invited the Commission 'to examine existing policies and instruments and to report to the Council on progress achieved' within six months (European Council 2008a: §50). In January 2008, a European Parliament resolution made an urgent call for a comprehensive 'European framework strategy on Roma Inclusion' (EP 2008: §6) and the following month, the Hungarian government, as then chair of the Decade of Roma Inclusion, invited other states to support a similar call. By June Hungary had been joined by the Czech Republic, Slovenia, Romania, Albania and Macedonia. The demand for such a strategy was repeated in March by a newly formed network of the most prominent national and international NGOs working to oppose discrimination against Roma, the European Roma Policy Coalition (ERPC 2008a: 1). Shortly before the main Commission report was due, a related report on Roma integration was presented by another EU body, the European Economic and Social Committee (EESC), and this, too, included a recommendation for a 'coherent and long-term umbrella policy strategy from the Commission' (Sigmund and Sharma 2008: 2).

This mounting pressure on the Commission to produce a new strategy for Roma inclusion focused attention on the long awaited restatement of its social agenda, updating the earlier Lisbon Strategy launched in 2000. Announced on 2 July 2008, this new social inclusion package comprised legislative proposals, studies and recommendations, coinciding with a Eurobarometer poll in which a large majority of EU citizens expected social inequalities to increase in the coming years. It also included a lengthy report reviewing instruments and policies for Roma inclusion, as had been required by the European Council, which contained a cautious opening statement about current perceptions of the situation of Roma populations.

> Although the European institutions, Member States and candidate countries as well as civil society have addressed these problems since the beginning of the 1990s, there is a widely shared assumption that the living and working conditions of Roma have not much improved over the last two decades. (European Commission 2008a: 4)

This was a strange and even misleading characterization since neither the EU, the candidate countries nor most NGOs had paid much attention to the employment situation and material conditions of Roma until the late 1990s, even though these had markedly deteriorated rather than 'not much improved' as implied (OSCE/ODIHR 2008: 11). Nevertheless, after noting this 'assumption', the tone of the report was optimistic with an upbeat conclusion, suggesting that existing structures were fundamentally sound and, together with certain modification, were sufficient for achieving the desired, long-term policy aims.

> The inventory and analysis of policies and instruments presented show that a framework exists at EU level for promoting Roma inclusion. It also demonstrates that the different tools available are being increasingly used by Member States, regional and local authorities, NGOs, social partners and individuals to promote inclusion and combat discrimination. At the same time many lessons can be learned from the experience to date and generate improvements across the board. (European Commission 2008a: 56)

The President of the Commission Barroso adopted a similar position in his speech at the Roma summit. After acknowledging the seriousness of the situation, he emphasized that the main responsibility for progress lay with Member States, while the Commission's role was to provide instruments for Member States and other agencies to utilize. In the Commission's view, its task was to facilitate rather than to implement.

> The instruments for creating change are mainly in the hands of the Member States. Key policies for the inclusion of Roma are the competence of Member States, though they are, or can be, coordinated at the Community level. [...] The Commission can also play an active role by providing policy guidance and stimulating the exchange of good practice between Member States. (Barroso 2008: 4)

These words of President Barroso appeared to reject explicitly the repeated call for a European framework strategy, though he moderated this stance by adding the suggestion that 'the idea of a European Platform for Roma Inclusion might be a useful one. Mutual learning and joint analysis can help to promote inclusion across the EU' (2008). However, what content might be given to this concept of a 'European Platform' remained unclear and not surprisingly, the Coalition found 'this message from the Commission to be ambiguous and insufficient' (ERPC 2008b: 1). According to the Coalition, the Commission was settling for the *status quo* since it 'did not seem to propose a more proactive role than it has in the existing policy framework, in which responsibilities lie with Member States supported by fragmented and ad-hoc Community instruments' (ERPC 2008b).

Given the pragmatic acceptance by the Commission of the basic structure of the present system, the July report understandably made much of relevant legislation and instruments available to Member States and gave numerous examples of projects regarded as good practice. The principal mechanisms included the PHARE (Poland and Hungary: Assistance for Restructuring their Economies) scheme – the main way in which candidate countries were given funding related to treatment of minorities, particularly 'substantial EU financial assistance to fund Roma inclusion' (European Commission 2008a: 49 §10.3). PHARE (now IPA) was a programme to support applicant countries during the accession process when their performance was regularly monitored and documented in annual progress reports. 'Under PHARE more than €100 million has been spent since 1998, targeting primarily education, infrastructure and other fundamental challenges for Roma communities' (European Commission 2008a: 49).

On accession, former candidate countries are eligible for structural funds such as the European Social Fund (ESF) and European Regional Development Fund (ERDF), which can be used to help recent entrants adjust to the EU environment and help reduce inequalities between them and established Member States. Furthermore, a few years before the first group of applicants were due to become members in 2004, the European Council launched a new policy package in 2000, the Lisbon Strategy, requiring states to promote social inclusion and prepare action plans. Both older and newer instruments were applicable to Roma populations, although by no means exclusively targeted at them, unlike a later World Bank/Open Society Institute initiative – the Decade of Roma Inclusion (2005–2015). Although not an EU scheme, the Decade programme closely resembles certain aspects of the Lisbon Strategy and is discussed briefly here since the EU became a formal partner of this initiative, supporting some of its projects with structural funds.

At this critical juncture, those most concerned with Roma issues hold widely divergent views about the best way forward to promote the social inclusion of Roma populations. The Commission is clearly wary of adopting a 'Europeanized' approach in the form of a European framework strategy, at least in the form that has been proposed, and would seem to prefer continuing and improving present policy and existing instruments, while the Coalition and others regard previous efforts as inadequate and ineffective.[3] Therefore it is a timely moment to reconsider the strategy pursued by the EU until now, particularly towards former Communist countries, where the great majority of Europe's Roma live.

EU expansion and Romani populations

One of the first international organizations to voice disquiet about the situation of Roma had been the Council of Europe in 1969. The UN and others followed suit.[4] But following the collapse of Communist regimes in 'Eastern European' countries from 1989, the centre of gravity for Romani issues increasingly shifted to the European Community (later Union) and its various constituent bodies (Mirga 2005: 2), though other organizations continue to play a significant role.

Newly elected, post-Communist governments sought both the protection and prosperity of Western European states and these desires coincided with expansionist plans within the European Community to push its boundaries eastwards. However, it was not until 1993 that a decision was made by the European Council about fundamental requirements to be met by applicants. The Copenhagen Criteria, as they are known, stipulated that candidate countries should have established a functioning market economy, adopted EU legislation, accepted goals of political, economic and monetary union, and ensured 'stability of institutions guaranteeing democracy, the rule of law, human rights and respect for minorities' (European Commission 1999: 3). Soon after, the Council of Europe, a broader-based European institution, called for a fuller and more explicit defence of national minority rights in its *Framework Convention for the Protection of National Minorities*. This required signatory governments to:

> undertake to adopt, where necessary, adequate measures in order to promote, in all areas of economic, social, political and cultural life, full and effective equality between persons belonging to a national minority and those belonging to the majority. (Council of Europe 1995, Article 4 §2)

Although almost all candidate countries with large numbers of Roma citizens had already recognized these populations as national minorities and furthermore went on to sign and ratify the 1995 Framework Convention, fulfilment of its requirements could hardly be made a binding condition of EU entry. Council of Europe conventions only possess the status of recommendations and indeed several existing Member States, for which ethnic diversity is a sensitive topic, ignored this instrument.[5]

In any case – and contrary to the view expressed by the Commission in its 2008 report – candidate countries neglected the economic and social rights of Roma until the late 1990s when more serious discussion about employment and housing eventually began. Instead, political and civic rights were highlighted, no doubt in part because these were emphasized in the Copenhagen Criteria. Meanwhile, as accession negotiations gathered pace after 1997, the Commission became increasing alarmed about the continuing, severely disadvantaged situation of Romani communities in several candidate countries.[6] Then, as now in Italy, this anxiety was aggravated by hostile media coverage of the arrival in Western Europe of Roma from these countries, at that time as asylum seekers.

Over and above political embarrassment and humanitarian concerns, there was an additional reason prompting reprimands from the Commission since the EU had been the main provider of substantial funds supporting a series of programmes to improve the conditions of Roma. This was part of the general financial and technical assistance provided by the EU to help candidate countries meet accession conditions by supporting them in administrative restructuring, capacity development and the introduction of measures to promote economic and social cohesion – mainly through the PHARE scheme (European Commission 2003: 6–9).

PHARE support played a key part in the accession process and projects funded by this programme were often part-financed by applicant countries, demonstrating their commitment. Within the overall requirement to satisfy the Copenhagen Criteria, the content of component programmes to meet these conditions was negotiated and formalized – principally in Accession Partnerships between applicants and the Commission. In addition, individual countries prepared action plans (NPAAs, National Programme for the Adoption of the Acquis) to relate their own initiatives, aimed at complying with EU norms, to wider national strategies. This structural arrangement had the advantage of allowing considerable flexibility by taking local circumstances into account, with individual EC (European Commission) delegations in candidate countries playing a prominent role. However, it had the drawback of making more difficult the formulation and application of a coherent policy by the main supervisory agency – the Commission's Directorate-General for Enlargement. This was not helped by the adoption of short-term, piecemeal programmes rather than developing an in-depth strategic approach, identifying and targeting the most important problems (EMS 2004a: 22–23).

Although the PHARE programme provided valuable financial and other aid and undoubtedly had the positive effect of heightening candidates' awareness of the need for substantial adaptation, 'its aims were too ambitious and the time allowed to achieve them too short' (Bailey and De Propris 2002). A 2004 review of PHARE programmes undertaken between 1999 and late 2003 found a third of all programmes had been evaluated as unsatisfactory. Those in the Economic and Social Cohesion sector (ESC) had proved 'the most disappointing' of all, largely due to 'insufficient support...provided to develop adequate strategies for economic and social development, and the instruments for delivering them'. Consequently, 'pilot investments were generally not made on the basis of proper needs assessments but were instead executed more on the basis of *ad hoc* allocations of funding with limited impact' (EMS 2004a: I).

Unsurprisingly, these same structural weaknesses also undermined the effectiveness of EU-funded initiatives intended to benefit Romani communities. Another comprehensive assessment of EU support – in this case examining PHARE Roma programmes between 1998 and late 2003 in the Czech Republic, Slovakia, Hungary, Bulgaria and Romania – acknowledged PHARE as 'the lever of change' in prompting governments to start taking action 'to fulfil the Copenhagen political criteria in relation to Roma' (EMS 2004b: 9). Significantly, this report also identified the 'absence, in any of the five countries, of a clear policy framework for social inclusion of Roma' (EMS 2004b: II). Instead, many PHARE programmes for Roma were seen as quite separate from the usual, mainstream responsibilities of ministries. To make matters worse, governmental bodies established to take responsibility for coordinating Roma programmes had insufficient status and authority to influence major ministries. Nevertheless, in spite of the lack of all-embracing, integrated strategies and although '[r]esearch ha[d] been almost totally ignored in PHARE programmes' (EMS 2004b: 27), attempts were often made to implement overly optimistic schemes in a top-down way without sufficient planning, adequate resources or appropriate consultation. Consequently, whenever 'PHARE tried to emulate complex socio-economic development schemes,...for various reasons [including] the short-term nature of PHARE, inexperience or lack of preparedness in the sector, the final outcomes of many projects fell short of their high expectation' (EMS 2004b: III). Furthermore, less ambitious efforts adopting 'a "bottom-up" and participatory approach', were more likely to produce positive results, albeit only at local level (EMS 2004b: II).

Negative effects of the absence of a comprehensive EU strategic approach are best demonstrated by the unsystematic targeting of PHARE funding. The criticism of PHARE programmes in the Economic and Social Cohesion sector, that they were not underpinned by viable strategies for economic and social development, was echoed in the review of Roma programmes. This highlighted the disproportionate and poorly directed use of PHARE funding. In all five candidate countries surveyed by the United Nations Development Programme (UNDP) in 2002, Roma asserted that their most pressing need was to find work (UNDP 2002: 31), while a World Bank study recognized that the widespread impoverishment of Roma was largely due to the loss of their former jobs in the Communist economy (Ringold et al. 2003: 1). Yet less than 10% of PHARE funding was allocated for projects 'to address long-term unemployment that is endemic in Roma communities' (EMS 2004b: 6).

Likewise, when Roma life expectancy is at least ten years less than the general population, 'only 3% [of PHARE expenditure was] on health related initiatives' (EMS 2004b: 6). The greatest proportion of these funds, a third, was devoted to education projects, while over a quarter (27) was spent on infrastructure (EMS 2004b: 16). This last item exemplified '*ad hoc* allocations of funding with limited impact' for almost two-thirds of expenditure in this sector was for a single, hastily prepared project in Slovakia to 'improve…drinking water supply, sewerage and road communications in thirty, out of a total of 620 Roma settlements' (EMS 2004b: 17).

There were also anomalies in differential take-up of PHARE aid in candidate countries, which the review suggested might be 'an indication of the level of political commitment' (EMS 2004b: 4). The Czech Republic was the most striking case for, in spite of a substantial Roma population estimated at around 200,000 (Czech Government 1999: 33), it accounted for only 8% of total PHARE funding for Roma programmes in these five countries in the 1998–2003 period. In comparison the share of Slovakia, with an official estimate of 320,000 Roma inhabitants (OPRC 2004), was 26%. The size of Czech projects was also relatively small and limited to low-level NGO initiatives at an average cost of €1.3 million, as opposed to larger, governmental schemes in Slovakia averaging €5.3 million each.

Although improved treatment of Roma minorities was a political criterion for membership, the EU-supported programmes designed to improve this situation had evident drawbacks. On the whole they were limited, piecemeal, short-term, ineffectual and lacked meaningful consultation with Romani communities. This was in spite of an Enlargement Strategy Paper from the Commission in 2000, which noted that 'Roma continue to face widespread discrimination and difficulties in economic and social life' and strongly recommended that 'programmes...[be] implemented in a sustained manner, in close co-operation with Roma representatives, and that appropriate budgetary support is made available in all countries' (European Commission 2003: 5–7).

Poor progress may be partly attributed to the weak political will of candidate governments, unwilling to jeopardize their electoral position by enforcing unpopular policies. But in any case, actual levels of financial aid offered by the EU and complemented by national government funding were inadequate to bring about significant change. This was the conclusion of the most systematic tracking of the enlargement process, the Open Society Institute's EU Monitoring and Advocacy Programme (EUMAP), which found that 'unfortunately,...policies [to protect Roma and other minority groups] are frequently more visible than effective. All too often, they have foundered due to insufficient political backing, low levels of public support, and even lower levels of funding' (Guglielmo 2002).

Paradoxically, other political developments associated with the Copenhagen Criteria had the effect of further hindering the potential of PHARE Roma programmes. Part of the required democratization process involved decentralization of the *dirigiste* governmental system characteristic of Communist rule. As a result, attempts to implement a national policy to promote Roma integration could now be frustrated by new powers devolved to regions and municipalities. This change had particularly profound implications for two key areas of PHARE funding – educational and housing infrastructure programmes.

An EU PHARE advisor, seconded to Slovakia, saw decentralization as posing 'a real risk of...a two-track educational system: one for the majority population and one for the Roma' (Bavoux 2003: 47). Likewise, the Slovak government's Plenipotentiary for Romani Communities, Klára Orgovánová, complained: 'Local government has been inactive [in helping the Roma] for years [and now] local government has the final word over whether it accepts assistance or not' (Balážová 2004). In the Czech Republic, and elsewhere, devolution in the form of privatization of state and municipal housing stock resulted in many Roma being forced to vacate their urban homes for inferior accommodation in more isolated places, deepening their social exclusion and worsening their job prospects.

As accession drew nearer, PHARE aid for Roma programmes increased, as was true of EU assistance in general. Yet, even in sectors where investment for Roma was concentrated, the EU saw relatively poor returns. This was by no means due to ignorance, as all PHARE programmes were frequently monitored and the results of these repeated interim evaluations were reflected in the annual reports assessing individual candidates' progress toward accession. Nevertheless, although comments about Roma integration were often highly critical in these Regular Reports, they proved ineffectual in bringing about substantive change. Yet, in spite of this apparent failure, it might be argued that attention paid to Roma during the accession process at least raised their profile, making their plight harder to ignore.

Whether any candidate countries were seriously at risk due to poor levels of compliance was dubious, since what would count as adequate progress by the time of EU entry had never been defined. As the date of accession neared, criticism in Commission reports abated, strengthening the impression that it was implausible that membership would be denied on the grounds that Roma were insufficiently integrated. In the end, no applicants were refused, even though there was no evidence that the situation of their Romani citizens had significantly improved.

After accession, the best prospects for progress lay in maintaining EU pressure on the new entrants through anti-discrimination and social inclusion policies. But a worrying concern is that while candidate countries are required 'to demonstrate respect for, and protection of, minorities', there are no equivalent EU constraints for Member States. As yet, minority rights remain excluded from EU-wide legislation and specific conditions uniquely binding former applicants simply lapse on accession.

Nevertheless, new measures offered hope. In 2000, the European Council adopted what was known as the Race Directive, requiring equal treatment of persons irrespective of racial or ethnic origin, which applied to all Member States and candidates. Also, a few months earlier in the same year, the Council launched the Lisbon Strategy, declaring that the EU should adopt the strategic goal of becoming by the end of the decade 'the most competitive and dynamic knowledge-based economy...with more and better jobs and greater social cohesion' (Atkinson et al. 2005: 17). Thereafter, for the new entrants and other

Member States, this broader but more focused policy was to become a main integrative mechanism for Roma, replacing the loosely defined terms of the Copenhagen Criteria.

The EU Lisbon Strategy

It has been argued that social policy had a relatively low priority for the EU, even though the European Social Fund had been established as early as 1957 in order to reduce disparities in prosperity and living standards across EU Member States and regions, thereby promoting economic and social cohesion (Potůček 2006: 2). However, in 2000, with the adoption of the Lisbon Strategy, the EU launched a new and urgent drive 'to make a decisive impact on the eradication of poverty by 2010' (European Commission 2006a).

Although fulfilment of the EU's economic potential – to be achieved through higher levels of more skilled employment – can be regarded as the main goal of the Lisbon Strategy, this was to be accompanied by a reduction in social inequalities. Consequently this initiative also focused on the key policy issue of poverty and other areas where social exclusion was prevalent, such as education, housing, pensions and health. Particular attention was to be paid to the most vulnerable groups and those suffering multiple deprivation with especially high risk of exclusion, such as the disabled, children and young people, women, ethnic minorities and immigrants, the homeless and the institutionalized.

To take account of the varied administrative and legal structures of individual Member States, a flexible approach to cooperation with the Commission was adopted. This Open Method of Coordination (OMC) is 'a mutual process of planning, monitoring, examination and comparison … on the basis of common objectives' where sharing experience and good practice is encouraged by peer review exercises (Atkinson et al. 2005: 33, 36–38; European Commission 2006b). The importance of social inclusion was reiterated at the March 2005 meeting of the European Council and a pragmatic approach to policy evaluation was advocated, placing even greater emphasis on 'effective monitoring and evaluation provisions' such as more efficient use of 'targets, benchmarks and indicators, [and] better links with economic and employment policies' (EPSCO 2005, European Commission 2005).

During the protracted period of the accession process, attention had been directed towards legal and economic reform, democratization and safeguarding of individual human rights to comply with EU norms. But beyond these aims, 'the fight against social exclusion did not form an integral part of the Copenhagen Criteria reform agendas' (Potůček 2006: 2). Even so, in preparation for their future responsibilities, candidates were asked in 2002 to identify problems and policies to tackle poverty and social exclusion and subsequently, as with existing Member States, to design a Nation Action Plan of Social Inclusion (NAPSI) for the period 2004–2006.

In this way 'social policy moved to the top of the EU political agenda of enlargement as late as one decade after setting up the Copenhagen Criteria of accession', although full participation in the Lisbon Strategy came only following EU entry (EMS 2004b). Hitherto, there had been 'no wider social inclusion agenda in the five countries covered in th[e] [PHARE Roma] review' (EMS 2004b: 27), which had found 'a lack of clarity about the term "social inclusion" ... [or] how a social inclusion strategy would guarantee a position of priority for the Roma in the future' (EMS 2004b: iii).

Soon after the first wave of ten candidate countries joined the EU in 2004, reservations were voiced about whether the Lisbon strategy was likely to be effective in increasing social inclusion. The commitment of individual governments was questioned after an EC-commissioned report had 'characterise[d] as "disappointing" the overall response of Member States to the [2002] Barcelona European Council's invitation to set targets' (Atkinson et al. 2005: 156). While this criticism was directed mainly against older EU members, several commentators raised doubts about the capacity for strategic governance in some new entrants (Kubánová 2005).

Agreement on specific targets was crucial for a realistic approach to increasing social inclusion and so, in 2006, the Commission's Social Protection Committee responded by adopting a set of common indicators to enable progress to be measured (European Commission 2006c). While this was adequate for the task of comparing standard categories of national statistics, the situation of the most excluded people of all – Roma – would still remain masked. Even in countries where they were most numerous, estimated Roma inhabitants amounted to less than 10% of the total population, and this situation was compounded by the fact that they were severely underrepresented in any ethnically disaggregated statistics that did exist, such as decennial censuses. On the whole, new Member States were disinclined to support any action to correct the mistaken picture given by official census figures, sometimes arguing that to gather separate statistics on Roma would be in breach of data protection legislation.[7]

The lack of sufficiently detailed information had also proved a major problem in attempting to evaluate PHARE Roma programmes, when governments and ministries in candidate countries had often listed targets whilst claiming elsewhere in other documents that relevant statistical information was unobtainable. The same was true of attempts to assess levels of discrimination to determine compliance with the EU's 2000 Race Directive.

Yet, towards the end of the accession process, new and more reliable information became available about living standards in Romani communities and the extent and depth of their impoverishment in post-Communist conditions by using large-scale, comparative surveys to gather evidence. Organizations such as the UNDP, the World Bank and the Open Society Institute were at the forefront of such exercises. In 2002, the UNDP's 2002 Human Development Report created shock waves when it claimed that 'most of the [CEE; Central and Eastern Europe] region's Roma people endure living conditions closer to those of sub-Saharan Africa than to Europe... [and] one out of six is "constantly starving"', prompting demands for further initiatives (UNDP 2003).

In mid-2003, the most substantial of these reports (Ringold et al. 2003) was published to coincide with a major conference in Budapest underpinning the call for a Decade of Roma Inclusion (2005–2015), eventually launched in February 2005 (World Bank 2005).[8] Although space does not permit discussion of this World Bank/OSI (Open Society Institute) initiative, the Decade resembles an overlapping, complementary process to the Lisbon Strategy. National action plans, developed with measurable targets and indicators, are monitored for progress on a regular basis using a comprehensive UNDP database (UNDP 2005). However, these action plans 'are intended to *complement and reinforce – and not duplicate – national strategies for Roma* that are in place in nearly all of the [participating] countries' (Decade 2005, emphasis in original). Unlike the Lisbon Strategy, the Decade applies only to Roma people and to former Communist countries.[9] Moreover, with the exception of a Roma Education Fund and some administrative support, no additional funding is provided by the sponsors. Instead, national budgets can be supplemented by structural funds or other donor aid to support Decade projects.

Limitations of EU Roma initiatives

The 2004 thematic report on five CEE countries with substantial Roma populations acknowledged the stimulating effect of the PHARE programme in placing Roma higher on the political agenda – both nationally and internationally – and prompting a variety of initiatives in candidate countries to promote Roma integration. Moreover, the Copenhagen Criteria for EU membership, including 'guaranteed…respect for minorities', were undoubtedly taken seriously by candidate governments, particularly when critical comments were made by the EU.

Nevertheless, the end result of this sustained monitoring was mainly formal compliance with required legislative changes and projects, which at most achieved localized improvements while leaving the bulk of the problems untouched. Certainly, these limited achievements did not begin to meet the Framework Convention's demand for 'adequate measures in order to promote, in all areas of economic, social, political and cultural life, full and effective equality'.[10]

Many weaknesses of the PHARE programme have already been discussed. Some concern the absence of a strategic approach in the design of this initiative resulting in a fragmentary collection of projects rather than a set of long-term, coherent plans for Roma integration, systematically addressing the main problems. Consequently, there was no firm requirement to target effectively the most pressing concern of most Roma and the main cause of their impoverishment – unemployment.

In this respect, the Lisbon Strategy seemed to offer more hope of progress, since improving employment prospects was at its heart and was seen as the most important factor in furthering social inclusion. Moreover, Romani issues were now the responsibility of the Directorate-General (DG) for Employment, Social Affairs and Equal Opportunities, a more appropriate DG than Enlargement with its wider remit. Furthermore, unlike the Decade, the Strategy included the Romani populations of older established Member States instead of only those in 'Eastern European' countries.

The Strategy also concentrated attention on the most vulnerable groups, addressing their multiple needs, and through the medium of NAPSIs presented a strategic approach to these complex and interlocking problems, avoiding one of the main criticisms of PHARE. However, with this broad scope, the Lisbon Strategy carried far greater risks that Romani communities would be overlooked than was the case with more targeted PHARE programmes.[11] Nevertheless, the 2004 Thematic Report emphasized the significant drawbacks of Roma-specific projects. It pointed to the practice of key ministries in sidelining Romani issues, rather than regarding them as part of their standard overall responsibilities.

Whether the Lisbon Strategy is performing better than the pre-accession instruments like PHARE can only be determined from monitoring studies and these depend on the availability of reliable data. Difficulties in this respect have already been mentioned and although there have been some improvements, serious deficiencies remain. Likewise there is no evidence that the situation in key areas such as employment, housing, education and health has noticeably improved, although there is a growing number of examples of good practice, albeit almost invariably on a small-scale, local level.

One revealing example of research looking at the application of national plans to Roma communities was a 2007 study of their impact in the Czech Republic, France and Portugal (ERRC/NÚMENA 2007). This detailed, comparative report presented a depressing picture, finding that many of the shortcomings of the PHARE programme were being reproduced. The promise of a more strategic approach seemed to have evaporated and instead, a 'cut-and-paste' culture, familiar to those dealing with PHARE project documentation, took the place of dynamic planning.

> The major problem with the NAP[SI]s to be noted in all three countries is the fact that little or no new policy specifically designed to address social exclusion issues experienced by marginalised groups such as Roma and Travellers are included in them. Rather, the NAP[SI]s are almost entirely an aggregate of existing policy in each country that fit within the framework of the European Social Inclusion Model. (ERRC/NÚMENA 2007: 14)

Likewise, opportunities for mainstreaming in both policy making and implementation had been missed. Although more progress appeared to have been made at the higher level, it was apparent that the NAP[SI]s had very little meaning in the day-to-day functioning of the social service systems in the target countries (ERRC/NÚMENA 2007: 15–16). Another fault afflicting some PHARE programmes was poor budgetary planning and the study found that both Czech and Portuguese NAP[SI]s for the 2006–2008 period were still being drafted long 'after the state budget [for 2006] had been approved' (ERRC/NÚMENA 2007: 17–18).

But the most disturbing reappearance of old problems was the 'apparent chasm between the national and local authorities' (ERRC/NÚMENA 2007: 18). Some measures in the plan were 'based on existing national policy documents not adopted or accepted at the local level' and national and regional authorities in all three countries frankly 'expressed their inability to influence the actions of public authorities at the local level. Indeed, certain measures...included in the NAP[SI]s lack any mechanism by which they could be legally enforced' (ERRC/NÚMENA 2007: 16–17). While there had been failure to cooperate in earlier years, this tendency had increased due to the progressive devolution of formerly centralized powers. This structural change was clearly identified as 'an inherent problem in social inclusion efforts':

> The reason why this gap appears is the fact that all countries have a decentralised system of governance that accords discretion on the part of the local governmental authorities to proceed with matters as they deem fit. Therefore, the national institution that oversees this process absolves itself of responsibility at the lack of/ partial implementation of the NAP[SI] provisions in these countries as it has fulfilled its responsibility in drafting the policy. (ERRC/NÚMENA 2007: 18)

This resulted in a stalemate whereby national governments complained that good policies were being blocked by local authorities, which in turn blamed central government for 'vague national policies without localised targets and an ever existing shortfall of funds to implement programmes' (ERRC/NÚMENA 2007: 18). But undoubtedly some local authorities simply disagreed with policies they were instructed to put into practice.

Another damaging effect of devolution stemmed from privatization of some social services, which resulted in 'very little coordination or evaluation by the governments concerned of the [social] work being implemented by NGOs' (ERRC/NÚMENA 2007: 19). Devolution also undermined another goal of successive policy instruments – that of Roma participation. 'Romani organisations in both Czech Republic and Portugal noted difficulties they experienced in accessing funding for initiatives within this [NAPSI] framework since most of the funding is given to longer established non-Romani organisations' (ERRC/NÚMENA 2007: 19).

Yet, while decentralization was limiting involvement of Roma activists at the local level, most governments in the region were recruiting Roma representation on national bodies charged with advising on Roma policies. These agencies, too, sometimes found themselves frustrated as a consequence. In 2008, another impact assessment, of the Commission's overall regulatory mechanism – the Open Method of Coordination for Social Protection and Social Inclusion [Social OMC], contained criticism that 'delivery on the common objectives has been too slow or inefficient' and suggested similar reasons.

> The analysis points to a lack of political commitment and visibility and a need for better horizontal policy coordination and mainstreaming of social protection and social inclusion concerns in all relevant policy areas. Furthermore, there is a need for a stronger analytical underpinning of policy and more involvement of regional and local actors in the Social OMC process. (European Commission 2008b: 2)

As regards what should be done to improve the situation, the Commission once more reiterated the basic statement that 'the Social OMC can only facilitate the achievement of those objectives, in a situation where the main responsibility for social inclusion and social protection policy remains with Member States' (European Commission 2008b: 3).

Justifying 'the need to strengthen the Social OMC' by emphasizing the importance of poverty eradication, the report presented three options for the future, characterized as the 'status quo', 'fundamental overhaul' and 'comprehensive and ambitious reinforcement within the present structure'. The feasibility of the first option was seen as 'high', since there would be minimal change but a high risk of 'process fatigue' was identified. The strong attraction of the second option was that measures envisaged would 'ensure almost "ideal" working of the system by means of a combination of considerably tighter procedures and a massive investment in resources'. Against this, Member States 'would probably be reluctant to accept some (or most) of the measures envisaged under this scenario', since 'at present, there are no treaty provisions on the basis of which individual recommendations could be issued' (European Commission 2008b: 4). Therefore, after outlining potential improvements, such as 'the evolution of a common analytical framework [that would] certainly lead to increased political visibility of the process' and 'quantified targets [which] can raise accountability of governments', 'the impact assessment conclude[d] by highlighting the third option as the best choice' (European Commission 2008b: 5).

This impact assessment dealt with the overall functioning of the Social OMC and the case for strengthening it was justified by a serious situation in which 'there are no signs of an overall reduction in poverty rates in the EU ... [where] 16 per cent of EU citizens (78 million) are at risk from poverty ... [a]mong them children at even greater risk: 19 per cent' (European Commission 2008b: 3). Yet reassurance for future progress lay in 'indicators [that] have already been agreed among Member States ... [and which] are sufficiently robust as a basis for the introduction of quantitative targets' (European Commission 2008b: 5).

Although the main report does refer to 'Roma communities' (only once), it is disquieting to discover that in the list of 'overarching indicators' – on which effective monitoring relies – there was no sign that ethnically disaggregated statistics were being considered (European Commission 2008b: 11 – Annex 2). Yet these are essential for analysing the situation of people who are acknowledged as among the EU's most impoverished and disadvantaged groups – Roma communities.

Conclusions: which way forward?

Given the undeniably faltering approach over the years towards the social inclusion of Roma populations, it is perhaps inevitable that this chapter focuses overwhelmingly on problems and the more negative aspects of initiatives intended to improve matters. Almost nothing has been said about examples of good practice, yet they do exist and can be inspiring.[12] Almost invariably, these are small scale, bottom-up initiatives, as was noted in the 2004 review of PHARE Roma programmes. However, sometimes 'good practices' are located within a broader policy framework.

The problem therefore is to discover which conceptual and institutional structures are more likely to foster schemes that, whatever their scope, must ultimately be local in their application. This is for the obvious reason that all Roma communities are sited in specific locations. To be successful such schemes must gain local non-Roma support, which is one of the most important lessons from many examples of good practice. Without such support, local authorities – the elected representatives – are likely to resist or sabotage instructions from central authorities. Indeed this has been the experience of all past large-scale attempts to integrate (or sometimes assimilate) Roma populations, ranging from the endeavours of Maria Theresa, those of Communist regimes and more recently, some policies of post-Communist governments with EU financial aid. The necessary counterpart to non-Roma support is local Roma involvement at every stage of initiatives. This has been a stated aim of various policy transformations over the years but largely remains an unfulfilled intention.

A natural solution to the substantial yet remarkably similar difficulties encountered when attempting to implement both PHARE programmes and the Lisbon Strategy would appear to be a more targeted, Roma-specific framework strategy, directed by a dedicated, centralized EU secretariat with its own budget. Yet, in spite of disappointing results to date, the alternative would be to persevere within the broader framework of an EU social cohesion agenda, where initiatives to improve conditions for Roma could be presented as benefits for disadvantaged citizens rather than ethnically labelled. Such a strategy would be more likely to diminish potential backlash at a time when global recession might impact disproportionately on more fragile post-Communist economies. The current discouraging situation underlines the urgent need for better access to and more effective use of EU structural funds.

However, whichever alternative strategy is pursued, a means must be found of making individual governments more accountable for the marginalized status and desperate condition of many of their citizens. The 2000 'Race Directive' is one such instrument whereby all Member States are required by the EU to transpose anti-discrimination measures into domestic law. The need for such legislation and for governments to have a positive duty to apply and enforce this was demonstrated by an ERRC study revealing widespread and institutional discrimination against Roma seeking employment (Hyde 2006, 2007).

The considerations mentioned above represent some of the main underlying issues at the September 2008 Roma summit. In a subsequent statement by the EU Roma Policy Coalition, NGO critics of the Commission accused it of empty rhetoric and called for a mandate for new structures and more targeted action.

> Despite… positive signals, we, the members of the EU Roma Policy Coalition (ERPC), believe that the European Commission has not lived up to the expectations of assuming a strong leadership and coordination role in setting up a framework for action that would see the rhetoric of the Commission officials translated into concrete steps and policy proposals. Furthermore, the shared responsibility of the Member States and the European Union for Roma inclusion was not promoted by the European Commission…. In our view, the European Commission made it clear that without a strong mandate from the European Council, e.g. the political commitment of the Member States, it will not be in a position to propose a progressive and long-term Framework Strategy for Roma Inclusion. (ERPC 2008b: 1)

This is exactly the point made in both the speech of President Barroso at the Roma summit and in the 2008 Commission report (European Commission 2008a: 4), which is that, as things stand, the Member States are in many ways sovereign bodies and that only they, through the European Council comprised of their heads of state, can collectively agree and impose binding policy measures.[13] Without such authority from the Council, the powers of the Commission to take action are severely limited.

Nevertheless some Member States – in their support for the proposals of the European Parliament and Policy Coalition for 'Europeanizing' Roma policy – might be suspected of seeking a way of having their cake and eating it too. For, should new proposals eventually involve shifting the main responsibility for Roma populations from individual governments to 'Europe', the result would be – without a new and strengthened mandate equivalent to a unanimously agreed directive – that the Commission would still lack adequate powers to enforce what might well become unworkable centralized policies.

And leaving the issue of Roma entirely to one side, the Commission believed that even in respect of their own 'ethnic majority' citizens in poverty, Member States 'are very attached to their prerogatives and powers in the social field, and would probably be reluctant' to see these diminished by passing more authority to the Commission, as envisaged in the second option in the Social OMC report (European Commission 2008b: 4).

In advocating the third option for a strengthened Social OMC, the Commission adopted the same pragmatic stance that it later presented at the 2008 Roma Summit. By doing so, it anticipated the equally cautious view of the European Council when it responded to the Roma report and Roma Summit in its Conclusions of 8 December. In a brief comment the Council called on the Commission and Member States, 'in close cooperation', 'to take account of the situation of the Roma when designing and implementing [general] policies', 'to identify specific actions for 2009 and 2010' and 'to make better use of the Structural [and other] Funds [...] to promote the inclusion of the Roma'. Tasks for the Commission were to produce a further progress report before July 2010, 'to continue and deepen the discussions and organise a further summit' and 'to organise, initially, an exchange of good practice between the Member States'. In addition, the Commission was required to 'provide analytical support and stimulate cooperation between all parties…including the organisations representing Roma, in the context of an integrated European platform' (European Council 2008b).

The same enigmatic phrase, 'European platform', had been used by President Barroso at the Roma Summit but on neither occasion was any content provided. Whether this was an empty cipher to placate the Policy Coalition, or alternatively, contained the suggestion that 'continued and deeper discussions' might possibly result in an institutional structure meeting some of the Coalition's demands remain an open question. What was evident was that the Council was not inclined to take the side of the Coalition in its continuing and strident criticism of the Commission.

The Policy Coalition was understandably disappointed with this 'ambiguous' response, but nevertheless resolved 'to be pro-active and provide recommendations to *enforce* the second option/ scenario' [author's emphasis]. This is for the Commission to 'use the mandate of the Council to its full extent', including the establishment of 'a dedicated structure within the European Commission, to act as secretariat of the integrated Roma platform', and presumably to implement a comprehensive European framework strategy (ERPC 2008c).

Yet whatever the outcome, much is at stake at this critical juncture. Adopting a mistaken course of action or 'neglecting implementation now [of any strategy] will cost more in the future, both in terms of social harmony and finances' (OSCE/ODIHR (2008: 9), in order to solve what George Soros bluntly called 'one of the European Union's most glaring deficiencies as an open society' (Soros 2008).

Notes

1. The author also a co-authored a comparative 2004 report reviewing EU programmes in five candidate countries. In 2006, he served as thematic expert in a Commission peer review to encourage other countries to learn from a Spanish example of good practice. See Guy (2006) and Guy and Fresno (2006).
2. The Decade of Roma Inclusion (2005–2015) is a World Bank/OSI initiative involving national governments of former Communist states.
3. See also interview with Mohácsi in this volume.
4. See Liégeois and Gheorghe (1995: 23–25).
5. France and Turkey maintained that they had no national minorities and therefore regarded the convention as not relevant to them, while Belgium, Greece, Iceland and Luxembourg signed but did not ratify the convention (Council of Europe 2008).
6. The countries specifically identified were Bulgaria, the Czech Republic, Hungary, Poland, Romania and Slovakia (European Commission 1999: 3).
7. See Guy and Kovats (2006: 17, endnote 2) and PER (2000).
8. Initial signatories were Bulgaria, Croatia, Czech Republic, Hungary, Macedonia, Romania, Serbia and Montenegro and Slovakia. Following the division of Serbia and Montenegro in 2006, the latter became a member in its own right. Albania along with Bosnia and Herzegovina joined in 2008. Spain is the newest member, signing up in February 2009 when it became the first 'old' European Union member to join the initiative. Slovenia has observer status (Decade 2008).

9. With the exception of Spain. See endnote 8 above.
10. See the full text of the Framework Convention for the Protection of National Minorities at: http://conventions.coe.int/Treaty/EN/Treaties/Html/157.htm.
11. In a review of 2003 Action Plans for most EU Member States, only Ireland mentioned 'Travellers' in relation to employment (Focus et al. 2004: 23, §25).
12. For example the Spanish Roma project, 'The eradication of shantytowns in Avilés', which was selected by the Commission for a 2006 peer review. See Guy (2006) and Guy and Fresno (2006).
13. The 'Race Directive' (European Commission 2000a) was an example of such a unanimous decision by the Council being translated into an enforceable directive, binding on all Member States.

References

Atkinson, A. B., Cantillon, B., Marlier, E. and Nolan, B. (2005) *Taking Forward the EU Social Inclusion Process*, Luxembourg: CEPS/INSTEAD Research Institute.

Bailey, D. and De Propris, L. (2002) *A Bridge too Phare? EU Pre-Accession Aid and Capacity Building for Regional Policy in the Accession Countries*, Birmingham Business School, Birmingham: University of Birmingham.

Balážová, S. (2004) 'Survey: Roma deprivation goes from worse to bad', *Slovak Spectator*, 11 October: http://www.slovakspectator.sk/clanok-17512.html

Barroso, J. M. D. (2008) 'Speech', *EC Roma Summit, Press Release*, Brussels, 16 September.

Bavoux, P. (2003) 'The strategy for integrating children from disadvantaged backgrounds, particularly from the Roma minority, into the field of education', *Final Report on Improvement of the Situation of the Roma in the Slovak Republic*, France/Slovakia Twinning Covenant, Paris/Bratislava: Racine/Government of Slovakia.

Council of Europe (1995) *Framework Convention for the Protection of National Minorities*, Strasbourg: CoE, 1 February.

Council of Europe (2008) *State Reports, Opinions, Comments and Recommendations*, Strasbourg: CoE.

Czech Government (1999) *Information about Compliance with Principles set forth in the Framework Convention for the Protection of National Minorities according to Article 25, Paragraph 1 of this Convention*, Government of the Czech Republic, April.

Decade (2005) 'Decade Action Plans', *The Decade of Roma Inclusion* [earlier version no longer available, but cited in Guy (2006: 60)].

Decade (2008) 'About the Decade', *The Decade of Roma Inclusion*, 25 September.

EMS (2004a) *From Pre-Accession to Accession: Consolidated Summary Report*, Interim Evaluation, Phare support allocated in 1999–2002 and implemented until November 2003, Brussels: European Monitoring Service (EMS),

Brussels: EC DG Enlargement, March, http://ec.europa.eu/enlargement/pdf/financial_assistance/phare/zz_pier_03020_e3_290304_en.pdf.

EMS (2004b) *From Pre-Accession to Accession: Review of the European Union Phare Assistance to Roma Minorities*, Thematic Evaluation, Phare support allocated in 1999–2002 and implemented until November 2003, EMS, Brussels: EC DG Enlargement, December.

EPSCO (2005) *Key Messages for the Spring European Council*, EU Council of Employment and Social Affairs Ministers (EPSCO), Brussels: EPSCO, 3–4 March.

ERPC (2008a) 'Discrimination against Roma in Europe', *Factsheet/Background Press Release*, European Roma Policy Coalition, Brussels: ERPC.

ERPC (2008b) *Shadow Conclusions of the EU Roma Summit*, Brussels: ERPC.

ERPC (2008c) 'Short analysis and envisaged action points for 2009', *Response to European Council Conclusion on Inclusion of Roma*, Brussels: ERPC, 17 December.

ERRC/NÚMENA (2007) *Social Inclusion through Social Services: The Case of Roma and Travellers, Assessing the Impact of National Action Plans for Social Inclusion in Czech Republic*, France and Portugal, Budapest: ERRC/NÚMENA.

European Commission (1999) *Enlargement Briefing: EU Support for Roma Communities in Central and Eastern Europe*, Brussels: EC DG Enlargement, December.

European Commission (2000a) *Council Directive 2000/43/EC*, implementing the principle of equal treatment between persons irrespective of racial or ethnic origin, (known commonly as the Race Directive), 29 June.

European Commission (2000b) *Council Directive 2000/78/EC*, establishing a general framework for equal treatment in employment and occupation, 27 November.

European Commission (2003) *Enlargement Briefing: EU Support for Roma Communities in Central and Eastern Europe*, Brussels: EC DG Enlargement, October.

European Commission (2005) *Working Together, Working Better: A New Framework for the Open Coordination of Social Protection and Inclusion Policies in the EU*, COM (2005) 706, Brussels: EC DG Employment, Social Affairs and Equal Opportunities, 22 December.

European Commission (2006a) *Social Inclusion*, Brussels: EC, DG Employment, Social Affairs and Equal Opportunities.

European Commission (2006b) *The Process: The Open Method of Coordination*, Brussels: EC, DG Employment, Social Affairs and Equal Opportunities.

European Commission (2006c) *Common Indicators*, Brussels: EC, DG Employment, Social Affairs and Equal Opportunities.

European Commission (2008a) *Community Instruments and Policies for Roma Inclusion*, COM_2008_420 CSWD 27[1].6.08, Brussels: European Commission, 2 July.

European Commission (2008b) *A Renewed Commitment to Social Europe: Reinforcing the Open Method of Coordination for Social Protection and Social Inclusion, Summary of the Impact Assessment*, Brussels: European Commission, 2 July.

European Council (2008a) *Presidency Conclusions – 14 December 2007,* 16616/1/07 REV 1, Brussels: European Council, 14 February.

European Council (2008b) *Presidency Conclusions on Inclusion of the Roma,* Brussels: European Council, 8 December.

European Parliament (2008) *Resolution on a European Strategy on the Roma,* adopted 31 January, P6_TA(2008)0035, Strasbourg: European Parliament.

Focus, ERRC and ERIO (2004) *The Situation of Roma in an Enlarged European Union,* Brussels: EC DG for Employment and Social Affairs.

Fraser, C. (2008) 'Italy police to protect Gypsies', *BBC News,* 14 May.

Guglielmo, R. (2002) *EU Enlargement: A Union of Values or a Union of Interests?* EU Monitoring and Advocacy Programme (EUMAP), Budapest: EUMAP.

Guy, W. (2006) *Discussion Paper,* peer review of Spanish Roma project: 'The eradication of shantytowns in Avilés', for EC Directorate-General Employment, Social Affairs and Social Inclusion, Vienna: ÖSB Consulting, October.

Guy, W. and Fresno, J. M. (2006) *Synthesis Report,* peer review of Spanish Roma project: 'The eradication of shantytowns in Avilés', for EC Directorate-General Employment, Social Affairs and Social Inclusion, Vienna: ÖSB Consulting, December.

Guy, W. and Kovats, M. (2006) *EU-funded Roma Programmes: Lessons from Hungary,* Slovakia and the Czech Republic, London: Minority Rights Group International.

Hooper, J. (2008) 'Violence as Italy expels migrants', *The Guardian,* 4 November.

Hyde, A. (2006) 'Systematic exclusion of Roma from employment', *Roma Rights Quarterly* 1, Budapest: ERRC.

Hyde, A. (2007) *The Glass Box: Exclusion of Roma from Employment,* Budapest: ERRC.

Kubánová, M. (2005) *The Missing Link: Monitoring and Evaluation of Roma-Related Policies in Slovakia,* EU Monitoring and Advocacy Programme (EUMAP), Budapest: EUMAP.

Liégeois, J.-P. and Gheorghe, N. (1995) *Roma/Gypsies: A European Minority,* London: Minority Rights Group International.

Milne, S. (2008) 'This persecution of Gypsies is now the shame of Europe', *The Guardian,* July 10.

Mirga, A. (2005) *Making the EU's Anti-Discrimination Policy Instruments Work for Romani Communities in the Enlarged European Union,* Princeton: PER.

OPRC (2004) *Rómovia na Slovensku: List faktov k sociografickému mapovaniu rómskych osídlení na Slovensku* (Roma in Slovakia: Fact List about the Sociographic Mapping of Roma Communities in Slovakia), Bratislava: Office of the Plenipotentiary of the Slovak Government for Roma Communities. Accessible at http://romovia.vlada.gov.sk/3554/list-faktov.php

OSCE/ODIHR (2008) *Implementation of the Action Plan on Improving the Situation of Roma and Sinti within the OSCE Area,* Warsaw: OSCE/ODIHR, 24 September.

PER (2000) *Roma and Statistics,* Project on Ethnic Relations (PER), Princeton: PER.

Popham, P. (2008) 'Italian tolerance goes up in smoke as Gypsy camp is burnt to ground', *The Independent*, 15 May.

Potůček, M. (2006) 'Does the Lisbon Strategy matter? The Czech experience', conference paper for *Reforms in Lisbon Strategy Implementation: Economic and Social Dimensions*, Zagreb, May.

Ringold, D., Orenstein, M. A. and Wilkens, E. (2003) *Roma in an Expanding Europe: Breaking the Poverty Cycle*, Washington, D.C.: The World Bank.

Sigmund, A.M. and Sharma, M. (2008) *Opinion of the European Economic and Social Committee on the Integration of Minorities – Roma*, (exploratory opinion), Brussels: European Economic and Social Committee, 20 June (adopted 9 July).

Soros, G. (2008) '"An unacceptable reality": The situation of Roma in the European Union', *Roma Initiatives*, Keynote address to the EU Roma Summit, 16 September, Budapest: OSI.

UNDP (2002) *Roma in Central and Eastern Europe: Avoiding the Dependency Trap*, UNDP/ILO Regional Human Development Report, Bratislava: UNDP.

UNDP (2003) 'Roma integration is key in an enlarged EU', *UNDP Press Release* on UNDP Roma report (2002), Brussels: UNDP, 16 January.

UNDP (2005) *Faces of Poverty, Faces of Hope: Vulnerability Profiles for Decade of Roma Inclusion Countries*, Bratislava: UNDP.

World Bank (2005) 'European leaders launch Decade of Roma Inclusion', *World Bank*, Washington D.C: World Bank, February.

3
The Romani Subaltern within Neoliberal European Civil Society: NGOization of Human Rights and Silent Voices

Nidhi Trehan

Introduction

The examination of both questions of power and positionality with respect to class, gender, ethnicity and other vectors of identity is fundamental to a deeper, more nuanced understanding of the hierarchies embedded within the domain of contemporary European civil society (cf. Kóczé, chapter 7). It is therefore not a coincidence that a Romani woman activist from an isolated village on the Hungarian-Ukrainian border has a decidedly different voice within the global human rights arena than an Ivy League-educated male lawyer who holds an American passport and works in Eastern Europe.

This chapter builds upon the Introduction to this volume, which emphasizes the hegemony of the prevailing neoliberal ideological lens vis-à-vis the broader post-socialist European framework structuring Romani political mobilization and policy generation. It begins by contextualizing the position of the Romani subaltern within a theoretical discussion of European civil society. It then weaves together some key strands surrounding the development of the Romani movement for human rights as a primarily NGO-driven vehicle.[1] Finally, it offers a synthesis of this knowledge in order to demonstrate the limitations and paradoxes of this dominant paradigm of Romani mobilization in Europe today.

The key questions explored in this chapter are the following: how does a primarily 'neoliberal human rights' approach manifest itself in the contemporary 'Roma rights' movement? What order does it (re)produce and whose interests are reflected therein? What happens to an emerging human rights/emancipation movement in an age of neoliberal policy hegemony? Furthermore, in focusing on human rights discourses in post-socialist Europe – and as NGOs have been the primary vehicles for the generation and diffusion of these discourses – additional questions revolving around NGOs are posed: Inherent to the neoliberal, technocratic policy approach towards NGO development, how has the 'NGOization' of human rights (Lang 1997; Stubbs 2007) impacted upon the development of an autonomous, democratic voice representing the needs of European Romani communities? And finally, are there any viable alternatives to the current trajectory of the INGO (International Non-Governmental Organization)-led 'Roma rights' movement?

In discussing 'neoliberal human rights' approaches, reference is made to phenomena wherein human rights concerns and campaigning operate synergistically within neoliberal capitalist democracies, becoming an arm of the contemporary global neoliberal economic and political order. Neoliberal economic theory has become the basis for the dominant socio-economic model in post-socialist Eastern and Central Europe – and indeed – the basis for a hegemonic socio-political order throughout the globe (Bourdieu 1998; AWID 2003; Trehan 2006). It is generally anti-statist in its trajectory, believing that the state should have a minimal role in the regulation of the private sector, and its appeal within post-socialist countries – at least until recently – unsurprisingly derives from the particular history of the 'passive revolutions' which led to the demise of communist one-party systems (Gill 2003: 52–53). Neoliberal thought, advocated most prominently by the 'Vienna' and 'Chicago' schools of economic philosophy, tailored itself well to a liberal political theory which was concerned about the development of modern, centralized nation-states and the erosion of individual autonomy (Chen and Churchill 2005: 15).

To a large extent, the neoliberal approach works hand-in-glove with the dominant discourse on post-socialist European civil society which began to permeate the region's fledgling NGO sector in the early 1990s.[2] Prominent neoliberals such as billionaire financier and philanthropist George Soros have long held that the 'twin pillars of the so-called open society are expansive individual rights and freedoms as well as unrestricted free markets' (Chen and Churchill 2005: 1; cf. Clark 2003). Specific mention of Soros is made here because, more than any other single individual, he has been responsible for the support and promotion of Romani NGOs (through the activities of the Open Society Institute) – organizations which putatively form the backbone of the movement.

'White civil society' and the Romani subaltern

> A different picture emerges if from the beginning one admits the coexistence of competing public spheres and takes account of the dynamics of those processes of communication that are excluded from the dominant public sphere.
>
> (Habermas cited in Jacobs 2000: 20)

With respect to the contemporary 'Roma rights' movement, a number of conceptual critiques of the (neo)liberal human rights framework apply to the interventions of the state and to the role of NGO actors, as well as the complex and dynamic interplay between the two. In examining the case of Romani civil society, it is instructive to look at the works of theorists who have identified lacunae in Habermasian (1989; 1992) theorizations of the public sphere in Europe. Whilst Habermas' insightful contributions focused on the interdependence of the *lifeworld* (public sphere) and *system* (the nexus of the state and market economy), and the negotiation of political power, other scholars have built upon his work to examine the role of subaltern groups *within* the public sphere itself (Calhoun 1992). Keane (1995, 1998) correctly emphasizes the multiplicities of public spheres which go beyond bourgeois conceptions of civil society (for example, the ethos of 'middle-class volunteerism'[3]). Similarly, Jacobs (2000) expands on the notion of 'multiple publics'; in other words, the public sphere (inclusive of organs of civil society) is not a monolithic entity, but represents a site of contestation of multiple, crisscrossing communities and publics. Nancy Fraser (1992) has coined the term 'subaltern counterpublics' to refer to those spaces within the public sphere which are staked out by subaltern groups and act as 'parallel discursive arenas where members of subordinated social groups invent and circulate counterdiscourses to formulate oppositional interpretations of their identities, interests, and needs' (123).

Jacobs' (2000) rich empirical study of the rise and role of black newspapers in urban America points to the limitations of inclusion within mainstream (white) civil society, and the resulting alternative public sphere created by Black Americans, in part to increase visibility within mainstream civil society. He reminds us of the early abolitionist press in the United States which was dominated by white Americans and their general indifference to the formation and success of independent Black media in the late 1800s and early 1900s (2000: 20–21). Similarly, the position of Roma in post-socialist Europe is today of a minority seeking visibility within a predominantly 'white civil society'. As Jacobs asserts, 'the challenge of multiple publics...suggests that civil society has a fractured quality which is not being overcome by some trend towards an integrated public sphere' (2000: 20). In illuminating the denials and limitations of 'white civil society' (cf. Jacobs 2000: 4–5), we are forced to confront a (re)conceptualization of the Romani movement in light of the reality of exclusionary mechanisms within contemporary civil society dominated by neoliberal agendas and policy priorities.

As elaborated upon in my doctoral work, Romani civil society is an embryonic and fragile sphere, as 'counterdiscourses' and dissident ideologies continue to remain marginalized (cf. Trehan 2009). Notwithstanding the critical contributions of an earlier generation of Romani activists (particularly those over 40 years of age, who began to organize during the days of Socialism[4]), the creation of a 'Roma movement' dominated by NGOs subscribing to a neoliberal agenda was itself an imposition from outside the Romani communities and has been an arena of strategic instrumentalization by elite participants (both Roma and non-Roma).[5] However, what is equally important to note is that the subalterity of Romani civil society functions at another level: that is, inside Eastern European civil society, which is itself embedded *within* a broader global civil society, dominated by neoliberal ideological and policy trajectories (Trehan 2006; cf. Guilhot 2005).

Connected to this point above, Gramscian and neo-Gramscian critiques (cf. Cox 1999; Trehan 2009) of contemporary civil society apply directly to the Romani NGO sector. Gramsci's observation that civil society is *a site for the hegemony of the established order, rather than a site for emancipation* applies to the hierarchies which abound in the Romani NGO sector, thereby reflecting the interests of global multilateral organizations and NGOs, as well as that of Eastern European elites, who are their willing partners (Cox 1999; Gramsci 1971, 2001; Trehan 2001). The influence of local Romani NGOs in the past decade were quickly supplanted by the interests of powerful INGOs, including national-level elite NGOs which become implementing partners for international projects such as the Autonomia Foundation of Budapest or Romani Criss of Bucharest. After the EU accession of Eastern European states, the establishment of Europe-level advocacy organizations such as European Roma Information Office and European Roma Policy Coalition (which includes Amnesty International) has served to solidify this trend (cf. Guy in this volume).

Gramsci's observation that civil society operates as an optimum site for the (re)production of hegemony by the bourgeoisie serves as an important corrective to prevalent neoliberal interpretations of civil society popular amongst both Western and Eastern European elites (cf. Cox 1999; Žižek 2005). Another critical perspective on civil society comes from Chandhoke (2003), who has analyzed the role of the subaltern within civil society at both the international and domestic levels of politics. Commenting on the limitations of formal democracy, she emphasizes that:

> [The] contemporary political aid industry is at its core…about system maintenance. Democracy, through and in political conditionalities, fits neatly with neoliberal agendas that have been pushed by donor agencies and multilateral funding agencies, particularly in the aftermath of the 'velvet revolutions' of 1989 in Eastern Europe. And neoliberalism is about system maintenance…. In effect, informed as it is by neoliberalism, democracy in its current avatar is safe, as it simply has no potential to pose a threat to entrenched power structures. (Chandhoke 2003: 6)

Few theoreticians of civil society in Europe have adequately examined the position of subaltern communities in their analysis, and moreover, despite the growth of NGOs putatively serving the 'Romani interest', few scholars have looked critically at their assumptions about the sphere being a space for emancipatory projects or the realization of active citizenship (see also Vermeersch 2005). Even established scholars of 'civil society' such as Cohen and Arato (1992) have not sufficiently interrogated the position of subaltern groups within Eastern European civil societies and polities. For various subaltern groups, these arenas may in fact be 'uncivil' (Keane 1998: 114–117). Therefore, the works of alternative theorists – Black, 'Third World' and feminists such as Chandhoke, Fraser and Jacobs mentioned above – offer us useful trajectories for the (re)conceptualization of civil society, including within the contentious sphere of NGO activity.

The emergence and growth of the 'NGOization of Roma rights'

> Witness the tragedy that has befallen the proponents of the concept: people struggling against authoritarian regimes had demanded civil society; what they got instead were NGOs!
>
> (Chandhoke 2003: 9)

As the Romani movement is at its core NGO-driven, it is necessary to examine key phenomena on NGOs and social movements in parallel. Inherent to the embrace of neoliberal policies in countries where the State became relatively weak during the course of the transition in tandem with privatization and de-regulation, social movements became institutionalized via the rapid growth and 'professionalization' of NGOs (Trehan 2001).[6] These developments ultimately led to the 'NGOization of human rights' and the creation of bureaucratic hierarchies within civil society (Lang 1997; Stubbs 2007).[7]

In examining how socio-economically marginalized communities attempt to organize strategically, and consolidate grassroots power in order to gain jobs and better access to education, health care and public transportation, the classical works on local level organizing by Alinsky (1946; 1971) and Fox-Piven and Cloward (1977) are instructive. In particular, works by social scientists who have examined the methods of the Industrial Areas Foundation (IAF) illuminate the structural obstacles encountered by poor and working class communities when they attempt to organize their communities into effective coalitions (Warren 2001: 40–45).[8]

There is a confluence of connecting phenomena accounting for the dramatic rise in the level of NGO human rights activity vis-à-vis Roma in the 1990s. First and foremost, the massive socio-economic changes within post-socialist countries resulting from the rapid shift from a command economy to neoliberal market capitalism laid the groundwork for the rising marginalization of Romani communities (Trehan 2006). During the 1980s, there was a weakening of the socialist state structures underpinning the region since the 1950s. This resulted in large-scale unemployment (and underemployment) leading to further impoverishment amongst Romani communities (Speder 2001: 240). Only a small number of Romani entrepreneurs fared well under the newly liberalized regimes. The widespread and increasing impoverishment of Roma further deepened anti-Romani hostility and exacerbated societal perceptions of Roma as a people who are 'by nature' work-shy, and engage in benefits fraud and other illegal activities.

In addition, by the early 1990s, there was a renewed emphasis on national identity, as well as a resurgence of ethnocultural boundaries spearheaded by political elites in the region (cf. Introduction in this volume). This new political *status quo* effectively excluded Roma from its version of the 'body politic', resulting in their further political marginalization. In the case of the newly 'democratized' Hungary for instance, the political ideologies emerging from both nationalist parties – such as the extreme right *Party for the Hungarian Truth and Life (MIÉP)*, an openly anti-Semitic and anti-Gypsy movement – and the liberals, who celebrated 'ethnic difference', created an environment in which ethnic consciousness was accentuated across the political spectrum. Kovats (1998; 2001) has correctly observed that the post-socialist left-liberal Hungarian government's policies were focused on a recognition of cultural differences of minorities at the expense of social solidarity with *all citizens* of the state.

Across post-socialist Europe, Roma, as particularly visible minority communities, became targets of discrimination and violence by large sections of society: not only by extreme nationalists (far-right politicians and members of neo-fascist youth groups) but also by police and state officials, especially at the local level. The old popular anti-Gypsy mythologies in the European *imaginarium* once again surfaced, and open intolerance and hostility towards Roma became widespread. The growing incidence of skinhead attacks in the early 1990s pushed indigenous advocates (both Romani and non-Romani) to mobilize and call for a stronger response by the State[9] (Human

Rights Watch 1993 and 1996; Vermeersch 2006). There were also a handful of social reformers and politicians who raised awareness of these issues nationally and abroad, urging governments to act decisively. The swift rise of the 'rights movement' for Roma can therefore be read as a response to the violence and hostility against Roma that grew in the early 1990s in the region, and the inability of the post-socialist States to respond effectively.

Secondly, the repudiation of state socialism, and the gradual erosion of attendant institutional structures in the 1980s, resulted in an ideological (as well as a material) vacuum. How this ideological space was filled is itself a complex narrative vis-à-vis the adoption of liberal human rights ideologies in the region. Former dissidents who had been vocal opponents of one-party rule in the previous regime, quickly adopted a liberal politics embracing classical Northern (or Western) human rights concerns rooted primarily in civil and political rights and a 'rule-of-law' framework modelled on the American and British experience (Carothers 1997; Guilhot 2005; Mutua 2002; Welch 2001). One example of the hegemony of the new liberal human rights ethos is how freedom of speech and political association came to be valued over the right to housing or employment at this time (during the 1990s).[10] Hence economic and social rights became either divorced from – or took a back seat to – this neoliberal human rights framework adopted within the broader context of the globalizing and increasingly capitalist economies of the region. Arguably, these very same practices – emanating from the liberal human rights paradigm – have done a disservice to those subaltern groups in Europe who continue to suffer the most severe forms of social deprivation.

In addition, strong anti-communist ideological impulses were also present, particularly amongst American private foundations and these were reflected in the interventions of key human rights entrepreneurs who had links to the broader Washington Consensus (e.g. Aryeh Neier of OSI (Open Society Institute), formerly of Human Rights Watch and Deborah Harding, formerly of the OSI and German Marshall Fund). Other US-based foundations such as the Project on Ethnic Relations (PER), led by Livia Plaks, explicitly emphasized 'security issues' in post-socialist Europe in their work (cf. Guglielmo and Waters 2005). Here, the role of key Western human rights entrepreneurs and their Eastern 'disciples' or partners was pivotal in setting the policy agendas on Romani communities, firstly in Eastern Europe, but then influencing the Western European discourse and policy as well (especially after EU accession of the post-socialist states). Connected to the point above about the ideological vacuum, and how it was filled by a particular brand of neoliberalism in post-socialist countries, the material means necessary to conduct 'rights' work became readily available[11] as Western philanthropic organizations and private donors (primarily, though not exclusively, from the United States) supported NGOs whose philosophies conformed to their own neoliberal ideologies about progress through 'democratization' – which for them meant an emphasis on strengthening the emerging civil society and human rights standards (Chandhoke 2003; Guilhot 2005; Trehan 2009).[12]

Furthermore, the increasing disillusionment of progressive Romani representatives with mainstream political parties and national electoral politics – particularly after 1995 – buttressed the role of the NGOs as vehicles for the promotion of the human rights of Roma. Therefore, the appeal of the NGO sector in post-socialist Europe is an organic result of the failure of the political integration of Romani politicians and representatives in mainstream political parties (Kovats 1998; Trehan 1999; Guy 2001; Vermeersch 2006). In other words, the careers (or interventions) of nearly all Romani politicians at the national level within their respective parliaments – particularly after the mid-1990s – have been fragile and contentious, with most elected (or party list selected) officials leaving after only one-term in office (see also Vermeersch 2006: 106–113; Sobotka 2003). Many were not invited to continue into a second term, and by the mid-1990s, the initial euphoria over the pluralistic democratic 'transition' began to wane considerably as the rise of ethno-nationalism became increasingly visible in Central and Eastern Europe, and Romani candidates came to be viewed as 'liabilities' to mainstream party electoral tickets rather than 'assets'.

Hence, Romani activists and intellectuals viewed civil society, and more specifically, the NGO sector, as an alternative arena in which to air their grievances and to influence the public sphere. Concomitantly, and even more fortuitously for some (who eventually reached top positions within the sector), Western philanthropic organizations interested in democracy promotion and strengthening civil society arrived in Central and Eastern Europe at this very time to support the development of NGOs (cf. Guilhot 2005; Trehan 2001). Their financial largesse and ideological capital was considerable, and by the late 1990s, the NGO sector, particularly as promoted by George Soros in the region, came to rival that of the State in terms of influence, especially in the area of Romani integration issues. All these factors ultimately led to the 'NGOization' of Roma rights.

To be sure, many of the post-socialist regimes did enact new (and in some cases, comprehensive) legislation on minority protections (drafted to a large extent with the aid and encouragement of Western legal consultants), and promoted minority cultures in media, culture and education (also with Western models in mind), and particular to the Hungarian case, created a system of minority self-representation (Kovats 1998, 2001; Guilhot 2005). This was part of a conscious effort at this time to conform to the Copenhagen Criteria and the EU accession agreements which mandated stronger protections for primarily civil and political rights. However, these emerged in two phases: first, under the influence of the American neoliberal ('Washington consensus') agenda, and secondly, with the arrival of the 'Europeanization' agenda (harmonization with EU). Nonetheless, this new politics revolving around liberal policy ideals embraced by former anti-communist dissidents proved far less effective at curbing anti-Gypsy racism and nationalist tendencies within society, than those of the previous Socialist regime (cf. Žižek 2005).

With respect to the influence of the Europeanization agenda, one astute observer had this to say about the impact of EU human rights accession framework on the Romani movement back in 2001:

> [T]he Romani issue is generally not understood on the ground as one of systemic human rights violations, and is rather only seen as an imposed condition for admission to the EU. I am concerned that this results in a situation in which our issues are addressed only out of a fear of exclusion from the EU, and therefore that solutions devised may never be efficient and may never address the real roots of the problem. That is, EU pressure may possibly create a new obstacle in the struggle (Kóczé 2001: 28).

The problems related to the rising precariousness of Romani citizens in post-socialist countries had a 'domino effect' on Western European

EU states as well. Here, the example of Italy is instructive, whereby the dislocation of thousands of Romanian Romani migrants has resulted in massive anti-Gypsy rhetoric which under Berlusconi has reached new heights with the *'emergenza rom'* (Romani emergency) directives (cf. Sigona and Guy in this volume). In other countries such as Germany, Austria, Holland, France, and the UK, the influx of Romani refugees from the Balkan wars and the xenophobic racial assaults in Czech Republic generated severe anti-Gypsy hostilities (cf. Guy 2001; Castle-Kanerova 2001; Matras 2000; Cahn and Guild 2008). These were among the primary factors that combined to make the scapegoating of Roma once again salient in post-socialist countries, thereby laying the groundwork for anti-Gypsy racism across Europe.

One offshoot of the hegemony of the liberal 'anti-discrimination' frame promoted by INGOs has been the discursive shift from 'Gypsy problem' to 'Roma rights' in mainstream European discourse. However, as my doctoral work demonstrated, this in itself was not an indicator of parallel changes in practices related to the treatment of Romani communities on the ground (Trehan 2009). The discursive changes were limited to the level of 'elite discourse', and functioned to conceal exclusionary practices at the societal level, and this gap between discourse and practise was particularly evident at the time of the European accession process (see also Simhandl in this volume). Moreover, with respect to developments in many countries of Western Europe, there was a clear preference for a self-construction of 'receiving' country for Romani migrations, despite the fact that nearly all countries have long established indigenous Romani communities whose condition is systematically kept out of the spotlight in order to legitimize the human rights/humanitarian discourse as a tool for influencing Central and East European states and regulating Romani migration (cf. Sigona in this volume).

Conclusion: listening to the Romani subaltern

The discussion above on the impact of neoliberalism and the resulting forms of structural oppression of Europe's Romani citizens – even within the realm of civil society – has highlighted the importance of understanding the limitations of the contemporary rights movement for Roma. The extreme example of the ethnic cleansing of

Roma in Kosovo witnessed by the International Community that literally 'watched on' as thousands of Roma lost their homes and livelihoods in the province highlights the structural weaknesses and vulnerabilities of Romani political efficacy today (cf. Mustafa and Salijevic interview, chapter 10). Who speaks for Roma in times of war? Who leads Romani communities in times of crisis (such as the socio-economic deprivation of today)? Who lobbies for them politically? Who offers guidance for a better future for Romani children? Certainly the past two decades of the NGO sector's interventions have been placed in doubt, and the liminal political spaces occupied by the few Romani individuals in mainstream governmental offices may not be influential enough to render any real structural changes within their respective polities.

Gramsci (2001), writing about the Italian polity of the 1920s, contrasted 'organic intellectuals' from primarily bourgeois backgrounds who had close links to their communities and were determined to organize them, with 'traditional intellectuals' (scientists, writers, religious orders, government, etc.) who continued to serve the ruling class as part of the dominant order. Citing the importance of organic intellectuals who would also emerge from working class backgrounds, Gramsci (1971) noted that 'the mode of being of the new intellectual can no longer consist in eloquence...but in active participation in practical life, as constructor, organiser, "permanent persuader" and not just a simple orator' (10). With respect to the emerging Romani movement, we see the rise of organic intellectuals from various ideological trajectories and broader national (Czech, German, Hungarian, Romanian, etc.) traditions; crucially, all share the common goal of organizing their communities to bring about social justice (Horváth 1999; Kawczynski 1999; Kóczé 1999; Kwiek 2008; Vesely 2005; Zoltan 2006). Moreover, even the few organic intellectuals amongst Roma who work in conventional intellectual professions such as academia or the law maintain strong linkages and share active responsibilities in their home communities. Within the Romani communities of post-socialist Europe, some of these organic intellectuals offer resistance to conventional neoliberal narratives generated within the NGO sphere, even as they may simultaneously work in the mainstream NGO or political sector. Nonetheless, their voices do not generally gain prominence at the European level, nor amongst institutional structures at the national level.

The 'NGOization' of human rights has been a key phenomenon in subordinating Romani voices 'from below', as many urban NGOs in the central and east European region have been structured along hierarchical, top-down models based on, for example, prominent Western NGOs subscribing to neoliberal interpretations of human rights (cf. Trehan 2009). Even if the subaltern can speak – as Spivak's (1988) provocative, rhetorical refrain reminds us – *who is listening?* Particularly in the case of the Romani victim or survivor of human rights abuse, her voice, her perspective and her vision for justice is many times missing today within the field of 'Roma rights' as too often, these are 'interpreted' for her by a human rights entrepreneur, legal expert, NGO worker or other person in a position of authority (cf. Bukovská 2006; Woodiwiss 2006; Zoltan 2006). This applies also to the movement as a whole, and this point was re-iterated by Dusan Ristic (2001), a Romani artist and activist from Serbia when he noted at a roundtable in Budapest reflecting on the Romani movement ten years after its inception:

> On a larger level, the Romani movement does not exist. To the extent that the movement does exist on the European level, it is full of outside influences. To be honest, in reality to me it looks more as if non-Romani people are presently making the Romani movement, with the participation of some Roma. So the Romani movement, in my opinion has an artificial (unnatural) appearance.... I think we need to change this situation.... It is time to start to build the Romani movement from the bottom up, with our own initiatives and resources. We need a lot of small-scale initiatives and all of them together will give us a signal as to the direction or directions we have to go. Of course we need to work together. But one more time I have to say the initiatives must be led by Roma, because only that way are we going to have a real shape and see our power and weaknesses. We will see what is reality.... Right now ... I don't see a Romani movement.... I believe that in 20 or 30 years we will have a Romani movement built mainly by Romani people. (2001: 22–23)

As my research confirmed, the bulk of reports, statistics and other forms of literature on policy vis-à-vis Roma (the 'raw materials' of discursive production) are generated by academics, governmental bodies and NGOs external to the Romani communities, with minimal or only symbolic input from Romani representatives themselves (Trehan 2009). This fact alone suggests the (re)emergence and (re)consolidation of asymmetries of knowledge-power (cf. Foucault 1972–1977; 1979) within post-socialist European civil society, suggesting as well the heightened potential for the perpetuation of 'epistemic violence' (cf. Spivak 1988), and this has profound implications for the autonomy and future of the 'Roma rights' movement itself (Trehan 2001; Trehan and Kóczé 2009).

This chapter has been a reflection on the genesis of 'Roma rights', and in particular, how it has been framed by the broader exigencies of neoliberalism and its impact on European civil society. It offered a critical assessment of the limitations of this particular framework for the rights movement. Whilst many elite actors in the movement justify their interventions on the basis of normative goals such as equality and non-discrimination for Romani Europeans, the actual practices emerging from a neoliberal approach to fostering civil and political rights for Roma leave too many troubling questions unanswered. Current human rights practices may actually be placing limits on the achievement of social equality as they do not offer possibilities for re-structuring power in society, and moreover, replicate hierarchies within European society (mirroring a type of structurally embedded oppression of Roma). Hence Romani people remain effectively cut off from active, participatory citizenship, trapped in symbiotic cycles of disadvantage and political muteness.

As detailed above, the NGO-led civil rights movement in the region has in many ways not addressed the core socio-economic issues of the Romani communities in part because the neoliberal discourse around which human rights issues are framed in Eastern Europe has neglected (and in some cases, been dismissive of) the importance of economic justice. In part, this may have stemmed from the new liberal, post-socialist nomenclatura's scepticism with older (and discredited) forms of political economy, that is, policy conceptualizations which considered workers' rights and reducing socio-economic inequalities. However, as mentioned above, this was also engineered to an extent by transatlantic neoliberals (and their Eastern European counterparts) who wished the region to develop according to their normative standards of 'liberal democratic capitalism'.

As progressive activists within the women's global emancipation movement emphasize, 'gender, race and class analysis is…essential to both understanding the impacts of neoliberal policies and for developing alternative policies that put sustainable development and human rights ahead of profits' (AWID 2005). What is needed, therefore, is a holistic analysis of the contemporary rights movement for Romani communities, an analysis that accounts for Romani diversity in Europe through an emphasis on privileging local level knowledge, as well as an emphasis on socio-economic justice as a central pillar within the contemporary human rights framework. This analysis would in turn contribute to making sound policy decisions with the input of Romani citizens themselves in the areas of education, employment, health care and childcare – all key areas where the human rights movement for Roma can have an emancipatory and transformative impact.

While the proliferation of projects within the actually existing 'Roma Rights' sector has become an important source of income for many NGO workers and entrepreneurs in Eastern Europe, it is also leading to a new kind of dependency for Romani subalterns within civil society. The marketization of 'Roma rights' has taken on a logic of its own, which in many cases is disconnected from the diverse needs of Romani communities. In addition, issues of accountability, transparency and the participation of Romani interlocutors (forming a diversity of social actors from activists to human rights victims to subjects of human rights litigation) are still contested sites within the *realpolitik* of human rights (Trehan 2001; cf. Rostas in this volume).

NGOs and the neoliberal human rights entrepreneurs who run them have became established forces for the putative promotion of the rights of Roma in Europe, and to some extent, they act as an alternative power base to that of the state-funded institutions and public foundations. Nevertheless, some of the classical normative distinctions in this 'emancipatory' human rights sphere seem to have been lost: between that of corporate versus public interests (for example, the interest of the World Bank in the Romani minority, and its programme 'The Decade of Roma Inclusion' with the Open

Society Institute and the EU (cf. Templer 2006)); the classic critique of colonizing interventions and exploitation of vulnerable communities; and the distinctions between grassroots mobilization and elite (vertical) power structures. All these issues revolving around discursive constructions, power and resistance in the human rights field are as vital to examine today in the heart of Europe as they were in the colonized 'Third World' over fifty years ago.

Notes

1. This chapter is based upon some of the theoretical insights and empirical findings of my own PhD work 'Human rights entrepreneurship in post-socialist Hungary: from 'Gypsy problem' to 'Roma rights' (2009).
2. 'Civil society' generally incorporates NGOs and non-profits, and broadly encompasses political parties, labour unions, workers' cooperatives, business associations, membership-serving organizations and religious bodies amongst other actors in society.
3. Canadian anthropologist Scheffel (2004) typifies this ethos when he ruefully points to the lack of volunteerism amongst Roma in eastern Slovakian ghettoes living in extremely deprived circumstances. This is symptomatic of a kind of 'middle-class' values projection upon particular communities which are racialized in this manner by Western anthropologists, who, along with other social scientists, subconsciously project their biases and fears, as well as their ideologies and value systems upon Romani communities whose lifeworlds they seek to make sense of.
4. See further the work of Kovats (1998), Vermeersch (2006) and Trehan (2009) for details on the political experiences of these earlier activists, as well as the constraints they faced within the new INGO-influenced arena.
5. See Zoltan (2006) and Trehan and Kóczé (2009).
6. This has been true of NGO development in Central and Eastern Europe. Little comparable work has been done regarding Romani NGO development in Western Europe; see Matras (1998) on Germany, Sigona (2006) on Italy and Gheorghe and Acton (2001). Hancock (1991) offers an insightful analysis for why Eastern Europe has historically been a fertile ground for Romani political mobilization; see further Nirenberg in this collection.
7. This insight on the institutionalization of 'causes' taken up by human rights entrepreneurs (see further Trehan 2009) seems to be a lacuna within the mainstream social movement literature, which tends to overlook or diminish these critical developments in the contemporary NGO sector (Fowler 1997; Ghosh 2006; Slater 2004).
8. I had the privilege of working for the IAF's Southwest division, headed up by Ernesto Cortes (a prominent disciple of Alinsky). I saw firsthand how schools, churches and unions, as well as community-based organizations

in working class communities could organize in the face of tremendous structural obstacles, not least of which was the growth of neoliberal policies. I witnessed the unfolding of leadership development skills amongst some of the poorest (Latino) communities in South Texas (cf. Warren 2001). This experience convinced me that there were clear alternatives to the ERRC's current model of human rights activism and organizing amongst Romani communities.

9. In addition, human rights lawyers and reformers on the police and judiciary took an early lead in demanding greater protections of minorities from the State.
10. There had been a well pronounced split in conceptualizations of 'human rights' between the Soviet Union and the American models – in the former, emphasis was placed on social and economic rights, whilst in the latter, civil and political rights took precedence. This was visible in early negotiations at the CSCE (OSCE; Organization for Security and Co-operation in Europe) as well (from the 1970s) between the USSR and Western countries, and in the United Nations as well (cf. Mutua 2002).
11. See further Diani and McAdam (2003) for an evaluation of resource mobilization theory and the nexus between how resources are accessed and mobilized and the emergence of social movements.
12. Here the umbrella term 'democratization' refers to the establishment and formalized functioning of civil society that aspires to be independent from the state. In addition, the term is also applied to state organs themselves. For an excellent discussion on the fluidity of this concept, see Carothers (1997).

References

Alinsky, S. D. (1946) *Reveille for Radicals*, Chicago: University of Chicago Press.

Alinsky, S. D. (1971) *Rules for Radicals*, New York: Vintage.

Association for Women's Rights in Development (AWID) (2003) 'Ten principles for challenging neoliberal globalization', *Women's Rights and Economic Change*, 6, December.

Bourdieu, P. (1998) 'The essence of neoliberalism', *Le Monde Diplomatique*, December, http://mondediplo.com/1998/12/08bourdieu

Bukovská, B. (2005) 'Dignitati memores, as optima intenti...? Some reflections on the human dimension of human rights work', *Human Rights and Public Interest Law Fellows Retreat*, Open Society Institute, 26–29 January, Cairo, Egypt, unpublished mimeo.

Cahn, C. and Guild, E. (2008) *Recent Migration of Roma in Europe*, Wien and Strasbourg: OSCE High Commissioner on National Minorities and Council of Europe Commissioner for Human Rights.

Calhoun, C. (1992) (ed.) *Habermas and the Political Sphere, Cambridge*, MA: MIT Press.

Carothers, T. (1997) 'Democracy assistance: the question of strategy' *Democratization*, 4(3), Autumn: 109–132.

Castle-Kaněrová, M. (2001) 'Romani Refugees: the EU Dimension', Guy, W. (ed.) *The Roma in Post-Communist Europe*, Hatfield: University of Hertfordshire Press.

Chandhoke, N. (2003) *The Conceits of Civil Society*, Oxford: Oxford University Press.

Chen, T. and Churchill, D. (2005) 'Neoliberal Civilization and the Economic Disciplining of Human Rights: Convergence of Models in the US and China', *Rhizomes*, issue 10, accessible online at www.rhizomes.net/issue10/chen.htm

Clark, N. (2003) 'George Soros, a profile', *New Statesman*, 2 June 2003.

Cohen, J. L. and Arato, A. (1992) *Civil Society and Political Theory*, Cambridge: MIT Press.

Cox, R. W. (1999) 'Civil society at the turn of the millennium: prospects for an alternative world order', *Review of International Studies*, 25(1): 7.

Diani, M. and McAdam, D. (2003) *Social Movements and Networks: Relational Approaches to Collective Action*, Oxford: Oxford UP.

Foucault, M. (1972–1977) *Power/Knowledge: Selected Interviews and Other Writings*, New York: Pantheon.

Foucault, M. (1979) *The Will to Knowledge: History of Sexuality, Volume One*, London: Penguin.

Fowler, A. (1997) *Striking a Balance: A Guide to Enhancing the Effectiveness of Non-Governmental Organizations in International Development*, London: Earthscan.

Fox-Piven F. and Cloward, R. (1977) *Poor People's Movements: Why They Succeed, How They Fail*, New York, Pantheon.

Fraser, N. (1992) 'Rethinking the public sphere: a contribution to the critique of actually existing democracy', Calhoun, C. (ed.) *Habermas and the public sphere, Cambridge*, MA: MIT Press.

Gheorghe, N. and Acton, T. (2001) 'Citizens of the world and nowhere: minority, ethnic and human rights for Roma', in Guy, W. (ed.) *Between Past and Future: The Roma of Central and Eastern Europe*, Hatfield: University of Hertfordshire Press.

Ghosh, S. (2006) Review of 'Social Movements: An Introduction by D. Della Porta and M. Diani', *Development and Change*, 38 (4): 771–772.

Gill, S. (2003) *Power and Resistance in the New World Order*, London: Palgrave Macmillan.

Gramsci, A. (1971) *Selections from the Prison Notebooks of Antonio Gramsci*, Q. Hoare and G. Nowell Smith (eds), New York: International Publishers.

Gramsci, A. (2001) 'State and Civil Society', *Selections from the Prison Notebooks*, (trans.) Q. Hoare, New York: International Publishers, http://www.marxists.org/archive/gramsci/prison_notebooks/state_civil/index.htm.

Guglielmo, R. and Waters, T. (2005) 'Migrating towards minority status: shifting European policy towards Roma', *Journal of Common Market Studies*, 43(4): 763–86.

Guilhot, N. (2005) *The Democracy Makers: Human Rights and International Order*, New York City: Columbia University Press.

Guy, W. (2001) *Between Past and Future: The Roma of Eastern Europe*, Hatfield: University of Hertfordshire Press.

Habermas, J. (1992) 'Further Reflections on the Public Sphere', Calhoun, C. (ed.) *Habermas and the Public Sphere*, Cambridge, MA: MIT Press.

Hancock, I. (1991) 'The East European roots of Romani nationalism', in D. Crowe and J. Kolsti (eds) *The Gypsies of Eastern Europe*, New York: ME Sharpe.

Horváth, A. (2000) 'The Future of the Romani Movement: What Shape? What Direction?' *Roma Rights Day* special roundtable, Central European University, 8 December, unpublished speech.

Human Rights Watch (1993), *Struggling for Ethnic Identity: the Roma of Hungary*, New York.

Human Rights Watch (1996), Rights Denied: the Roma of Hungary, New York.

Jacobs, R. (2000) *Race, Media, and the Crisis of the Civil Society*, Cambridge: Cambridge University Press.

Kawczynski, R. (1997) 'The Politics of Romani Politics', *Transitions*, 4 (4), available at http://www.geocities.com/~patrin/politics.htm

Keane, J. (1995) 'Structural transformations of the public sphere', *The Communication Review*, 1(1): 1–22.

Keane, J. (1998) *Civil Society: Old Images, New Visions*, Cambridge: Cambridge University Press.

Kóczé, A. (1999) 'Taking control of our identity', *Roma Rights*, 3: 69.

Kóczé, A. (2001) 'The Romani movement: what shape, what direction?' *Roma Rights* no. 4, accessible online at http://www.errc.org/cikk.php?cikk=769

Kovats, M. (1998) *The Development of Roma Politics in Hungary 1989–1995*, PhD thesis, University of Portsmouth.

Kovats, M. (2001) 'Hungary: politics, difference and equality', in Guy, W. (ed.) *Between Past and Future: the Roma of Central and Eastern Europe*, Hatfield: University of Hertfordshire Press.

Kwiek, G. (2008) *Any Rom Will Do? The Processes of Implementation & Recruitment in the Struggle for Roma Inclusion*, B.A. dissertation, Department of Ethnology, Stockholm: University of Stockholm.

Lang, S. (1997) 'The NGOization of feminism', in Kaplan, C., Keates, S. and Wallach Scott, J. (eds) *Transitions, Environments, and Translations: Feminisms in International Politics*, London: Routledge.

Matras, Y. (1998) 'The development of the Romani civil rights movement in Germany 1945–1996' in Tebbutt, S. (ed.) *Sinti and Roma in German-speaking society and literature*. Oxford: Berghahn.

Matras, Y. (2000) 'Romani migrations in the post-Communist era: their historical and political significance', *Cambridge Review of International Affairs*, 13(2), Spring-Summer: 32–50.

Mutua, M. (2002) *Human Rights: A Political and Cultural Critique*, Philadelphia: University of Pennsylvania Press.

Scheffel, D. (2004) *Svinia in Black and White: Slovak Roma and their neigh-bours*, Toronto: Broadview Press.

Sigona, N. (2006) (ed.) *Political participation and media representation of Roma and Sinti in Italy*, Florence: OsservAzione/OSCE, http://www.osservazione. org/documenti/osce_italy.pdf.

Slater, D. (2004) *Geo-politics and the Post-Colonial: Re-thinking North-South Relations*, Oxford: Blackwell Publishing.

Speder, Z. (2001) 'Poverty dynamics in Hungary during the transformation', *Transformations in Hungary: Essays in Economy and Society*, Heidelberg: Physica-Verlag.

Spivak, G. (1988) 'Can the Subaltern speak?', Nelson, C. and Grossberg, L. (eds) *Marxism and the Interpretation of Culture*, Urbana: University of Illinois Press: 271-313.

Stubbs, P. (2007) 'Community development in contemporary Croatia: globalization, neoliberalization, and NGO-isation', in Dominelli, L. (ed.) *Revitalising Communities*, Aldhershot: Ashgate Press.

Templer, B. (2006) 'Neoliberal strategies to defuse a powder keg in Europe: the '"Decade of Roma Inclusion" and its rationale', *New Politics*, 10(4), Online Journal, available at http://www.wpunj.edu/~newpol/issue40/ Templer40.htm

Trehan, N. (1999) 'The vicissitudes of Romani rights: racism, legal reform and popular discontent', paper presented to the *Rights, Identities, and Communities of the European Union Conference* at University of Leeds (Law Department & Centre for the Study of Law in Europe), UACES, 30 April.

Trehan, N. (2001) 'In the name of the Roma? The role of private foundations and NGOs' in Guy, W. (ed.) *Between Past and Future: the Roma of Central and Eastern Europe*. [citation information for the book?]

Trehan, N. (2006) 'The genesis of "Roma rights" in contemporary Europe: the "public interest" and (neo)liberal global order', *Human Rights: Genesis and Justification*, workshop by Irmgard Coninx Foundation/Max Weber Center for Advanced Social and Cultural Studies, Berlin/Erfurt, 27 April–1 May, unpublished mimeo.

Trehan, N. (2009) *Human Rights Entrepreneurship in Post-Socialist Hungary: From 'Gypsy Problem' to 'Roma Rights,'* London School of Economics and Political Science, unpublished thesis.

Trehan, N. and Kóczé, A. (2009) 'Racism, (neo)colonialism, and social justice: the struggle for the soul of the Romani movement in post-socialist Europe', in Huggan, G. and Law, I., *Racism Postcolonialism Europe*, Liverpool: Liverpool UP.

Vermeersch, P. (2005) 'Marginality, advocacy, and the ambiguities of multiculturalism: notes on Romani activism in Central Europe', *Identities: Global Studies in Culture and Power*, 12: 451–478.

Vermeersch, P. (2006) *The Romani Movement*, London: Bergahn.

Vesely, I. (2005) 'Where are the Romani organizations?', *Transitions Online*, February 3, http://www.tol.cz/look/TOL/article.tpl?IdLanguage=1&IdPubl ication=4&NrIssue=101&NrSection=2&NrArticle=13467.

Warren, M. (2001) *Dry Bones Rattling: Community Building to Revitalise American Democracy*, Princeton: Princeton University Press.

Welch, C. (2001) NGOs and *Human Rights: Promise and Performance*, Philadelphia: University of Pennsylvania Press.

Woodiwiss, A. (2006) 'The law cannot be enough: human rights and the limits of legalism', in Meckled-Garcia, S. and Çali, B. (eds) *The Legalisation of Human Rights*.

Žižek, S. (2005) 'Against Human Rights', *New Left Review*, 34, July/August. Available at http://www.newleftreview.org/?view=2573

Zoltan, F. (2006) 'Citizens or denizens? The future of Romani integration in Europe', Panel presentation, London School of Economics, *Centre for the Study of Human Rights* and *Central London Europe Group (CLEG)*, June.

4

Beyond Boundaries? Comparing the Construction of the Political Categories 'Gypsies' and 'Roma' Before and After EU Enlargement

Katrin Simhandl

> What is familiarly known is not properly known, just for the reason that it is 'familiar'.
>
> (Georg Wilhelm Friedrich Hegel)

Introduction

The situation of Roma in Europe is the subject of prominent discussions within the institutions of the European Union today, proving those voices that expected the 'Roma issue' to fade away from the political agenda after EU enlargement wrong. Since the EU enlargement to include Central and Eastern European states, the European Parliament (EP) passes resolutions every year calling upon the European Commission and the Member States to improve the situation of Roma (EP 2005, 2006, 2007 and 2008).

Upon the request of the European Council (2007), the European Commission examined its policies and instruments with respect to Roma (European Commission 2008). An EU high-level group of experts analysed the situation of ethnic minorities with respect to social inclusion and in its consequent report, focussed on the situation of Roma in particular (High Level Advisory Group of Experts 2007). Moreover, the Commission set up an internet platform[1] in 2006 informing the public about the institution's Roma related activities and organized, together with the French Presidency, a European Roma Summit in September 2008. Furthermore, it was over the Roma topic that the extreme-right EP political group 'Identity, Tradition, Sovereignty' (ITS) split up, following offensive remarks by Alessandra Mussolini, a member of the group, in November 2007.[2]

The question therefore remains whether any changes in debating these matters can be observed since enlargement, and if so, what kind of changes. Taking a discourse analytical approach which examines the 'politics of representation' (Shapiro 1988), the analysis reveals that the EU discourse on Roma has consists of three phases: a first phase – largely overlooked – began in the 1970s, a second phase commenced with the eastwards enlargement process in the late 1990s, and finally, the present one began with the implementation of EU enlargement. While looking for shifts as well as continuities in the EU debate on Roma matters, it is essential to include all three phases in the analysis.[3]

What language tells us: a discourse analytical approach

Taking a post-positivist approach, I fundamentally call into question what is usually taken for granted in the discourse under investigation. Accordingly, I do not take the category of 'Roma' as an unchallenged starting point for further considerations. Rather than taking 'categories of practice as categories of analysis' (Brubaker 1996: 15), and thereby subscribing to a 'realism of the group' (Brubaker 1998: 292), this chapter explores precisely the process of constructing this category. It aims to tear 'realities' off their quasi-evident nature (Foucault 1969), making visible what is usually too visible to be seen.[4]

Based on the ontological assumption that the social world is not externally and objectively given, but constructed through a process of human interaction (Rorty 1989), the analysis focuses on language as the most important means in this process. Language is not simply a mechanical transmission belt linking the physical and the social worlds. Hence, as Connolly suggests, the 'language of politics is not a neutral medium that conveys ideas independently formed; it is an institutionalised structure of meanings that channels political thought and action in certain directions' (1974: 1). In the course of language interaction, the structure of meaning evolves. Discourse, as used here, is understood as the articulation of a specific set of ideas and categorizations that evolve around a central concept that itself is developed through the discourse.[5] Discourses are generated in particular social, economic and political contexts and therefore reflect the power and policy of the times, in other words they are not generated in a vacuum. Taking such a theoretical approach, the chapter is interested in the way a political category is generated by language.

Revealing the unspoken assumption of the discourse

The most obvious result of the analysis, and frequently not even realized, is that discourse is constituted by an unspoken assumption: the category of 'Gypsies', 'Roma' or whatever term is used, is taken for granted. This assumption remains largely unarticulated, but must necessarily be shared for the statements that constitute the discourse as a whole to be meaningful. Regardless of what terminology is used, it is beyond doubt that the category *per se* exists and can be clearly distinguished from others. Consequently, a decision is possible on whether a person is to be assigned to this category or another. The process of assigning people to a category is, however, not articulated, so that the difficulties that arise from this are hidden from sight.

The unspoken agreement to treat 'Roma'/'Gypsies' as an objective category is the foundational moment of the discourse, and the preservation of this category is decisive. Consequently, any challenge to the existence of this category itself represents a challenge to the discourse as a whole. To prevent the discourse from being put at risk, such lines of argumentation must be silenced: the 'limits and boundaries of a particular discourse are established by the exclusion of a discursive exteriority that threatens the discourse in question' (Torfing 1999: 43). The success of such a procedure determines the persistence of the discourse. It is therefore no accident that only one articulation can be found in the relevant EU documents that calls into question the essentialist nature of the category by stating that attempts 'to analyse the specific features of this ethnic group run into problems of definition [...] since there is no objective category for deciding who is and who is not a member of the Romany population' (European Commission and Government of Hungary 2003: 10). In only one interview during my research, did a Commission official question the essentialist assumption thus: 'One of the difficult things about the whole Roma issue is of course what and who is [a] Roma. [...] It's not so black and white being a Roma' (Post 2004). Despite this ontological problem, however, the category forms the basis on which political instruments such as action programmes are built. These run into trouble if the category as a whole is challenged.[6]

The most obvious example of how the idea of Roma as an objective category manifests itself in the discourse is the *strategy of numbering*, that is, the ubiquitous search for numbers, data and facts about the purported 'object.' It is only the shared assumption that 'Roma' form an objective category that allows – and at the same time requires – the search for the objective facts constituting this category. This demand for facts was present at the very beginning of the EU institutions' 'discovery' of 'Gypsies' in the 1970s when a Member of the European Parliament (MEP) asked the Commission:

> Does the Commission know: (a) how many itinerant people there are in the Community? (b) whether they are concentrated in any particular countries or regions and what origins they have? (c) what nationalities they have and whether they have any problems in relation to nationality? (d) to what extent they benefit from social services in the Member States? (Kavanagh 1975)

And this fact-finding mission has been ongoing ever since. In 2007, the EU's Agency for Fundamental Rights (FRA), for example, complained about the lack of statistics on ethnic origin in the EU Member States (FRA 2007: 49–50).

In this line of thinking, the fact-finding bias and the turning of human subjects into objects of discourse go hand in hand.[7] Thus, in the early days of EU discourse formation, knowledge was to be gathered *about* 'Gypsies,' not *from* them. For example, Jean-Pierre Liégeois, a consultant on Roma matters for the Commission for some 20 years, stressed that there are special 'Gypsy education methods' within the Romani community and that finding out more about these methods 'is a task for ethnographers' (Liégeois 1987: 160). Making the people themselves participants in the discourse by asking *them* about such issues was not even considered as an option at that time. Instead of a communicative *interaction* between different kinds of political actors, Gypsies/Roma were written out of the discourse as potential partners, making it a discourse exclusively among different EU institutions. This discursive pattern has only recently begun to change.

The interpretative pattern of the early phase of discourse: 'nomadism – the relevance of a lifestyle'

On closer examination of the discourse, it emerges that below the general level mentioned above, there are shared, but changing, premises guiding it. Indeed, analysis reveals that there are three phases of discourse within the EU discourse on Roma, each of them guided by different interpretative patterns.

In the first phase, starting with the emergence of the 'Gypsy'/'Roma' topic in the context of the European institutions in the 1970s, the discourse was structured around the category of geographic mobility. 'Nomadism' was the dimension that enabled and at the same time limited the trajectory of the discourse.

Most tellingly, this interpretative pattern reveals itself from the labels used to name the central category of discourse during its gradual emergence from the inchoate mass of the overall societal discourse: in the mid-1970s, MEPs started to raise an issue, that centred on a category diffusely named 'itinerants,' 'travelling people' [*sic*], 'gypsies' [*sic*] and to a lesser extent also 'nomads' or combinations of these terms. Of course, none of these designations was coined by the actors under investigation themselves; all of them were taken from broader discourses in society.

Two of these designations – 'traveller' and 'itinerant' – refer, in their literal sense, to a social phenomenon: a mobile way of life. These people travel and can consequently be contrasted with 'settled people,' as for example MEP Desmond (1991) did. In this sense, everyone who lives a Traveller's lifestyle can be named a 'traveller.' But the terms 'traveller' and 'itinerant' carry a second dimension of significance: they may also imply historical depth, applying only to people whose travelling way of life is understood as traditional.

The semantic multidimensionality of the terms 'traveller' and 'itinerant' became relevant within the discourse itself: when the Commission was questioned on the progress of a project on 'itinerants,' the Commission explained that it was a 'project on the rehabilitation of itinerants' and that 'this project is not concerned with itinerant communities such as the gypsies [*sic*] but with individuals without a settled way of life, mainly single men' (Answer of the Commission to Kavanagh 1978). The difference imposed here is that the former live an itinerant way of life in a social group, whereas the others do so individually, implying that individual itinerants should not be part of the central category of discourse. Using the very same formulation of 'rehabilitation of itinerants', another MEP, O'Connell (1980), again combined both categories, before the category of individual itinerants was finally banished outside the boundaries of the discourse.

Utilizing the term 'gypsies' [*sic*], the EU discourse employed a widely shared linguistic usage. Although different derivations of the term are offered in the literature, it is beyond dispute that it is an exonym, a name imposed by people who do not consider themselves to belong to the group. Thus, the term also imposes boundaries on the group from the outside. While these boundaries are conceptualized in different ways, most of the time little evidence is provided as to where they are drawn from. As a result, the central category of discourse remains indefinite in shape: 'There seems to be a *communis opinio* about who they are' (Willems 1998: 17).[8] The general silence regarding the *criteria* employed to determine the course of the category's boundary corresponds to the unspoken assumption that an objective category exists. As the underlying assumption that 'Gypsies' (as well as 'Roma') form an essentialist category is not revealed, neither do the criteria for distinguishing this category from others need to be disclosed. The assumption that agreement exists on who is and who is not a 'Gypsy' can only be sustained by an eloquent silence on this issue, which itself offers the basis for the perpetuation of this *communis opinio.*

Another expression, adopted in the discourse in the mid-1980s, was people 'with no fixed abode' (EP 1984). This expression, taken from different national legal contexts, was used in the drafting process for a resolution that was initially intended to deal with 'educational problems of circus and fair children' (Hoff, Viehoff and Malangré 1982). As the drafting process continued, the group was enlarged to 'caravan dwellers'. Nomadism, as a characteristic that these groups were *assumed* to share, was seen as demanding a common policy approach. Thus, nomadism was employed to constitute a broader group: 'the educational problems confronting circus and fair children affect all children whose parents have no fixed abode. We can distinguish three categories of children within this group: children of caravan dwellers, fair and circus children and barge children' (Explanatory Statement, EP 1984).

Looking also for terms standing in opposition to the term designating the central category of discourse, it becomes clear that in the first phase of the EU discourse, hardly any contrasting terms were used. As the meaning of a word is also fixed by its complement (Williams 1999: 39), maintaining silence with regard to the complement keeps the term itself elastic. Moreover, the absence of a complement serves implicitly to keep the group in question in isolation from its surroundings: applying a contrasting term would establish a connection with the surroundings, albeit through negation.

While the heterogeneity of designations keeps the boundary flexible from the inside, the near total failure to designate what stands in opposition to the main term does the same from the outside. Together, both procedures create a conceptual border *corridor* rather than a clearly defined boundary *line* between people considered to be objects of the discourse and those who are not. Attempts were sometimes made to narrow the corridor (as shown in the case of 'itinerants' where 'individuals without a settled way of life' were moved from the border corridor to the outside of the discourse). However, a grey area remained.

While nomadism served to create categories broader than 'Gypsies,' it was at the same time emphasized as the most prominent particularity of 'Gypsies' – an element that distinguishes them from the rest of the population. In this respect, nomadism was not regarded just as 'a key element in the lifestyle of caravan dwellers', but as a fixed constant of identity, thus 'it determines not just the conditions in which they live but also their way of thinking and way of life' (Explanatory Statement, EP 1984: 9). This line of argumentation was a recurring feature of European level discourse. Liégeois for example, the long-standing advisor to the Commission already mentioned, stated in a study carried out on behalf of the Commission: 'A Traveller is someone who remains detached from his surroundings, who is able to pick up and move whenever it is useful or necessary to do so, when he needs to or simply feels like it.' He summed up: 'A Traveller – even a "housed" Traveller – is a Traveller still.' Conversely, a 'settled person,' when moving about, remains 'settled' in spirit' (Liégeois 1987: 34–35). The interpretative pattern ascribes to the object a sense of space that is entirely relative. This relativity was then generalized to an entire lifestyle (see e.g. Explanatory Statement, EP 1984: 9).

The assumed mobility of lifestyle was even more enhanced by anchoring it in history as well. In the EU discourse, as well as in the academic literature (see e.g. Braham and Braham 2000: 99), hinting to the origin of 'Gypsies' in India has regularly been the starting point of narration on this group. In line with the theoretical approach of this article it is not meant to place judgment on whether this 'fact' is 'right' or 'wrong.' It is rather telling that this origin – in which the literature suggests that the ancestors of the Roma left South Asia during the eleventh century – is still considered relevant in the context of the contemporary situation of Roma in Europe, while simultaneously, a lot of other facts and developments are skipped. Hinting to an Indian origin is consequently the result of a specific selection from a pool of historical events. It is the construction of Roma as 'immigrants,' which is selected and retold for centuries, resulting in their '"permanent migrant" status' (Guglielmo and Waters 2005: 778). The narrative implies the diagnosis that these people do not originate from 'here,' although this 'here' is itself vague and fragile. It results in a *discursive expatriation* from the home state of currently living Roma.[9]

My analysis of the first phase of the discourse suggests that mobility was in some instances regarded as the common ground on which 'Gypsies' were lumped together with other groups. But at the same time, it was the dimension of mobility, which was stressed as a special characteristic of 'Gypsies' and thereby as the decisive dimension for differentiation. While the arguments made on the basis of a mobile lifestyle, were different, sometimes even contradictory, it was the very same dimension, which was regarded to be relevant. With the beginning of EU enlargement, the dominating interpretative pattern of EU discourse changed substantially.

A new interpretative pattern arises: 'Roma – the minority in Eastern Europe'

In the mid-1990s, a second interpretative pattern developed: the term 'Roma' was increasingly used, the characterization as 'minority' gained importance, and the boundaries of the discourse were geographically re-drawn, this time, around 'Eastern Europe.' From its confines as a *niche* topic, the Roma issue now became increasingly prominent and after its incorporation in the Commission's Progress Reports in the course of enlargement, it reached the everyday political agenda of the EU.

With the emergence of the term 'Roma' in the EU institutions, a new designation appeared and gradually gained importance since the middle of the 1990s.[10] The most noticeable shift in terminology was the Commission's use of 'gypsies' [*sic*] in its opinion on the accession applications of the candidate countries in 1997 to 'Roma' in the first Regular Reports from 1998 onwards. In contrast to the formerly used exonym 'gypsy,' an endonym was now employed.[11] Adopting the endonym allows for a new mechanism in drawing the category boundaries: it provides justification for shifting responsibility for the task of boundary drawing to the designated group itself. As the term is taken from the Romani language, Roma themselves are now expected to define the extent of the term's application. The fact that no exact definition is provided by 'the Roma' is presented as an anomaly, even though struggles over the definition of group membership and outsider status are common in other communities as well.[12]

Underlying the call for a precise decision is a pre-existing implicit idea that an exact borderline exists and runs in a certain direction. The group is constructed *a priori*, the boundary is drawn in advance. This procedure is such a necessary precondition that it can appear odd if the group does not constitute itself according to this boundary; only then can the following judgment on Romani political structures be passed: 'divisions among the Roma population and corruption hamper successful political organisation' (ESC Delegation to the EU-Bulgaria Joint Consultative Committee 2002: 8). Just as in the case of 'gypsies,' no criteria are provided for drawing the boundary between 'Roma' and 'non-Roma'.[13]

As a corollary to the increasing importance and eventual dominance of the term 'Roma,' the previous variety of terms was substantially reduced during this second phase of the discourse. With the dying off of the multitude of shifting designations, the border corridor narrowed to a precise – though nowhere explicitly defined – line, which is no longer open for negotiation. The central category of discourse was constructed as more internally homogeneous and more clearly distinguished from the outside. Put in another way, heterogeneities within the group and homogeneities with outsiders were reduced or written off. The designation 'Roma' was not used in combination with other terms to establish a broader category based on a more broadly shared characteristic any more.[14]

While the combination of different terms observed under the first pattern of the EU discourse ceased to exist, a supplement to the term designating the central category of the discourse – used only rarely before – gained prominence: as a consequence of the growing prominence of a discourse centring around the category of 'minorities' in the first half of the 1990s, it was the term 'Roma minority' that became important. In the EU context, the new interest in minority situations became manifest in the Copenhagen Criteria (1997), which required from candidate countries, among other things, 'respect for and protection of minorities'. The Copenhagen Criteria set the framework for the Regular Reports, and Roma were, from the very beginning, clearly positioned in the minority section of these annual documents accompanying the accession negotiations. As a result of the overarching presence and legitimacy of the discourse on minorities in these days the ethnic conceptualization of Roma as 'minority' prevailed over alternative ones, such as the social category 'disadvantaged group.'

Looking again for contrasting terms in this second pattern, the terms 'majority' and 'other national minorities' are the most prominent. Both point to the discourse on minorities. While all minorities are clearly distinguished from the majority population, there is a striking dichotomy between 'Roma' on the one hand and 'other minorities' on the other. While Roma are sometimes subsumed under the category of 'national minorities,' the formulation 'national minorities' is more often used in contradistinction to 'Roma.' Symptomatic were contrasting characterizations, such as the following: 'While the situation of other minorities continued to be satisfactory, the situation of the Roma has not really improved' (European Commission 1998: 10). The term 'other minorities,' used in contrast to 'Roma,' does not carry any meaning on its own. It only receives meaning when combined with 'the one' minority and is therefore not a self-contained conceptual category. The difference between 'Roma' and 'other minorities,' a difference which is clearly emphasized, is only explicated at the level of appearance and not on a conceptual level.

Although the Copenhagen Criteria refer to the situation of minorities in general, the situation of 'the Roma minority' came to the fore within the EU discourse. While in 1997, the situation of 'gypsies'/'Roma' was already highlighted in the Commission's opinions on the candidate countries' applications, from 1998 onwards, the Roma issue dominated the minority sections of the reports.[15] On the eve of enlargement, 'minority' was quite often used as a synonym for 'Roma' (e.g. ESC Delegation to the EU-Bulgaria Joint Consultative Committee 2002). Moreover, the rise to prominence of the category 'Roma' within the discourse on minorities was revealed through the use of contrasting terms: 'other minorities' were labelled 'non-Roma minorities' (e.g. European Commission 2001: 24), which is a makeshift designation by negation. The category 'Roma' was not only used to define people placed inside the boundary of the target group, but also those who were placed outside. 'Roma' or 'non-Roma' – reality was hence classified according to this binary schema. In this regard, the second term does not provide any clarification of its complement, but merely refers back to it.

As indicated above, the regional focus of the discourse in this phase was entirely on Eastern Europe. Following the localization of 'Gypsies' within a nomadic 'nowhere' in the first phase of discourse, Roma were now discursively 'settled' in the eastern part of the continent. Numbering – as one of the most powerful procedures of modern thinking – strongly supported this regional focus: large numbers of Roma in Eastern Europe were taken as arguments *per se* that the Roma issue is important (only) to this region (e.g. European Commission 1999: 3).

Reflecting on the evolution of the discourse on Roma within the EU institutions until the eve of enlargement, the discourse exhibits a striking history, characterized by clear discontinuity separating two different phases. Hardly any continuities are to be found between the first interpretative pattern of 'nomadism' and the second pattern of Roma as 'the minority in Eastern Europe.' Terminological continuity was broken; 'nomadism' ceased to be a point of reference. The dimension of culture present (though not dominant), under the first interpretative pattern, also vanished, let alone any explicit reference to the first phase. Instead, the two interpretative patterns were kept strictly separate.[16] As a consequence, the geographical association of 'Roma matters' with 'Eastern Europe' allowed the establishment of 'Roma' as a category that refers exclusively to 'the East.' Building on this separation, 'Eastern Roma' could be portrayed as obstacles to EU enlargement and more generally as obstacles for 'pre-modern Eastern Europe' to draw level with 'post-modern Western Europe,' while rendering the situation in Western Europe itself largely invisible.[17]

Entering a third phase of discourse: 'Roma – from object to subject?'

With the day of enlargement, the new Member States of Eastern Europe had – at least on the formal, institutional level – 'caught up' with the western part of the continent. However, the embedded structures of discourse continued to exist in many respects while changing in some others: building on the general modern idea of the relevance of numbers and the consequent logic that size matters, mentioning high numbers of Roma is still a constant of EU discourse. This discursive routine results in a continuing focus on Eastern Europe. The 2005 annual report by the EU Monitoring Centre on Racism and Xenophobia (EUMC) is only one of many examples: 'The fact that substantial Roma populations live in a number of the new Member States of Central and Eastern Europe means that issues of discrimination against Roma are now reinforced as a theme within EUMC reports' (EUMC 2006a: 3). Apart from the regional focus on Eastern Europe, also the terminology connected to the second pattern continues. The European Parliament, the Council and the Commission continue to use the term 'Roma' nearly exclusively. As the term was introduced in the EU discourse in the context of enlargement, its sustained use supports the special link to Eastern Europe.

Apart from these continuities, some modifications can be observed. The EUMC, and since March 2007 its successor the European Union Agency for Fundamental Rights (FRA), for example, uses not only the term 'Roma' but also combined terms. Thereby, it follows a procedure also detected under the first pattern of the discourse. Hence, this EU institution breaks with the apparently precise, although undefined, construction of the central category of discourse expressed by the term 'Roma' under the second pattern. In its annual reports, for example, the combination label of 'Roma, Sinti and Travellers' is used (e.g. EUMC 2006a: 78, FRA 2007: 101). Moreover, the institution uses combined terms not only within documents but also in the document's title 'Roma and Traveller in Public Education' (EUMC 2006b). What continues indeed is the unexplained nature of the terms. Using the formulation 'Roma, Sinti and Travellers' in the headings of several chapters, the texts within these chapters stick to the rule of neither defining the terms nor explaining why they are lumped together. The meaning becomes even more unclear as the term 'Sinti' is not even picked up within the texts, and the term 'Traveller' only rarely. Characteristically, the heading 'Roma, Sinti and Travellers' is immediately followed by a subheading entailing only 'Roma' (see EUMC 2006a: 78; FRA 2007: 101). In other cases, some headings refer solely to 'Roma' (EUMC 2006a, FRA 2007).[18] Thus, the dominance of 'Roma' persists, while at the same time the combination of terms points somewhat to the border corridor of the first phase of the discourse, where overlapping designations resulted in a grey area of which groups were considered to be part of the central category of discourse. The present ethnic context of the terms, however, prevents confusion of the kind the category 'itinerants' had created in the 1980s.

While sporadic references to the first interpretative pattern at the level of terminology can be detected in the third phase of the discourse,[19] a more salient difference can be identified at its most profound level. It is a change in discourse that distinguishes the third phase from the two former ones: at the beginning of this chapter, it was stated that positioning 'Gypsies'/'Roma' as *objects* and not as *subjects* of the discourse formed the basis of the discourse under investigation. Although this procedure of turning human subjects into objects of discourse is far from disappearing within contemporary EU discourse, slight modifications can be observed. The statement of MEP Christopher Beazley is illustrative:

> It seems to me, Commissioner, that rather than us devising a strategy and telling others what to do, it would perhaps be wise to ask representatives of the Roma community [...] to ask them how we can best further their prospects, rather than telling them how they can integrate into our society and how we can best accommodate their social needs. (Beazley 2008)

Appeals for such *subject-turning* strategies reinforce a trend, which could occasionally be detected before.[20] Such kinds of appeals call for an end to a situation, in which the institutions guiding the discourse dispose themselves of the physical 'Roma' and replace them with a mythical image. It is a plea to end the 'absent presence' (Delaney

2001: 57) of Roma and replace the image by real people. Such a process is developing slowly by the emerging presence of some Roma at the EU level: following the first Romani MEP (from Spain), Juan De Dios Ramírez-Heredia, who served as MEP for 13 years from 1986 to 1999,[21] two other Roma have become MEPs since 2004 (Lívia Járóka and Viktória Mohácsi). Moreover, in the High Level Advisory Group of Experts drafting the report on ethnic minorities in the labour market for the EU are two members of Romani origin (FRA 2007: 139). Furthermore, since 2005, the European Commission provides further access to the discourse by providing internships for Roma; different parties of the EP (SPE, ALDE) have similar programmes. The Commission has contracted the European Roma and Travellers Forum (ERTF) for different projects (FRA 2007: 140; cf. Nirenberg in this volume). Also other NGOs explicitly addressing the European institutions have emerged, and collectively, all these developments are discursive practices that enable the role of Roma to shift from an object to a subject position in the discourse. However, this trend to no longer systematically ban Roma from speaking by ascribing them an object position in the discourse, and thereby diminish the most fundamental act of discrimination, does not imply that challenges do not remain.

Racist articulations are still found within the sphere of the EU institutions. Though extreme-right articulations tend to be excluded (Simhandl 2007),[22] populist right-wing narratives still enter into mainstream EU discourse. Although there was a strong critical response to then EU Justice Commissioner Frattini, advising the Italian government to dismantle camps inhabited by Romani migrants from the Balkans (to prevent their return after a forcible expulsion),[23] the acceptance of amendments tabled by the EP right-wing group 'Union for Europe of the Nations' (UEN) during the adoption of the EP Roma resolution in 2008 is an example of right-wing narratives entering EU mainstream discourse. While all other demands of the resolution ask for more support for Roma by the Commission and the Member States, the UEN amendments accepted by EP majority vote shift the focus, asking the Commission and the Member States to stop supposed misbehaviour among Roma. Within the amendments, typical racist notions are found, such as the connection to crime (EP 2008: Para. G), or the conceptualization of Romani neighbourhoods as breeding grounds for diseases, with 'no hygiene [...]

standards' (EP 2008: Para. 20) and where 'vaccination plans for children' (EP 2008: Para. 18) are not in place. Another amendment which was accepted by the EP calls on the Member States 'to solve the problem of camps' – leaving the way to do this up to the imagination of the reader (EP 2008: Para. 20).[24] Typically, racist discourse[25] is not formulated in a blunt racist way, but is depicted, for example, as a concern for the situation of children und women.[26] Among the minority of MEPs rejecting the UEN amendments, it was Viktória Mohácsi who was most sensitive about the fact, that, through this mechanism, racist narratives enter mainstream EU debate. Her critique (see The Parliament 2008) exemplifies the necessity of having MEPs with a finely-tuned awareness of the racist patterns in the European Parliament – in order to realize EU's aim of anti-discrimination and social inclusion.

Conclusion

In this chapter, I traced the discourse on 'Gypsies,' 'Travellers,' 'Roma' – and other terms used to designate its central concept – within the sphere of the institutions of the EU since the beginning of the discourse in the 1970s.[27] Analysis reveals that the conceptualization of 'Gypsies'/'Roma' as an essentialist category forms the overall basis of the discourse. The most obvious discursive practice following from this conceptualization is the ubiquitous search for exact statistics of the seemingly objective category. Building upon the most general, essentialist foundation of the discourse, three different phases of the discourse guided by different interpretative patterns were revealed.

Under the first pattern, a mobile way of life, i.e. a sociological category, formed the basis on which the central category of discourse was conceptualized. It served as the relevant dimension to lump together 'gypsies' [*sic*], as was the terminology in these days, with 'other travellers' [*sic*], including circus and fair people. Consequently, seeking solutions for practical problems of nomadism was the focus of EC discursive practices in that period (cf. Sigona in this volume[28]). At the same time, and in contrast to sociological understandings, nomadism was taken as an argument to differentiate 'gypsies' from the rest of society. Both conceptualizations were biased by the idea of 'helping' people that were conceptualized as passive objects of discourse. Non-Roma 'Gypsy experts' were placed in a position to develop aid programmes, for example programmes for distance learning, for these people.

Under the second pattern, 'Roma,' as per the new label, were conceived of as *the* ethnic minority in Eastern Europe. In this phase, hardly any reference to the first phase of the discourse was made. Holding the two interpretative patterns separate resulted in a separation of 'Eastern Roma' and 'Western gypsies and travellers.' This allowed for the establishment of 'Roma' as a category that refers exclusively to 'the East' (cf. Simhandl 2006). Consequently, ethnicity was inscribed as a category relevant to Eastern Europe, while avoiding it with regard to the 'Western' part of the continent. Including support for Roma in the extensive PHARE (Poland and Hungary: Assistance for Restructuring their Economies) programmes aiming to prepare Eastern European countries for EU accession was one of the consequent political outcomes (cf. Guy in this volume).

Entering a third discursive phase after EU enlargement took place, the focus on Eastern Europe persists. The main characteristics of the discourse present in the second pattern continue. However, a slight change can be observed at the most fundamental level of the discourse: although the discursive procedure of turning human subjects into objects of discourse identified at the beginning of this chapter is far from disappearing today, it can be observed that Roma increasingly enter the discourse as subjects instead of being the objects talked about. Modified discursive practices come to the fore: instead of designing aid programs for passive objects of discourse, EU politics is at least formally committed to develop Roma policies by involving Roma themselves, accepting Roma as subjects of discourse. Interactive workshops and stakeholder conferences point in this direction. To ban Roma from speaking was – and in many instances still is – the most fundamental, and one of the most subtle, ways of discrimination. Fundamentally changing this mode of discrimination is the most important prerequisite to reach the EU's self-declared aim of anti-discrimination and social inclusion.

Notes

1. See further http://ec.europa.eu/social/main.jsp?catId=518&langId=en.
2. Mussolini made the remarks in the course of a debate centring on the group expulsion of Romanian Roma from Italy following a murder in 2007. She told the Romanian newspaper *Cotidianul* on 2 November, 2007 that 'breaking the law has become a way of life for Romanians'. The leader

of the far-right Greater Romania Party (ITS member) found it to be 'a sacrilege' that Mussolini did not distinguish between Romanian Roma and other Romanians.

3. I use the term 'European Union' in this text, though prior to 1993, it was known as the 'European Community'.

4. For a detailed description of the approach taken, see Simhandl (2007).

5. Rather than a crystal grid, a discourse is a fragile chain of statements that can endlessly be amended and altered (Diez 2001: 15).

6. In the interview, Roelie Post described how, on the one hand, the category of Roma had to be part of a certain action programme in order to fit into the conditionality of accession, but, on the other hand, she and her colleagues were unhappy at designing programmes exclusively for Roma, as this raised the problem of defining who is and who is not Romani. They did not want to 'oblige people to put a stamp 'Roma' on their head in order to benefit from programmes'. Eventually, the proposed education project was re-labelled as a programme 'for disadvantaged groups with a special focus on Roma' (Post 2004). In 2008, the European Commission admitted that there are 'fluid boundaries of who is or is not considered to be a 'Roma' in particular contexts' (European Commission 2008: 4).

7. Of course, turning human beings into objects is not unique to the case of 'Gypsies'/'Roma'. It is rather an essential component of modern thinking in general (Deleuze and Guattari 1980), which reveals its power in this case.

8. Willems' diagnosis refers to the academic curriculum rather than to political actors. So, taking the category of political practices as a category of analysis is a widespread exercise in 'Gypsy studies.' For further critical reflections on 'Gypsy studies' see Willems (1996) or Baldauf (2000).

9. It has to be stressed that returning 'Gypsies' to India was not mentioned as an option in any EU document. However, it is the idea of India as the 'home country' of these people that enables this idea in the first place. It is only this kind of thinking that enables the note found at the site of a deadly crime against Roma in Austria in 1995: 'Roma back to India' (Österreichischer Rundfunk 2008).

10. Although use of the linguistic endonym 'Roma' is intended to be politically correct, not all the people who feel themselves covered by the term subscribe to this usage. Instead, some have adopted 'Gypsy' for self-designation, a term that others regard as insulting.

11. 'Roma' means 'man' or 'human being' in Romani.

12. See for example differences of opinion in Germany on whether 'Russlanddeutsche' should be considered German or Russian.

13. The only exception in the large volume of documents analysed is when the term 'Roma' was footnoted with the explanation that it is used as a 'generic name for the group of people who speak a Romani tongue and/or share a common ethnic identity, culture and history' (European Commission 2003: 4).

14. It is striking to note that this change repeated at high speed a development that the discourse once underwent gradually. In his analysis of the historical construction of Gypsies, Maciejewski (1996) shows how 'Gypsies' were lumped together with other socially marginalized people in edicts of the sixteenth and seventeenth century before these other groups were gradually extracted from this constellation in the eighteenth century, resulting in 'Gypsies' as a stand-alone category provided with specific stereotypes.

15. Only with regard to the Hungarian minority in Slovakia and the Turkish minority in Bulgaria do we find regular reporting on minorities other than Roma at all.

16. For a comparison of the two interpretative patterns see also Liebich 2007.

17. The construction of Eastern Europe as being at a 'racist' backward stage, a stage which Western countries have overcome long ago, can also be observed in the US imaginary. African Americans were recommended as consultants for Eastern European Roma on how to resolve the 'racist' situation in the eastern part of Europe. In making such a proposal, racism is effectively relegated to the annals of US history (see Atanasoski 2006).

18. Sometimes, however, 'Travellers' are also dealt with under this headline (FRA 2007: 81).

19. See EP (2005) and Mohácsi (2008) for examples of such terminology.

20. In 2003, for example, Commissioner for Employment and Social affairs Anna Diamantopoulou stated: 'we need to be sure that we listen fully to those who have most at stake – the Roma themselves and their organisations. [...] We cannot allow decisions to be taken by policy-makers, or educationalists, or doctors, on behalf of Roma people, without their being closely involved in the decision-making process' (Diamantopoulou 2003: 6–7).

21. According to the rules of discourse, his presence in the EP is largely forgotten today.

22. As MEP Járóka put it: 'It's not very fashionable here to admit you are a racist' (2004).

23. He made this statement in the context of a group expulsion of Roma from Romania, i.e. EU citizens, following a murder of a Rumanian Roma on Italian soil. The statement was harshly criticized by the EP stating that it 'believes that the recent statements to the Italian press by Franco Frattini, Commission Vice-President, in connection with the serious incidents in Rome were contrary to the spirit and the letter of Directive 2004/38/EC, a Directive with which he is called upon to comply in full' (EP 2007: Para. 14).

24. In the only amendment not accepted by the EP, the UEN wanted to call 'on the Roma to respect human rights, in particular with regard to women and children, avoiding forced marriages and traditional practices' (Angelilli 2008).

25. Some commendable works on racist discourse analysis are Gotsbacher (2001), Reisigl and Wodak (2000), and Wodak and Van Dijk (2000).

26. This strategy can be observed also in other UEN articulations within the EU discourse, e.g. Francesco Speroni (MEP) stated in a debate in 2000: 'Many of them [Roma] abuse their women and, more importantly, their children'; 'of course, the Roma have rights and should not be discriminated against, but many of them, and I am not saying the majority, but certainly a large number of them, as has been statistically proven, do not live lawful lives' (Speroni 2000).
27. For an overview of activities of other European institutions, especially in the transition period, see Kovats (2001).
28. Sigona's work shows how these three discourses are not chronologically bounded, and coexist and overlap in a country such as Italy where the 'nomadic' frame continues to guide national and local level policies and practices, despite demographic change in the Roma and Sinti population as a result of immigration, and pressure from EU level policies (see also Sigona [2003]).

References

Secondary Literature

Atanasoski, N. (2006) '"Race" Toward Freedom: Post-Cold War US Multiculturalism and the Reconstruction of Eastern Europe', *The Journal of American Culture*, 29(2): 213–26.

Baldauf, M. (2000) 'Lustig ist das Zigeunerleben...?', *Zur Konstruktion des stereotypen 'Zigeunerbildes' in der österreichischen Wissenschaft vom 18. bis ins 20. Jahrhundert*, Graz: Diss.

Braham, M. and Braham, M. (2000) 'Romani Migrations and EU Enlargement', *Cambridge Review of International Affairs*, 13(2): 97–116.

Brubaker, R. (1996) *Nationalism Reframed: Nationhood and the national question in the New Europe*, Cambridge: Cambridge University Press.

Brubaker, R. (1998) 'Myths and Misconceptions in the Study of Nationalism', in Hall, J. (ed.) *The State of the Nation: Ernest Gellner and the Theory of Nationalism*, Cambridge: Cambridge University Press.

Connolly, W. E. (1974) *The Terms of Political Discourse*, Oxford: Blackwell (2nd ed. 1983).

Delaney, P. (2001) 'Representations of the Travellers in the 1880s and 1900s', *Irish Studies Review*, 9(1): 53–68.

Deleuze, G. and Guattari, F. (1980, Engl. 1987) *A Thousand Plateaus: Capitalism and Schizophrenia*, Minneapolis: University of Minnesota Press.

Diamantopoulou, A. (2003) 'World Bank Roma conference', Budapest, 30 June 2003. Accessible at: http://info.worldbank.org/etools/docs/library/32321/Diamantopoulou.pdf

Diez, Th. (2001) 'Europe as a Discursive Battleground: Discourse Analysis and European Integration Studies', *Cooperation and Conflict*, 36(1): 5–38.

Foucault, M. (1969, Engl. 1972) *The Archaeology of Knowledge*, London, New York: Routledge.

Gotsbachner, E. (2001) 'Xenophobic normality: the discriminatory impact of habitualized discourse dynamics', *Discourse & Society*, 12(6): 729–59.

Guglielmo, R. and Waters, T.W. (2005) 'Migrating Towards Minority Status: Shifting European Policy Towards Roma', *Journal of Common Market Studies*, 43(4): 763–86.

Kovats, M. (2001) 'Problems of Intellectual and Political Accountability in Respect of Emerging European Roma Policy', *Journal on Ethnopolitics and Minority Issues in Europe*, November 2001.

Liebich, A. (2007) 'Roma Nation? Competing Narratives of Nationhood', *Nationalism and Ethnic Politics*, 13(4): 539–54.

Maciejewski, F. (1996) 'Elemente des Antiziganismus', in Giere, J. (ed.) *Die gesellschaftliche Konstruktion des Zigeuners. Zur Genese eines Vorurteils*, Frankfurt, New York: Campus Verlag.

Österreichischer Rundfunk (2008) *10. Jahrestag des Roma-Attentates*. Available at: http://volksgruppen.orf.at/kroatenungarn/aktuell/stories/25591.

Parliament, The (2008) *EU Roma resolution attacked over education and crime link*. Available at: http://www.theparliament.com/latestnews/ news-article/newsarticle/eu-roma-resolution-attacked-over-education- and-crime-link/.

Reisigl, M. and Wodak, R. (eds) (2000) *The Semiotics of Racism: Approaches in Critical Discourse Analysis*, Vienna: Passagen.

Rorty, R. (1989) *Contingency, Irony, and Solidarity*, Cambridge: Cambridge University Press.

Shapiro, M. J. (1988) *The Politics of Representation*, Madison: University of Wisconsin Press.

Sigona, N. (2003) 'How can a "nomad" be a "refugee"? Kosovo Roma and Labelling Policy in Italy', *Sociology*, 37(1): 69–79.

Simhandl, K. (2006) ' "Western Gypsies and Travellers" – "Eastern Roma": The Creation of Political Objects by the Institutions of the European Union', *Nations and Nationalism*, 12(1): 97–115.

Simhandl, K. (2007) *Der Diskurs der EU-Institutionen über die Kategorien 'Zigeuner' und 'Roma': Die Erschließung eines politischen Raumes über die Konzepte von, Antidiskriminierung' und, sozialem Einschluss'*, Baden-Baden: Nomos.

Torfing, J. (1999) *New theories of discourse: Laclau, Mouffe, and Žižek*, Oxford, UK, Malden, Mass.: Blackwell Publishers.

Willems, W. (1996) 'Aussenbilder von Sinti und Roma in der frühen Zigeunerforschung', in Giere J. (ed.) *Die gesellschaftliche Konstruktion des Zigeuners. Zur Genese eines Vorurteils*, Frankfurt, New York: Campus Verlag.

Willems, W. (1998) 'Ethnicity as a Death-Trap: The History of Gypsy Studies' in Lucassen, L. et al. (ed.) *Gypsies and other Itinerant Groups: A socio-historical approach*, Hampshire, New York: Palgrave.

Williams, G. (1999) *French Discourse Analysis. The Method of Post-Structuralism*, London, New York: Routledge.

Wodak, R. and van Dijk, T. A. (2000) *Racism at the Top: Parliamentary Discourses on Ethnic Issues in Six European States*, Klagenfurt: Drava.

Documents

Angelilli, R. (MEP), on behalf of the UEN Group (2008) *Amendment 9 to the Joint Motion for a Resolution by the PPE-DE, PSE, ALDE, Vets/ALE and GUE/ NGL Groups, European Strategy on the Roma.* 31 January 2008.

Beazley, C. (MEP) (2008) *Statement in the Debate on 'A European Strategy on the Roma',* CRE 16/01/2008 – 14. 16 January 2008.

Desmond, B. (MEP) (1991) 'Question no. 63: fire hazards for caravan dwellers', *Debates of the European Parliament,* 4–405/213, 15 May 1991.

Diamantopoulou, A. (2003) 'Nothing for the Roma without the Roma', address at the *World Bank Roma Conference,* Budapest, 30 June 2003.

ESC Delegation to the EU-Bulgaria Joint Consultative Committee (2002) *Social Policy Issues in Bulgaria Against the Background of Accession: The Partial Closure of the Kozloduy Nuclear Power Plant and the Minority (Roma) Issue,* working document prepared for the Seventh Meeting of the EU-Bulgaria Joint Consultative Committee, DI 39/2002 fin.

European Commission (1998) *Regular Report on Czech Republic's Progress towards Accession.* COM(98)0708-C4-0111/99.

European Commission (1999) *Communication from the Commission: Countering Racism, Xenophobia and Anti-Semitism in the Candidate Countries,* COM (1999) 256, 26 May 1999.

European Commission (2001) *2001 Regular Report on the Czech Republic's Progress towards Accession,* SEC(2001) 1746.

European Commission (2003) *European Union Support for Roma Communities in Central and Eastern Europe.* Brussels: Enlargement Information Unit.

European Commission (2008) *Commission Staff Working Document accompanying the Communication from the Commission to the European Parliament, the Council, the European Economic and Social Committee and the Committee of the Regions: Non-Discrimination and Equal Opportunities: A Renewed Commitment: Community Instruments and Policies for Roma Inclusion,* SEC(2008) 2172.

European Commission and Government of Hungary (2003) *Joint Memorandum on Social Inclusion of Hungary.* Brussels, 18 December 2003.

European Council (2007) *Presidency Conclusions – Brussels European Council 14 December 2007.*

European Monitoring Centre on Racism and Xenophobia (EUMC) (2006a) *The Annual Report on the Situation Regarding Racism and Xenophobia in the Member States of the EU.*

European Monitoring Centre on Racism and Xenophobia (EUMC) (2006b) *Roma and Travellers in Public Education: An Overview of the Situation in the EU Member States.* 16616/1/07.

European Parliament (1984) 'Education for children whose parents have no fixed abode' Report drawn up on behalf of the Committee on Youth, Culture, Education, Information and Sport, *Working Documents,* 1–1522/83, PE 87.789/fin., 12 March 1984.

European Parliament (2005) 'Resolution on the situation of the Roma in the European Union', *OJ* C 45 E, 23 February 2006: 129–33.

European Parliament (2006) 'Resolution on the situation of Roma women in the European Union', *OJ* C 298 E, 8 December 2006: 283–87.

European Parliament (2007) *Resolution on Application of Directive 2004/38/ EC on the Right of EU Citizens and Their Family Members to Move and Reside Freely within the Territory of the Member States*, P6_TA-PROV(2007)0534, 15 November 2007.

European Parliament (2008) *Resolution on a European Strategy on the Roma*, P6_TA-PROV(2008)0035, 31 January 2008.

European Union Agency for Fundamental Rights (FRA) (2007) *Report on Racism and Xenophobia in the Member States of the EU*.

High Level Advisory Group of Experts (2007) *Ethnic Minorities in the Labour Market – An Urgent Call for Better Social Inclusion*. Brussels: European Commision.

Hoff, M., Viehoff, Ph. and Malangré, K. (1982) 'Motion for a resolution: education problems of circus and fair children', *Working Documents* 1–1522/83, PE 87.789/fin., 12 March 1984: Annex II.

Járóka, L. (2004) 'I owe it to my people – Interview with Stephen Moss', *The Guardian*, 15 December 2004.

Kavanagh, L. (MEP) (1975) 'Written question 126/75 to the Commission: community policy on travelling people (Gypsies)', *OJ* C 192, 2 August 1975: 17.

Kavanagh, L. (MEP) (1978) 'Written question 1350/77 to the Commission: Gypsies in the community', *OJ* C 157, 3 March 1978: 10.

Liégeois, J.-P. (1987) *School Provision for Gypsy and Traveller Children: A Synthesis Report*, Brussels, Luxembourg: Commission of the European Communities.

Mohácsi, V. (MEP) (2008) 'European strategy for Roma: the EU must tackle this issue urgently', Press release, 31 January 2008.

O'Connell, M. (MEP) (1980) 'Written question 1566/79 to the Commission: itinerants', *OJ* C 126, 27 May 1980: 64.

Post, R. (European Commission, DG Enlargement) (2004) *Interview conducted on 19 April 2004 in Brussels*.

Speroni, F. E. (MEP) (2000) *Statement in the Debate on 'Human Rights, Racism, Xenophobia and Anti-Semitism'*, 15 March 2000.

5
Romani Political Mobilization from the First International Romani Union Congress to the European Roma, Sinti and Travellers Forum

Jud Nirenberg

Introduction

Roma have never united behind or been led by one political body in Europe, nor do they suffer from a lack of political diversity today. Still, there is now more coordination among Romani political activists than ever before. There is one consortium in Europe which provides a political voice to several hundred Romani-run non-governmental organizations (NGOs) across the continent. With the voluntary participation of hundreds of organizations across most of the continent, the European Roma and Travellers Forum (ERTF) is the closest thing that Roma and other 'Gypsy' communities have ever come to a unified voice communicating with European or international institutions. To understand the relationship between Romani civil society and European institutions requires critical reflection upon the ways that Europe addresses and in some cases manipulates Romani politics, and the extent to which Europe listens to Romani political bodies at all. One could discuss at length whether various European bodies take the ERTF seriously. But first, one might ask whether the ERTF merits being taken seriously. One should perhaps look at how the ERTF organizes its own house; does it represent the views and

94

concerns of its affiliated organizations and how are its policies and priorities determined? How does it unify NGOs that were previously in competition with one another and how is it a manifestation of a new fragmentation? How is its style influenced by earlier efforts at pan-European Romani cooperation such as the International Romani Union?

One can understand the international Romani organizations in general and the ERTF in particular by looking at their opportunities, their restrictions and many other factors. In this text, the focus is on how the ERTF and its forefather institutions have been shaped – how their corporate culture and norms for decision and policy-making are better understood by considering certain aspects of Romani political history.

Early Romani political life

There are those that would argue that the Roma have never lived in a political vacuum and have never lived without political actors. Although it may be true that Roma have always been subject to the politics of the countries in which they live, nonetheless, this does not mean that there were no political actors seeing to the political interests of those they represented. For centuries, there was a division between leadership *within* Romani communities and Romani *representation to* power structures and the outside world. For politics within, some groups of Roma (in particular, the *Vlach*) had a strong tribal court tradition; the *kris* was a committee of male elders who arbitrated disputes amongst members of a community (Weyrauch 2001). The disputing parties' acceptance of *kris* judgments was necessary for the system to function, and so it has never been relevant to relations with the majority (non-Romani) society. For relations with outsiders, in many cases a go-between figure emerged, who claimed a variety of royal titles as necessitated by the practical need to negotiate with the broader society's power structure. Historically, local nobility or power structures in Europe expected each group of Roma to have a leader with whom to communicate and, at times, from whom to collect taxes. These 'kings' or 'barons' were either self-appointed or appointed by the non-Roma. They were not necessarily people of high standing *within* their communities (Kaminski 1980: 134–138).

One often hears in Romani activist circles that Roma tradition-ally reacted to oppression by migration and were therefore slower than other peoples to develop politically. However, to my mind, this belief employs a false assumption, thereby generating a false conclu-sion. It assumes that emigration was a specifically Romani response to majority hostilities (see Fraser 1992). It was neither a model used *only* by Roma, nor the method *most* used by Roma. Sedentary life has been the norm for most of Europe's Roma for centuries, and empir-ical evidence contradicts the nomadic stereotype commonly associ-ated with Roma (cf. Matras 2000).

State policies often aimed at forced sedentarization.[1] This pol-icy of turning middle-class traders and artisans, whose profession required mobility, into peasants tied to land, was a deliberate impov-erishment of the Roma. People's most valuable assets and work tools, such as horses and wagons, were confiscated in order to leave them with no livelihood but sharecropping. 'Gypsy kings' – as professional intermediaries – were in the difficult position of serving non-Rom-ani objectives to some extent whilst also helping Roma to resist and avoid *full* compliance with states that sought to strip them of their assets and livelihoods.

The long history of Roma playing king to an audience of non-Roma has made an impact on how many Romani people view the self-proclaimed leadership today. Many Roma neither expect polit-ical activists to be chosen by, nor to set an agenda according to, the views of any polity. They also do not expect honesty or altruism, though they expect that the successful 'king' will not eat alone or monopolize all gains. This belief suggests that Roma have been able to live outside of politics; on the contrary, the community's needs have shaped and formed its go-between leaders. Thus, Roma have always applied various models for politics and diplomacy with non-Romani power structures.

Looking to more familiar (or 'modern') models of community organization apart from Gypsy kings or tribal courts, the first Romani political steps emerged during the beginning of the twentieth cen-tury. In 1906, Roma in Bulgaria submitted a petition to the national Parliament demanding equal rights (Hancock 2002: 113–114). The first formal Romani community organizations in Europe, founded in Russia and Czechoslovakia, were ostensibly focused on culture, arts and sports.[2] Although many of these early Romani organizations dealt with literature and areas related to the arts or culture, none-theless, they were models of community organizing and they were arguably political, at least in the sense that they sought and received public funding.

During the same period, the first overtly political Romani NGOs were formed in Bulgaria (in 1919) and in the United States (Hancock, Dowd and Djurić 1998: 60). In 1927, a one-member non-profit organ-ization in the US aimed to convince the federal government to give Roma territory. Steve Kaslov, the activist concerned, was inspired by the freedoms he perceived indigenous Americans had on reservations (Hancock 1987). Furthermore, earlier attempts at political organiz-ing were made prior to the First World War, for example, in 1879 in Kisfalu, Hungary, but not until after the war's end did the flourishing of Romani organizations begin to take shape (Hancock 2002).

In the period between the World Wars, the nation-state was raised up, eventually to become hegemonic. Fascist movements were not alone in treating minorities as impurities within the ideal nation-state. Large states worried considerably about members of their nation beyond their borders. Every people proclaimed the right to territory. It is unsurprising in this context then, and given the breadth of discrim-inatory legislation and norms in Europe, that some Roma – similar to some communities of European Jewry at the time – believed their safety would be best assured by separation and the establishment of a Romani territory. In 1937, Michal Kwiek, who carried the Polish state title of 'King of the Gypsies' called a 'Romani World Congress' in order to announce his plan that Roma demand a land of their own. It is difficult to assess today whether the idea gathered any supporters outside of Poland, or even among Roma within Poland.[3]

The Second World War's aftermath and the International Romani Union (IRU)

In any case, the spread of fascism and the Second World War brought chaos and destruction to the Romani communities that prevented any significant political life for several years. After the Holocaust, where an estimated half a million Roma perished alongside European Jews, there were new constraints (Friedlander 1995). Roma in Central and Eastern Europe were subject to communist authoritarian regimes that did not leave much room for ethnic minorities to express their own agendas, with the notable exception of Tito's Yugoslavia.[4] The much smaller Romani communities of Western Europe were slow to develop their own institutions. While in a few countries there were important efforts by and for nomadic groups to defend their right to preserve their way of life, there was little effort to address larger questions of integration or to draw attention to discrimination against the sedentary majority of Europe's Roma and Sinti.

In 1971, the first World Romani Congress was held in London (Liégeois 1986). Activists there began to discuss ways to provide their trans-territorial ethnic group an international voice. The event gave Romani activists and non-Roma interested in their cause a chance to meet, but it was not a Romani-inspired meeting; the Congress would not have been held without the organization and financial backing of non-Roma. It was not until 1978 that the participants reconvened for a second congress (Crowe and Kolsti 1991). At that meeting, IRU was formed. The IRU's creation was in some ways the birth of the international Romani political environment that dominated for years to follow and continues today (Acton and Klímová 2001).

The IRU is an NGO and so it is worth reflecting on what an NGO is, and why NGOs are viewed as such an important piece of the puzzle in achieving equality for minorities. NGO stands for non-governmental organization and in common usage is virtually synonymous with NPO, or non-profit organization. Private, non-profit associations have been crucial actors in the Anglo-Saxon world's history of human and civil rights efforts. Labour unions are a type of NGO. The emancipation of slaves, the push to end institutional racism and desegregate schools, suffrage for women and many other major causes were led mainly by such organizations. NGOs are one vehicle for a group of people outside of government to pressure the government to change policy. However, the original model is member-driven. A large number of people join the NGO and it runs on members' donations of money and labour. An organization like the American Jewish Congress is not representative of *all* Jewish Americans but it does reflect the concerns of thousands and is certainly more focused on serving members, who are Jewish Americans, than serving any other interest. It is an imperfect expression of the will of a certain community and it has some merits. The value of an NGO as a representative of an ethnic constituency tends to decrease when an NGO is not membership-driven or 'grassroots'.[5] When an organization has activities or events generated only from outside donations, especially from a short list of funders, the NGO may be more a service provider to a donor than a vehicle for the expression of an ethnic group's aspirations or ethos. The more efficient the institution, the better it serves its donor-clients.

The IRU and most Romani NGOs formed since 1971 are based, like European NGOs in general, on models other than membership. If they have membership at all, it is not based on dues and thus is passive. Many NGOs use the term 'member' to mean anyone on a mailing or email list and one can be claimed as a member without knowing it. In my own experiences of working with the IRU, it has always had an engaged membership limited to less than one hundred persons. In fact, as the organization has gone years at a stretch without a meeting for its general membership, its active members were typically less than ten people. While its 2008 meeting in Zagreb, Croatia had hundreds of participants, it is debatable how many were indeed included in any consistent way or given the chance to participate fully at that meeting (Sebestyen 2008). Dr Ian Hancock, a founding member, and representative of the IRU to UNICEF, publicly resigned from the body in November 2008, stating that '[the] leadership has been controlled by a handful of pre-1989 remnants whose mentality has not adjusted to the times' (Hancock 2008).

Lack of accountability to any Romani constituency was not the IRU's only limitation in the early years. Its members were, naturally, mainly from the countries with the largest Romani communities. As these were places from which one could only travel with special permission from an authoritarian regime, the members were mostly employed by or beholden to their governments. The IRU was hindered at its onset from any serious vocalization of the rights abuses in the countries where most Roma lived and where the most severe abuses were perpetrated. As for the few members from the Western world, there were few professional political activists or community organizers among them. When one IRU member in the United States was invited in the 1990s to speak before the US Congressional Committee for Human Rights, the author listened as this member was asked what the US Congress could do to help Europe's Roma. The author listened in disbelief as this IRU member proposed sending Coca-Cola machines to Romani slums. Given the skills, experience and constraints of the membership, the organization's general focus was on symbols of nationhood such as the creation of a national flag, anthem, etc. It did not – until very recently – develop concrete plans for addressing discrimination or poverty.

The 1990s and the explosion of Romani political life

As communism came to a close in Eastern and Central European countries during the late 1980s, numerous Roma found themselves free to express their ideas and to form associations. The number of Romani NGOs and Romani political parties exploded in the first few years of the 1990s. Private foundations entered Eastern Europe to stimulate civil society with donations and training. While new freedoms and funders might have invigorated the IRU, its most skilled members were quite occupied with work in their own backyards. They were creating their own local NGOs, parties, newspapers, etc. Some were attempting all these ventures at once. Emil Sčuka of the Czech Republic held onto his leadership of the IRU while chairing a political party, running an NGO, and producing a television programme.

Activists were in a political system that was new to them. There were various strategies and mechanisms for NGOs wishing to influence policy or secure public funds. While Romani political parties needed to make strategic choices based on discussions amongst members, most NGOs were sole proprietor ventures. While some countries had rules requiring a board of directors, most NGOs had such oversight only in theory. Decisions were made by individuals. It is the author's experience that many NGO leaders were strongly influenced by donor interests. The author also observed that most of the new NGOs, having neither broad-based membership nor an engaged board of directors, became strongly influenced by the stakeholders they *did* have: their donors. International cooperation among Roma was often on the donors' initiative and terms. Various international charities set up their own international Romani organizations. Their process of decision-making was overtly subordinate to their parent institutions (cf. Trehan 2001).

The largest private donor to Romani civil society in the 1990s was the US-based Open Society Network of foundations, founded by George Soros. This organization became the primary donor for hundreds of Romani NGOs. The top leadership was comprised of Americans with shared views of how a 'rights movement' should be organized. The Open Society system funded a number of competing institutions and initiatives for Roma but only one institution is relevant here: the Roma National Congress (RNC). Created by Rudko Kawczynski,[6] an activist in Germany, the RNC was originally a German Romani NGO focused on the concerns of immigrant Roma. After Kawczynski spent a year running the Open Society Institute's Roma Participation Program in 1997–1998, he turned the RNC into a broader international network comprised mostly of activists whose NGOs were funded by that same OSI (Open Society Institute) office. The RNC as a new, international umbrella group of NGOs was formally established at an OSI-arranged event in Łódź, Poland attended exclusively by OSI grantees. The RNC capitalized on the inaction of the IRU, and a sense of disappointment amongst Roma that, at the international level, there was nothing more functional. Holding frequent meetings with Open Society Institute's logistical and financial assistance, the RNC had a short-lived burst of activity in the late 1990s. It was overtly critical of the IRU and a rivalry emerged between the two organizations. RNC members were typically more active in community organizing, petitions and advocacy than the IRU. Still, the organization had much in common with its competitor. Whilst the RNC initially called itself a coalition of NGOs and not individuals, insisting on a contrast with the unrepresentative nature of the IRU, the RNC in practice was just a collection of individuals that had their posts and positions no different from that of the IRU. And the RNC too relied heavily on its funder and had, for most of the time, just one. When the Open Society Institute stopped funding it, the RNC became – like the IRU was for many years – dormant.

No shortcoming of the two best-known international Romani groups could discourage the vision of a more significant actor. The European Union was set on expansion and Roma were, as a cross-border constituency, as well as a people in need, catching the interest of new, and powerful, benefactors. Western governments and inter-governmental agencies thus joined the melee.

The impetus for Romani organizations to move beyond competition

Those organizations seeking to be the international voice of Roma were inherently in competition for attention and sponsorship, thus generating strong distrust between the organizations' leadership.

Nonetheless, all Romani leaders dreamed of being seen as leaders of their people rather than leaders of just a certain NGO. There was a motivational force towards unity.

When governments feel the need to get a non-governmental or 'community' view on a policy, they know what views they wish to hear. Presented with a variety of self-selected ethnic community representatives, governments tend to choose the parties with whom they wish to meet. Romani activists have complained for years that governments have had their favourites.[7] Just as the IRU had once monopolized the role of Romani leadership and lost its monopoly in the 1990s with the growth of the RNC, the old guard of the IRU and RNC now lost their place. Governmental bodies ignored them, opting to speak with NGOs led by younger and more educated Roma. The RNC and IRU protested that they, the 'grassroots Romani leadership,' were being ignored and that Roma with no real ties to their communities were being treated as legitimate spokespeople. Other cultural and demographic differences between IRU and RNC personalities and the new voices also were factors; some activists used 'grassroots' to mean rural and Romani-speaking Roma, and thus accused their competitors of being 'assimilated' urbanites. In short, the unelected (IRU and RNC voices) accused the unelected of having no right to speak for the masses.

Governments and international organizations like the Council of Europe, European Union, etc. were the conveners and sponsors of meetings and hence decided who came to the table. They were the buyers and it was a buyer's market. At their beckoning, the supply of 'Roma leaders' increased. The Council of Europe (CoE) paid for and built up two international Romani NGOs; an International Roma Women's Network (IRWN) and the Federation of European Romani Young People (FERYP). The World Bank, in cooperation with the Open Society Institute, created a network of 'young Romani leaders' specifically to serve as the Romani civil society input to their Decade of Roma Inclusion. Other funders created their own ever-more-grassroots Romani leaders.

The Organization for Security and Cooperation in Europe (OSCE) has a small office focused on Roma, the Contact Point for Roma and Sinti Issues, housed within the OSCE's Office for Democratic Institutions and Human Rights (ODIHR). The key person in this office, Nicolae Gheorghe[8] became a major source of funding for activists and international initiatives. Gheorghe's attempts to establish new groups tended to have only temporary results and limited mandates. Perhaps his main achievement was that he was able to impress upon the RNC and IRU that they could no longer demand to be treated as more than *just* competing claims upon the 'Romani voice,' until and unless they proved that they could speak in unison. In the year 2000, he used an OSCE conference in Warsaw as an opportunity to invite the two organizations to sit together and find common ground. He proposed they draft a resolution outlining their common positions, touching on any and all common ground but especially on refugee rights. This paper could be presented to diplomats from concerned nations at the conference. The exercise showed the two organizations that they had as much in common with each other as they held amongst their own respective memberships. It also demonstrated a mutual belief that a common position was a prerequisite to being heard by diplomats and political powers. Thus, the RNC and the IRU had begun to combat the frequent claim that one cannot work with Romani community leaders on an international level because Roma lack consensus. Gheorghe insisted at various diplomatic events that the RNC and IRU were the two most credible international Romani institutions and that they were prepared to enter a common structure.

The desire for an elected pan-European Romani body

Since the late 1980s, Romani activists had called for an elected European body of Romani leaders. The people calling for such a body had different visions of its values and none were specific about its structure. Rudko Kawczynski believed the end goal to be the establishment of a European-wide charter that would commit all European governments to affording the Roma certain collective rights. He saw a unified and legitimate (elected) European-level body of Roma as the best means of drafting and arguing for such a charter. Other people talked about an elected Romani 'state without territory' that would become an aid beneficiary and channel resources to the poor. Still others saw such an elected body as an end in itself, a tool for raising Romani national consciousness. Governments and European structures began discussing the idea in earnest.

One can find several reasons why, from a cynical viewpoint, politicians became open to pan-European Romani representation.

Politicians from some countries with large Romani communities may have believed that internationalizing the discussion of how to help Roma could relieve domestic politics of responsibility. Some countries in the West were concerned about immigrant Roma and about the root causes of their departure from their countries of origin; therefore, stopping Roma from migrating from East to West had to be addressed internationally. Whatever the reason, some governments accepted the premise that more discussion of Roma at the European level was needed and that this discussion would be easiest with one Romani dialogue partner (cf. Guy in this volume).

Finland and, in particular, President Tarja Halonen was this idea's greatest advocate and friend. By 2001, the Finnish government became committed to developing a new European approach to solving Roma's problems. Finland used the CoE as the staging ground for its advocacy of a democratic and representative institution for Roma that could help Europe and its Member States to understand Romani needs. The CoE and Finland invited a small number of prominent Romani activists to a series of meetings to explore the shape that a Romani 'forum' might take (cf. McGarry 2008).

In 2002, the CoE helped these Roma to call a 'Second World Roma Congress' in Łódź, Poland. The organization of the venue and other logistics were mainly handled by the RNC. IRU members were present at the event and many of them had not been together since their own 'Fifth International Roma Congress' in Prague the year before, arranged with the support of the Czech government. Participants agreed to disagree about how to count previous global meetings. According to the press releases, this was the largest gathering of Romani NGOs ever in Europe. Though this claim was dubious, it was an unusually diverse group, with more than thirty NGOs in the room. The meeting's purpose was to win legitimacy for the team of Roma who had been negotiating with the CoE. Discussions over the creation of a European Romani forum were gaining momentum. While the Roma could not choose their negotiation partners – they had to deal with the CoE – the non-Roma could choose which Roma to talk to. The meeting in Łódź aimed to allow a wider community of Romani civil society a chance to approve the idea of a forum and to select the people who should be entrusted to represent Roma in negotiating its eventual shape.

This was, for all its limitations, a crucial event. Rather than allow non-Roma to treat any party they liked as the voice of Romani opinion and rather than simply appoint themselves and hope that non-Roma would agree, these Romani activists were attempting to create a process of representative selection. Furthermore, even if it was not the largest gathering ever of Romani NGOs, it was the first true attempt to welcome all. The invitation to the event had been publicized in a variety of ways with the intent of allowing any and all Romani organizations to attend. Even those interested and unable to travel could participate through videocam, and two representatives did so in this manner. The participants nominated and elected a team who would be mandated for a certain time to continue talks with the CoE. The election confirmed that those people who had been going to the talks so far were trusted to continue.

The significance of this meeting was apparently not grasped by the CoE. In subsequent meetings in Strasbourg to discuss the details, the CoE identified Roma they would like to see included in the project and simply invited them to join the Romani negotiation team. It was hard for Roma to know exactly who was on their team and their complaints about this fell on deaf ears. Apparently, the mandate won by the negotiation team at a CoE-funded and arranged event negotiating mattered little, not even to the CoE itself.

Eventually, the will of Finland and a few other countries to see a Romani forum established won over the concerns of the few governments with doubts. Where the Roma and the non-Roma disagreed on the structure or role of the forum, the Roma acquiesced. A common understanding was reached, after a few years of wrangling. On 15 December 2004, the Council of Europe's Secretary General signed an agreement with the provisional president of the European Roma and Travellers Forum, or ERTF, and in January of 2005 the organization began its work, opening an office and soliciting the involvement of NGOs across the continent (Council of Europe 2004).

The ERTF[9] would be formed as an NGO in France and would receive core funding from the CoE (which, in turn, would get this money from Finland) for a minimum period of three years. During this time, the ERTF would be able to develop an office and staff with in-kind contributions from the CoE. The agreement assured that various organs of the CoE would be open to dialogue and cooperation with the ERTF and it was hoped that the ERTF would build relationships with other European institutions, like the EU and OSCE. According to the agreement, the ERTF was to be a CoE-funded, independent NGO that would 'maintain special relations with the Council of Europe'. The CoE would 'have recourse to the expertise of the Forum' (Council of Europe 2004, Section 1, para 3, 4). We will return to the significance of this wording shortly.

The unique shape of the Forum is simple, yet remains unclear to many. It has already been noted that members of the RNC and IRU often misunderstood or misrepresented their role in and relation to those organizations. The pattern continues in the ERTF. Most ERTF participants do not know the structure, rules or terminology of the organization.

In principle, members of the European Roma and Travellers Forum are *national fora*. In each CoE country, all Romani organizations are welcomed to *affiliate* with the ERTF. These affiliated NGOs may then form a national forum, appointing a select number of people to attend the general assembly of the ERTF. The functioning of the ERTF should be a matter of representative democracy, with all Romani organizations (including NGOs, parties, etc.) to join and take part at the national level. However, its complexity is further compounded by the fact that not every member institution of the ERTF is a national forum. The ERTF also allows for certain international Romani NGOs to become members as well. Therefore, an NGO with less than ten members may have as many seats and votes in the ERTF general assembly as a national Romani umbrella group encompassing hundreds of NGOs and, indirectly, thousands of activists. The process for admitting international Romani NGOs is also based on the willingness of existing members to accept a new member. Fully one year after the ERTF's establishment, at its second annual meeting of elected representatives of the member organizations, one could see that most of the representatives ('delegates' in ERTF parlance) did not understand the relationship between the organization's secretariat, elected leadership, members, and members' delegates.

Of course, understanding the relationships is no easy task. Like in the case of the IRU, the ERTF rapidly developed honorary titles for every ego. There were soon many positions having no written job description or obvious purpose. The roughly twenty persons who had been the original founders and board members of the ERTF were meant to hold their special status only until the day of the ERTF's first general assembly, when the delegates elected by their national fora would choose the organization's leadership. But in a decision made just days before that first meeting, the original board deemed that its members would have permanent seats in the general assembly. So, like in older international Romani bodies, the ERTF general assembly is theoretically full of people representing various constituencies and is, in practice, made up largely of individuals with a kind of emeritus status.

And so the ERTF has adopted some of the habits of the people and organizations that gave birth to it. Still, it became during its very first year of existence that which its founders hoped for – the single largest and most representative Romani institution in Europe. Several hundred local organizations spread over almost every CoE country chose to affiliate to it and at least indirectly participate. Even today, while many of these member bodies are uninformed of ERTF workings and may complain about the procedures, they do not generally withdraw their membership. No other Romani entity can claim nearly the same level of participation. This is true even if one argues that the ERTF exaggerates its membership. It claims to have the participation of over a thousand organizations and this is stretching the facts. One Romanian organization, *Partida Romilor*, was allowed to register all its field offices (in truth, individual party activists), separately, thereby adding up to a total of more than 700.

The language of the ERTF's partnership agreement with the CoE was noted earlier, and this too is reminiscent of the past. The CoE vaguely calls the ERTF 'special,' but neither does it recognize, nor refer to it as *the voice* of the Romani people. Rather, it grants itself the right to turn to the ERTF for expertise – when it so chooses. It makes no promise to seek that expertise on all occasions, let alone base its work upon the recommendations. In practice, CoE policies toward Roma are still made by a panel of government-appointed experts, the MG-S-ROM. This body has had its meetings on the same days and in the same building as ERTF general assemblies, and despite this, has not sought much working cooperation. In sum, the ERTF is formally recognized as nothing more than one of many Romani NGOs out there which may at times be asked for an opinion. The ERTF, like Gypsy kings of the past and like the IRU (in regard to its relationship with the ECOSOC), uses the little influence it has with officialdom to suggest that there is something more. ERTF leaders have frequently referred to their organization as *the voice* of the Romani people, and have criticized intergovernmental agencies and Romani activists for not respecting the ERTF as more than it truly is.

Kawczynski's speech at the EU Roma Brussels summit in September 2008 is a recent example, and he made these very points there.[10]

Meanwhile, European institutions, their member-state governments and private philanthropies have continued as before 2004 to foster a wide array of new international Romani fora and umbrella groups and to work with them as much as with the ERTF.

Governments' and intergovernmental institutions' influence on shaping the ERTF

There was an imbalance of power between Roma on one side and the European institutions and national governments on the other when the organizational form of the ERTF was being debated and negotiated. Roma held little bargaining power. Towards the end of the process, certain CoE officials and Finnish diplomats had spent so much time pushing for the ERTF's creation that they too needed to see the negotiations brought to a successful close. This might have given the Roma at least the power of refusal, the threat that they might just walk away if a satisfactory arrangement could not be found. However, this threat was not credible. At a negotiation session in Strasbourg in 2004, the author saw the Romani negotiators cheer when Rudko Kawczynski expressed their frustration and told the CoE representatives that Roma would concede on any point to bring the ERTF to a start. What bothered Romani negotiators more than specific compromises was that they found the rules of the negotiation process unclear. The people at the table representing the CoE could not explain exactly what the concerned countries' positions were. When the suggestions of Roma were rejected, they were unable to gain information about which country or person had held objections to them. The Roma, perhaps having no habit or tendency towards inclusion of their stakeholders or constituents (prior to their negotiations with non-Romani structures), never tried the 'We would need to present this to our people' as a strategic means to block a proposal. Even a mid-level professional from an international organization could turn his or her personal suggestion into an ultimatum by saying that the idea could not be given up without approval higher up. The Roma never responded in kind by saying that they could not make a compromise without holding another expensive international congress to make sure their constituents agreed.

The Roma also complained that they were playing a game in which they were not allowed to choose their own team. Governments and the CoE chose their own representatives at the meetings and the Roma could not object. This issue has already been noted in the earlier section on the pan-European Romani body.

In the end, the Romani negotiating team was only one of many interested parties in the discussions and had the least influence, partly due to its inherently weak position and partly due to unfamiliarity with tools of negotiation.

Does the ERTF reflect members' interests and views?

With respect to policy-making within the ERTF, the theory diverges from practice. In theory, ERTF delegates form specialized committees or focused working groups which determine the ERTF's positions and actions on issues. In practice, this has generally not been the case. The policies and statements of the ERTF are almost always decided by a small circle of top function-holders, such as the president, two vice presidents, treasurer and secretary general.

When the ERTF's policy-making has involved the ongoing participation of delegates outside this circle, it has been the result of outside initiative and pressure. For example, when Nicolae Gheorge was the head of the ODIHR's Contact Point on Roma and Sinti issues within the OSCE, he took the initiative of creating a working group on Roma in Kosovo composed of ERTF delegates. As the funder and convenor of this group, he gave them some voice in various international meetings about refugee concerns.

Does the ERTF, then, reflect its members' interests and views? There are two ways of approaching this question and the first would be to look at whether ERTF's statements are developed *after* communication amongst its membership. This is generally not the case. Member organizations, as represented by their delegates, meet rarely, often not communicating with each other between meetings. The ERTF usually chooses its policies, advocacy strategies and priorities without its membership.

However, there is a second way of seeing the matter. There are some people involved in the ERTF who see its real value in the credentials it gives and not in the work of its secretariat. In other words, the purpose of the ERTF is not to take action or have positions at all. Its most valuable role is that it makes NGOs in each country meet in a national forum and select spokespersons. Those people's abilities to carry out advocacy locally, nationally and even internationally is strengthened by the prestige of having been elected at a national meeting. The ERTF does not need to reflect members' concerns in this case, as it acts as a tool to help them get attention for their views. The ERTF is, in this way of thinking, a modernized form of the Gypsy king model. Special titles demand the attention of governments, donors or journalists and the ERTF gives special titles. While every activist can label himself a president of his or her own NGO, the ERTF offers at least some brand recognition.

At the 2006 annual assembly, delegates repeatedly asked the ERTF's top leadership to give out identity cards that delegates could use to prove that they 'represent the ERTF.' The board members explained again and again – without success – that delegates do not represent the ERTF. They represent their national fora *to* the ERTF. No matter; the requests show how delegates and members see their relationship to the ERTF and its value to them.

Unifying groups previously in competition and exemplifying new factions

The ERTF's intent is to bring together a wide cross-section of Romani civil society and it does so successfully. The organization has the participation of NGOs and parties. There are secular charities and faith-based, proselytizing groups. There are NGOs from both Eastern and Western Europe. Roma are a majority but other groups, such as Manouche, English Travellers, Irish Pavees and Finnish Kale take part. There is no other Romani organization with the same diversity.

The organization's main purpose is – for many of its founders – to speak on behalf of all Roma (or at least Romani civil society) rather than just one organization or faction. A few years ago, policy-makers could choose not to work with Roma by saying that it was impossible; the conventional wisdom was that if you worked with the RNC, the IRU would complain. If you worked with the IRU, the RNC and the IRWN would cry foul. These excuses no longer hold. Now there is one institution in which the RNC, IRU and several other international Romani groups have co-ownership.

At the start, the shift from competition to cooperation proved difficult, particularly for the RNC and IRU. Over a short time, they have learned to live together. By the end of the second year, the RNC and IRU were behaving somewhat like parties within the parliamentary environment of the ERTF general assembly. Delegates at the 2006 assembly who were not aligned with one of the big international groups complained that they were not included in all discussions. Several delegates opined that proposals and voting in the general assembly were a formality to approve decisions made in smaller RNC-IRU talks held behind closed doors. In the coming general assembly, it is the author's expectation that delegates wishing to have any influence or position will either associate with one of these groups or work in advance of the meeting to form their own coalitions. The session will more and more mirror a parliamentary process.

While the ERTF has ended some animosity and created healthy, constructive cooperation for some factions, it has also generated and/or demonstrated new schisms. So far, evangelist Christians and observant Muslims in the ERTF have cooperated well together. Tension is not between people of different faiths but rather between people who believe in a separation of politics from religion and those who do not. Many delegates expressed frustration during the second general assembly in December 2006, though not on the record, that so many of the key speakers and position-holders brought religion into their speeches. There was concern about the use of religion in official ERTF ceremonies. In future, if a balance is not found, delegates and by extension the national organizations they represent may well lose interest and enthusiasm.

The greatest gap is not among participants in the ERTF. It is between those who have chosen to affiliate with the ERTF and those who shun it. In early 2005, the ERTF began to inform NGOs across Europe on the affiliation process with the ERTF, how the organization would work, and what it would attempt. Information was sent in several languages to thousands of activists. Over time, a few hundred organizations signed on. Others ignored the call.

One can see broad distinctions between the two groups. Activists affiliating to the ERTF feel excluded from CoE, EU and OSCE meetings about Roma and want to find a space in which to speak. NGOs remaining outside the ERTF are those with access to CoE, EU or OSCE meetings and not frustrated by a lack of inclusion. Activists affiliated to the ERTF wish to travel internationally. Those disinterested in joining the ERTF are often invited to international events and have no need for the ERTF to create such opportunities. ERTF participants are uninformed about CoE; many assume it to be a source of grants. Those who choose not to affiliate with the ERTF often understand the role of the CoE and how to apply for intergovernmental funding. Many ERTF participants first joined the organization assuming that the ERTF had money to distribute; they had little formal education that would help them make sense of European politics and institutions. Thus, those who chose not to affiliate are more likely to have attended higher education in politics, law or other relevant fields, and read lengthy, wordy documents before choosing to subscribe to an organization.

In sum, the ERTF gathers Roma who are generally not a part of international policy discussions, who may not fully understand the opportunities and limitations of an international consortium like the ERTF, who may not know the mandates and natures of the international organizations with which the ERTF communicates, who are relatively unprepared for international advocacy, and who do not tend to review materials much before making decisions. Roma already in regular contact with the MG-S-ROM or other CoE bodies do not tend to join the ERTF. One may fear for the future of an ERTF that fails to attract the Roma most prepared to comprehend and influence international policy-making.

This division is to be expected. The ERTF offers a certain hope of participation to those who feel excluded and is less attractive to those leaders who are already engaged. At the same time, it is an indication of a current and growing trend among Romani political organizers. There is a division between those who consider themselves educated, capable of working within professional and non-Romani institutions and determined to 'mainstream Romani issues' on one hand and, on the other, those who focus on community organizing and claim the misnomer 'grassroots leaders.'

Impact of governments and international organizations

Governments' actions and inaction are the context in which all Romani politics occur. Governments and international organizations (IO) have always used their power to invent some Romani leaders and draw attention away from others. Lately, they have been effective in steering Romani activism. NGOs, especially those which are not membership-driven and funded, are easily re-directed. Romani NGOs prioritize their attention and pick causes to advocate based on what conferences and discussions governments or IOs invite them to attend, or based on what initiatives governments and IOs are willing to fund. A movement of NGOs is led by those activists who show a talent for drawing funds, which means that those who cater to the funding tastes of governments and IOs tend to rise to the top.

The ERTF does not combat this tendency as much as demonstrate it. This chapter reflected on how the history of Romani political culture shapes the largest umbrella groups in Romani civil society today and their interaction with European policy-makers. It has indicated some current fractures in the Romani political community; these obvious divisions will either be addressed by community organizers or exploited by governments wishing to minimize the Romani community's political influence.

This chapter, begun in 2008, expresses a desperate wish that the ERTF, as was its original purpose, could be the genuine unifying voice of Romani community organizers. That hope might no longer be realistic. Because the ERTF failed to fully include and represent its members (as manifested partly in debates within the organization over management and use of funds), and because the European institutions did not treat it as the voice of the Roma, the organization's credibility has largely deteriorated amongst Roma. In conversations with many activists who had once participated enthusiastically in it, the author has heard strong doubts. Still, Roma need some form of collective advocacy and European-level policy-makers concerned with Roma need some way of speaking with a large, diverse assembly of Romani community organizers and aspiring leaders. Perhaps the look backward provided here can assist future efforts in seeing and avoiding pitfalls.

Notes

1. See also Olmazu (2006).
2. The Pan Russian Romani Union, for example, was an organization made up of artisan cooperatives (Hancock 2002: 115).
3. See also Marushiakova and Popov (2004).
4. Except for state-sponsored cultural organizations and quasi-state consultative bodies as alluded to above.
5. The frequent misuse of this term within the Romani NGO context will be addressed later in this chapter.
6. Kawczynski, founder and board member of the RNC, was the original director of the Open Society Institute Roma Participation Program and the first and current president of the ERTF.

7. The selection of which Romani representative(s) non-Romani institutions choose to work with is not handled in the same way across all European states. Countries such as Sweden and Finland seek Romani representation in two very different ways (Kwiek 2008). Finnish authorities in their work with the Romani language have sought linguistic competence in the academic sense, while Swedish authorities sought to integrate the community to a broader extent in their work. Arguments made behind closed doors regarding the issue of representation have varied.
8. This post was taken up by Andrzej Mirga at the end of 2006.
9. See the Statute of the ERTF: http://www.ertf.org/en/statutes.html.
10. Kawczynski's full speech can be heard at http://romasummit.ning.com/video/2335464:Video:46 (in German with English subtitles).

References

Acton, T. and Klímová-Alexander, I. (2001) 'The International Romani Union: An East European answer to West European questions?' in Guy, W. (ed.).

Council of Europe (2004) *Partnership Agreement between the Council of Europe and the European Roma and Travellers Forum*, 15 December 2004, Strasburg: Council of Europe. Available at: http://www.coe.int/t/dg3/romatravellers/FERV/partnershipagreementscan_en.pdf.

Crowe, D. and Kolsti, J. (1991) *The Gypsies of Eastern Europe*, Armonk: M.E. Sharpe.

Fraser, A. (1992) *The Gypsies*, Oxford: Blackwell.

Friedlander, H. (1995) *The Origins of Nazi Genocide from Euthanasia to the Final Solution*, Chapel Hill: University of North Carolina Press.

Guy, W. (2001) *Between Past and Future: the Roma of Central and Eastern Europe*, Hatfield: University of Hertfordshire Press.

Hancock, I.F. (1987) *The Pariah Syndrome*, Ann Arbor: Karoma.

Hancock, I.F. (2002) *Ame Sam e Romane Dzene/We are the Romani People*, Hatfield: University of Hertfordshire Press.

Hancock, I.F. (2008) 'Resignation from IRU', *Roma Virtual Network*, 16 November 2008.

Hancock, I.F., Dowd, S. and Djurić, R. (1998) *The Roads of Roma: A Pen Anthology of Gypsy Writers*. Hatfield: University of Hertfordshire Press.

Kaminski, I. M. (1980) *The State of Ambiguity – Studies of Gypsy Refugees*, Gothenburg (Sweden): University of Gothenburg Press.

Kwiek, G. (2008) *Any Rom Will Do? The Processes of Implementation & Recruitment in the Struggle for Roma Inclusion*. B.A. dissertation, Department of Ethnology, Stockholm: University of Stockholm.

Liégeois, J.-P. (1986) *Gypsies: An Illustrated History*, London: Al Saqi Books.

Marushiakova, E. and Popov, V. (2004) 'The Roma – a nation without a state? Historical background and contemporary tendencies' in Streck, B. (ed.), *Segmentation und Komplementarität – Organisatorische, ökonomische und kulturelle Aspekte der Interaktion von Nomaden und Sesshaften*. Available at: http://www.nomadsed.de/owh/owh6marushiakova.pdf.

Matras, Y. (2000) 'Romani migrations in the post-Communist era: their historical and political significance', *Cambridge Review of International Affairs*, 13(2): 32–50.
McGarry, A. (2008) 'Ethnic group identity and the Roma social movement: transnational organizing structures of representation', *Nationalities Papers*, 36(3): 449–470.
Olmazu, L. (2006) *Roma/Gypsies in Europe – Exodus or Invasion?*, Draft research paper. Available at: http://www.policy.hu/olmazu/IPF%2029%20July%20 short.pdf.
Sebestyen, A. (2008) 'A personal report of the 7th Congress of the IRU (Zagreb)', *Roma Daily News Service*, 31 October 2008.
Trehan, N. (2001) 'In the name of the Roma? The role of private foundations and NGOs', in Guy, W. (ed.).
Weyrauch, W.O. (2001) *Gypsy Law: Romani Legal Traditions and Culture*, Berkeley: University of California Press.

6
Contentious Politics in Europe: Experiences of Desegregation Policy in Hungary and the Push for an EU-Level Strategy on Romani Integration

Nidhi Trehan in conversation[1] with MEP Viktória Mohácsi

Since 2004, Viktória Mohácsi has been a Member of the European Parliament (MEP) with the ALDE group (Alliance of Liberals and Democrats for Europe), representing the Hungarian Liberal party SZDSZ (Szabad Demokraták Szövetsége [Alliance of Free Democrats]), thereby becoming one of the first (and youngest) Romani MEPs in the history of Europe.[2] She serves as a member of the committee on Civil Liberties, Justice and Home Affairs as well as being a delegate to the EU-Croatia Joint Parliamentary Committee. In 2008, she was appointed to be the chairperson for the UN Forum on Minority Issues (UNFMI), and since 2004, has been a co-chair for the board of the European Roma Rights Centre (ERRC). From 2002 to 2004, she was Ministerial Commissioner for the Integration of Disadvantaged and Romani Children at the Hungarian Ministry of Education, and conducted both research and advocacy work in several domestic and international projects vis-à-vis Romani issues including with the World Bank and the Soros Foundation. She has worked actively in the area of educational desegregation for Romani children in Hungary.[3] Her term as an MEP ends in July 2009 after the upcoming June elections for the European Parliament. In the following interview, she reflects on her experiences working in Hungary for the NGO sector, as well as being a government minister responsible for Romani children's integration within the school system, and then connects them to her current work within the EP. She is a strong advocate for a Council Directive that would curb anti-Romani discrimination across the EU.

> *NT: You have been actively lobbying the EU for funds for the desegregation of schools, and you mentioned that to date nearly 300 million euros have been allocated for desegregation programmes in Hungary.[4] Give us some further insights into this problem.*

VM: Money was actually not the most difficult issue – it was *the law* – getting the law passed and enacted was the first and most critical obstacle. In 2002, my staff and I [at the Hungarian Ministry of Education] started working on the issue of public education. We prepared the draft amendments to the Public Education Act, identifying and defining the term 'segregation' itself. The amendments were eventually enacted as law on 1 September 2003.[5] From that day onwards, it's *illegal* to have segregated classrooms and facilities in all schools in Hungary – public schools, private schools, church [religious] schools, everywhere, it's illegal.

We have approximately 400 'ghetto' schools in Hungary, and this figure itself does not account for the segregated classrooms within schools or other educational institutions. Thus far, only five of these schools have been closed, two of them only because I threatened them individually. I personally travelled to see the mayors of these towns, and I told him or her that if they did not close down their ghetto schools within three months, I would file official complaints against them, and make press statements that to the effect that they were operating illegally. But the remaining 395 schools still continue to operate as segregated schools to this day.

> *The 300 million euros which have been allocated for desegregation purposes by the EU, is this money supposed to help teachers, mayors and local institutions for achieving desegregation, and then assist them in developing new projects, develop[ing] a new curriculum, new materials, etc.? What exactly is this money used for?*

The money is for a mixture of uses: closing down the segregated illegal schools, spreading the kids according to the 'freedom of choice' principle for the schools [according to existing education laws in Hungary]. And, of course, this gives the right to Romani parents also … first of all they should select another [mainstream] institution, and if they do not select one, then their children should be spread equally amongst other institutions; and of course, this money is to be used for busing, for 'catch-up' programmes, etc. Usually in ghetto schools, children do not learn foreign languages, but in a mainstream school, by the time your child is 12 years old, he or she would be learning English for more than three years. Therefore, the 'catch-up' programme in the segregated schools would enable the children within, say one year, to reach the same level of English as other children; the money is used to finance the provision of English teachers, and they use similar criteria for other aspects.

> *Are there some good models or examples where the mayors or the local institutions and power structure have said, 'OK, we agree, we are going to desegregate these schools, and bring in a better educational system to include Romani children'? And what about the mechanism of desegregation, if the other ghetto schools or the local communities there don't know what they need to do in order to de-segregate effectively?*

Yes, the five schools I mentioned above – only these have closed down in the past five years – I guess one per year is a good result [*laughing ironically*] when we have 400 such schools. With respect to the mechanism, it doesn't have to do with the [local] Romani people, it has to do with legal compliance. When we prepared the law, I was seriously thinking about how far we should include the Romani communities in it; but then I realized that so many Romani organizations, including Orban Kólompár, the Head of the Gypsy National Minority Self-Government wouldn't support it [at the beginning]. But nowadays, the whole political atmosphere has changed, both from the Hungarian [majority] side and the Romani side. Orban Kólompár asked me why I wanted to create such a programme. Then, with my staff, I presented my ideas at key Ministerial meetings. I also shared my information with Romani organizations, all the key actors and people like Orban Kólompár, Florian Farkas and others in FIDESZ [Fiatal Demokraták Szövetsége/Magyar Polgári Szövetség (Alliance of Young Democrats/Hungarian Civic Union coalition)], etc. who are important and playing an active part in the whole movement. And at that time [in 2002], I remember both Farkas and Kólompár – and they are both in opposition to me [*she laughs*] – said that I would be 'killing the community' if I push for desegregation. My response was that 'maybe, it will have some negative impacts on the community, but it would be more important to receive quality education than taking care of cultural issues'. Of course, these are important as well, but there already exists a lot of support for cultural activities and community organizing and so on.

At the beginning, in the first round of EU funds [2004–2007], we received 8 billion HUF, and now it's 70 billion HUF in the second EU budget [2007–2013]. So that's why, for example, if a local authority decides that they want to close down their ghetto schools, all they have to do is to apply for these funds. However, if they are not doing that, we will file a complaint against them if I have time and energy. I lobbied for my sister Erzsebet to create an organization called 'Chance for Children'. So if I go to threaten a mayor, then they come immediately after me, and take the complaint forward to all the offices, telling the local authorities that they are operating the school illegally. So that's how we managed to close five schools.

What about the Hungarian politicians' and the mainstream society's perspective, do they understand the importance of this? If Romani children are disadvantaged at a young age, then how can they compete on the labour market? When I was living in Hungary in 1997, I was familiar with the Gandhi school, and there were many Hungarian teachers around the school interested in Romani children's education, for example, Tibor Derdak and Peter Heindl – would they also work to create alternative models for desegregation? What you said earlier about the legal aspects is important, but what are the next steps towards implementation of desegregation policy?

In the first and second years of our desegregation initiative, we did not threaten the mayors; we started this only about a year ago. So, for almost four years, we spent time lobbying for such things, but not those who founded the Gandhi school, because this is a 'ghettoized' school too, even if they are Hungarian teachers. You shouldn't mix these two types of issues. One is minority education: teaching pupils who belong to a particular minority community. There are many minority schools in Hungary, for example, for Serbians, Croatians,

Germans and Chinese as well. The Gandhi School is an example of minority education: keeping your identity, learning back your language, producing good quality of education and the conscious creation of an elite.[6] But desegregation has really nothing to do with 'minority education', it is a different [matter].

It begins at the primary school level and is universal education.

Yes, it means, for example, that if you have 20% Romani children in a school or classroom, then they should be spread to other schools, and it doesn't have to do with any pedagogical issues. We expressed ourselves for four years on this issue, and many, many people – 12,000 teachers have been re-trained already, and another 14,000 will be re-trained in the next few years. A huge amount of money is being spent for creating clubs for parents, preparing extra materials, using cultural issues, and it has everything in it, it's all in one big package. If you [as a mayor] decide to desegregate your city, and not only close down one school, but all the schools in your city, then you receive 150 million HUF at the beginning. This amount is far more money than the annual budget of many local municipalities, and this is really a lot of money, and is given to the local authorities who then have to buy this big box, this package, with all the elements: after-school programmes, cultural issues, busing, clubs, interest-making, community organizing, everything that's in the package. I gathered Romani people together and we brainstormed, and I put this into the EU funds, and we received it. And now you don't see anything from this money. *Nothing*, like nothing, only five schools have been shut down, and probably they are stealing this money. I mean before the electoral campaigns.

So is there a village or municipality which has a particularly good record or experience with desegregation?

Yes, Hódmezővásárhély, it's in southern Hungary. They have a FIDESZ mayor, which is unbelievable actually. They decided three years ago to desegregate themselves, because one member of the education committee participated in a conference where we were speaking about this; we organized hundreds of conferences around this issue, so many people attended these events. Nowadays, I am not active in these issues as I am more involved at the EU level, because the rise of neo-Nazism and other such issues are more important for me these days [the Italy crisis was on-going at this time, with Berlusconi's *emergenza rom* directives in the Fall of 2008; cf. Guy's and Sigona's chapters in this collection].

So the Mayor and other local politicians in Hódmezővásárhély, they heard that this was good for the future, and learned how to involve local Romani people, and we lobbied for this. Then they prepared the application, which is a very difficult process. You have to make a timetable, a detailed plan on how to desegregate, but you cannot focus on Romani kids specifically, you focus on kids who are 'disadvantaged,' as according to the Hungarian law on 'freedom of identity', you cannot single out persons on the basis of ethnicity. Children are defined as 'disadvantaged' if their parents do not have more than an eighth grade elementary education.[7] Unfortunately, this applied to 90% of Roma in Hungary in 2002, and we shall be monitoring this to see if this changes in the upcoming years.

It seems that whenever there is a programme or policy with respect to Roma, there are rarely any measurements for goals, like what you just said, that in 2008, that X% of children whose parents don't have eighth grade education – but there can be goals set, like for example, 'by 2015, we should aim for x, y, z'. How did you ensure this in your programme?

Yes, the desegregation programme referred to everything: we had indicators, goals, we calculated how many kids, how many teachers and how many teachers' training programmes were required etc. It's very complex, and thousands of documents went into its production.

The political problem was that when the Socialists in Hungary realized what they had done, what they had actually *voted for*, they received a huge shock and began to think that they had taken on too much. Then they changed the whole EU programme, replacing the original goal of closing down *all* ghetto schools, with only *a reduction* in the number of segregated schools. The goal was effectively downgraded, and the language reflected this. This means that – if within ten years – you close down only one school, this is a reduction [and therefore, meets the requirements of the law]!

One of the biggest questions now is that after almost 20 years of 'transition,' and all the rights that are there on paper for Roma, including human rights, all the desegregation issues, etc. – and indeed, especially

> *the Government of Hungary has adopted these human rights measures –
> when we contrast this to the real situation on the ground, in the daily
> life of Roma, in terms of equal opportunities, in terms of socio-economic
> opportunities, in terms of employment/labour market inclusion, Roma
> are still…in fact, Roma are worse off than before, except for a few.
> There might be a small number of Roma who may be doing better in
> the new system, a tiny minority, but the vast majority have lost their
> job and incomes are declining as you are aware. There are a lot of people
> [activists, policy-makers] now who are promoting an 'EU Roma policy,'
> including you, so how will this benefit Roma?*

I have a very simple answer to this question. In Hungary, when I
created the governmental programme for the legal treatment of persons with mental disability, desegregation initiatives and other programmes, I designed these with both the law and budget in mind.
If people do not want to integrate Roma in general, why would they
do it, just because the sun is shining [*laughs*]? No, so under these
circumstances, we have to force them to do it through the law. You
need to bind this to a programme of legal compliance, to do everything within the law. For programme development and implementation, you need money, and then these three elements can work,
but you need all three elements, if you are missing one, of course it
will not work. So that was my dream when I received my mandate at
the EP, to create a 'horizontal directive' on this issue, to create an EU
Roma strategy, to create EU funds, but separate funds from Brussels,
not giving them to the member-states who would then decide what
to do with the money.

We lost the initiative for the Directive. Until 2 July 2008, I thought I
was very successful, as I had been before in the Hungarian Parliament,
where we had organized the political parties, lobbied, changed amendments [even if I didn't have the right]. We had tremendous success in
creating new laws, new paragraphs, etc. Here, at the European level
it has been more difficult. Initially, I thought it would be easier here
at the European level because more people understand human rights,
but that's not true. I thought more people would think the Romani
issue is an important issue, but that's not true [*laughing*]. I was like
a little girl when I arrived here, and I thought everything would be
ok if I did the same things I had done in the educational field in
Hungary, and then I realized that nobody – including my girlfriend

Lívia Járóka [MEP for centre-right FIDESZ] – wants a horizontal directive on this issue. In the end, I realized that the EU Vice-President Barrot [in charge for Justice, Freedom and Security] and Commissioner Spidla [EU Commissioner for Employment, Social Affairs and Equal Opportunities] had been lying to me the whole time – let's say the truth – they said to me that the horizontal directive would be helpful, suggesting it would be a collection of the legislation to fill the gaps of the other EU directives, for example, the Race Directive. As I have always stated in EP plenary sessions to negotiators, and to everyone who I work with, it's true that the Race Directive says that there shouldn't be discrimination in education, but what it does not say is that *segregation is equal to discrimination*, which is the key point from a legal perspective. In fact, we need only one statement, that segregation exists, and that it's illegal, and that it is a form of discrimination, but we failed to do this. And on 2 July 2008, they proposed a Council Directive,[8] and although they chose Article 13 as a basis for this directive,[9] in the end, the Parliament did not mention this [ethnicity or racial discrimination] at all – they are afraid, and therefore don't want to do this. I initiated eight Parliamentary resolutions which asked for those three elements [law, budget, programme implementation], I put this forward *eight* times. I mean even if the Parliament gave an order to the Commission on how to do Roma integration at all, it would just be neglected – 100% – from the whole integration package. But for Member State governments, they [European Council] have generated horizontal directives for homosexual rights and access to health care. For example, if you are travelling from England to Hungary, you will have access to health care insurance and you can see a doctor, which is of course good for the future, but at the same time, there is not a word on Roma, not a word on segregation, not a word on any such thing.

> *As you know, there are some criticisms against creating an EU-level Roma Policy, there are people who are critical of this trend presently. For example, there are Spanish and Greek Romani leaders who feel that they have a better chance to work within their national policy frameworks.*

So, how come their national level interventions have not worked so far? Did they reduce the number of unemployed Roma in their country? Have they improved educational achievements for Romani children in their schools?

Actually, in Spain yes, but they are not active at the EU level.

Come on, you're pulling my leg [*expresses disbelief*]! Come on, how come I don't see [Romani] judges, lawyers, etc. from these countries then?

Yes, they are there, but they are concentrated at the national level. You are right, your question about why they are not active at the EU level is a good one. But within Spain, Roma have a high degree of professional standing compared to other countries [in Western Europe].

I don't believe this. I doubt there is any evidence for this.

Well, that's the story inside Spain.

Come on! I have seen the EU programme in Spain, it's just a small amount compared to what we did [with 300 million euros in Hungary]. I've seen what they have done, they received only one-third of the money for Romani integration from the EU [100 million euros] of what we received, and they gave the whole amount of money to one civil organization run by *gaje* [non-Roma]. One of their programmes gave '12 pregnant Gypsy women access to internet'; another programme gave legal advice for those people who were discriminated, but there were no clients in the office; there was an employment generation programme, but because the people implementing it abused the funds, it failed; there was another programme for monitoring education at higher levels. At that time, I was working for the Hungarian government [2002/2003], and they ordered us to go to Spain, to observe 'best practices,' and adapt them to Hungary. After observing for two days, I left early, in total frustration, and said 'I am not part of this delegation, I am not going to listen to these silly ideas for projects'. In Hungary, similar types of projects were initiated for example, 10 to 15 years ago – cultural issues/language protection, offering computer literacy training to pregnant women, etc. I am absolutely sure that they have not used money from EU funds for successful Romani integration, that's for sure. Maybe for some other reasons, they have, I don't know. But there is no Spanish person at the level of Rudko's [Kawczynski] movement [ERTF], there is no Spanish Gitano judge in Europe in any of the courts, if there were, we would have heard of them in the international movement. And Greece? Have you seen the ECHR judgments against Greece?[10]

> *You are right, these people are absent from the European level, but what I am suggesting is that the Roma communities in these two countries, many of them want to work within the nation-state framework, that's exactly why you will not see them at the EU level, because they are working at the local, county and regional levels.*

Yes, in Hungary, it is the same philosophy, but look around, have you seen any results? In Hungary, all you hear is the mantra, 'let's mainstream, mainstream…don't do separate Romani programmes', but what have been the results so far? Mainstreaming and all of this is just a big zero. What are the results? What have they done with Roma in these projects? They just gave everyone the position of 'advisor,' and then [we] Roma are relegated to only being 'advisors' [without any executive power] who are unable to design policies ourselves. But where do you gain the most in terms of rights? In Greece? A country which is known for its segregation practices and human rights violations?

> *I am not saying that the human rights situation of Roma is better in Greece, what I am saying is that the connection between the Roma and state is stronger, in terms of identifying with their nation-state.*

But it cannot be stronger than in Hungary. Today in Hungary, there is actually a discussion at the moment about whether a Romani person could be a Prime Minister or not, and every party is fielding Romani candidates in their European and national lists, including right-wing parties, left-wing parties, liberals, everybody has placed a Romani candidate forward.[11] If they are so successful at Romani integration, why is the Spanish government not fielding Romani candidates, and why don't we see them?

> *That's a good question for the Spanish government.*

At the end of the day, an EU Roma Policy doesn't exist today, so I don't know why people are even criticizing it. I am just saying, we have to identify four areas [like in the Decade for Roma Inclusion] – housing, education, employment and health care. And what does it mean, in the four sections of the programme? Nobody knows, for example, I myself only know about education, I worked with 120 people for two years, to prepare this programme, it was very massive, it's unbelievable the work we did. I have never worked this hard in my whole life, in all 33 years of my life. I know what I am speaking about, and it is not a 'separation' programme, as Lívia [Járóka] claims. We are not separating ourselves, neither at the programme level, nor the budgetary level. It's not a question of separating ourselves or not, the results will speak for themselves. If she or anybody else has not created such programmes, it would be difficult for them to understand. For example, I created desegregation programmes, and we need the same process for employment and other sectors. Health care, for example, what does it mean, integration of Roma in the health care sector? But now we will never know, as there is no chance to even think about this anymore. Commissioner Spidla and other politicians have collected statements suggesting that we don't want to separate ourselves in our programming. Then, who should create the programmes? Therefore, the EU policy will merely be reduced to 'best-practice' collection. This is very effective [*sarcastically*]. We see many lawyers, political participants, you see equal access to quality education in all countries, everywhere, we never see the illegal treatment of persons with mental disabilities, oh no, never, never, especially in Spain, especially in Greece [*sarcastically*]! I mean how can this ever be effective? If this is effective, then 27 Member States could prove it, because we live for enough years in Europe, we are living in Europe for hundreds of years, we are 10 million people. I would be very curious to see if they have any effective programme, mainstream or separate, any programme. If we are not preparing programmes with indicators, goals, with those things, without an EU Roma Policy, I don't think 'best-practice collection' will lead anywhere.

But let's take for example Ivan Vesely of Czech Republic, who's known as a critical Romani activist, he might say that compared to the EU level, the understanding of Romani issues is more advanced in Eastern European countries, because Hungarians live with Roma [laughing]. In contrast, the segregation in Holland, UK, Germany and France is more severe in terms of spatial segregation, it's true what you said, for example both Sweden and Germany have many educational activities for Sinti and Roma minorities in the school system, but the social distance is severe. In contrast, if you have been to Macedonia, you know that the social distance between Roma and non-Roma is less in social settings. I am not talking about marriage, I am talking about social mixing. In Western Europe, there is more social segregation.

Shutka[12]? What is this if not social segregation? Do they provide quality of education in Shutka? There are so many people who are unemployed.

That's true, but today, at the Ministerial level, there is a Rom, and in other government offices, there are top officials who are Roma. In Hungary, David Daroczi also has a top post. You will not find this is Germany, Sweden, France....

That's true.

If you create an institutional framework where Europe is giving money towards Romani integration, for desegregation, or for other issues, OK, that's fine, but that money is not forever, the ultimate responsibility is at the national level, not at the EU level. [...] Is it something truly sustainable?

I don't understand this question fully. If we have a) an Act, b) a programme and we also have c) money, then [*points to two piles*], here is the money, and here we have a programme which can be called either a policy or integration package, it doesn't matter. *The most important thing is to have a directive which can be forced upon [which is legally binding for] the Member States.* Not these two elements, the money and the programme, these are not key issues, but this one is [the directive]. If the EU [Directive] requires all 27 Member States to act to implement the measures by 2013, then that's it, that's the deadline. The Directive will work like this: 'Let's see what you have to do till 2013 according to the programme: the State shall reduce the 90% unemployment rate to 25%, which is the average Hungarian unemployment rate. That's the goal. In the field of education, the Member State shall reduce the number of ghetto schools from 400 to 0. In the field of health care, the state shall provide insurance for the Romani people.' And so on. We do have estimated data related to these issues from most of the Member States, and if not, then we should obtain it. I mean, that's the programme-creator's job – to find out how many Member States have ghetto schools for Romani and non-Romani kids, for the most disadvantaged, those children always placed in lower quality education. I do not want communism, I don't believe that 'everyone can eat equally from the plate.' What I would like is that the most disadvantaged – regardless of whether they are Roma or not – must not remain there [in low quality education]. They have enough space within mainstream education. That's the key point in the EU Roma policy – that you have to pump them [integrate them] into the majority society. But if you don't elaborate a programme for integrating that 20% of the population, then nothing will happen, because the majority never wants you, never. You have to force them. If there is no directive, then it's irrelevant whether they intend to make 'best practice collection' or not. That means nothing, because if the Member State could make it [integration], we [the EU] would not have to show the way forward for integrating Roma, they could do it on their own. But without the law, if there is only 'best-practice collection,' that would only make the situation easier from a technical perspective, and they can browse for those programmes on the internet, and that's all. And money is not the question, since the EU itself monetarily supports all of its programmes. That would be the ideal scenario from my perspective – maybe not for Ivan Vesely or for Lívia [Járóka] – if the legislative act would be in line with programme and funding as well.

There are some dangers also in my opinion.

It would be dangerous if there is only 'best practice collection.' That would be very dangerous. If we set up some indicators and goals, then it wouldn't be as risky. You just cannot cheat if you have to present concrete data on schools, on unemployment. You can see the hard data, it is either 90% or it's not; either you have 400 schools or you don't. If we de-ethnicize this issue, and we just pray every day to be mentioned as a target group in the Funds, then it will never happen, never ever. I realized how the Hungarians have dealt with these issues, how they have ignored the problems, how they thought that this 300 million euros is the easiest to steal. And they have stolen it, and they will spend it for the EP electoral campaign and for the national electoral campaign as well, however they will not close down even one Romani ghetto. It seems that nobody intends to respond, so I have to take action against my own country [*chuckling*].

But you know the other thing is the socio-economic policies in Hungary, they've been moving in the last ten years towards – let's say – a neo-liberal agenda. For example, the privatization of the health sector is on the rise, so this is affecting the poorest people in Hungary including Roma of course. It's a broader issue in Eastern Europe where the economic system changed from being a socialist, social welfare-system to a capitalist, privatized system of economic development and social policy. So the question is that within the new system itself, are there are any solutions offered at the EU level?

No, no. I don't think it's about this. Equal opportunity exists as a ground principle [a horizontal goal] which should be mainstreamed in each of the programmes financed by the EU. If you are preparing such a programme – let's say you have to represent Roma, people with disabilities, women and other groups as they are represented in the society. These are the rules for all programmes. I think neither you nor Lívia [Járóka] have had the chance to see how these have been set up. They implement the rules, and they take it seriously. However, though you can find quotas for, say, 10% women, 15% disabled and 30% Roma in those programmes, you cannot reach the target group, neither the women, the disabled, nor the Roma. So we can say that though they try to 'mainstream' equal opportunities in the programmes, the success of these programmes depends on the rules of application and on the partners who cooperate with the government [depending for example, on whether or not they are Romani organizations]. It also depends on the political situation, on the government's will: how far they are willing to go in order to steal money. Because most European governments think that EU money is 'money that I found on the street and I don't have to give it to anybody'. Everybody thinks this way, especially the new Member States. For example, in the highway construction tenders, they set up a quota for the long-term unemployed, for those who have not worked in the past 8, 10 or 15 years. What do the Hungarian [contracting] companies do? They go to non-Roma asking them to sign a statement which identifies them as Roma; this then enables them to get the job [despite the affirmative action policies]. They think they can solve it in this manner, but they should not have to prove the ethnicity of the employee, only the fact that the person is a long-term unemployed individual. Therefore, ethnic monitoring does not deal with this issue either, because Romani participation in the programme is not a priority for the contractor, and of course, every other actor works for the government: the monitors, sponsors, evaluators, etc. Everybody works for the government. These are the reasons for the misuse of EU funds. The question is whether they will let civil organizations apply for these funds; otherwise, nothing will change, and money will continue to disappear.

I was reading the report about the votes in the Parliament on the finger-printing crisis, and saw who voted for and against the finger-printing resolution. You can see that the EPP-ED [European People's Party-European Democrats] which is conservative, neoliberal and centre-right, they voted in one solid block; Professor George Schöpflin, like Lívia [Jaróka], abstained in the vote, but nearly all of them voted against the resolution[13]. The Socialists, the Greens and the Liberals voted in the other block, in favour of the resolution to stop the finger-printing. You [ALDE] are in the minority, because the EPP is currently in the majority within the European Parliament. So, in your opinion, what do you think about the EU level, the Parliament in particular, what does it represent for you in terms of a political platform?

I can tell you how this resolution against the finger-printing measures [in Italy] was made. First, I drafted the text and sent it to my Liberal policy advisor, asking him to spread it around to the LIBE [Committee on civil Liberties, Justice, and Home Affairs in the European Parliament] committee members for their response. The Greens, the Socialists and a few members of the EPP responded positively.

Yes, I noticed there was one EPP member from Romania who voted in favour of your resolution.

Yes, but the majority [in the EP] supported the resolution. I didn't have to struggle to convince Lívia [Jaróka] or György Schöpflin, because I knew that I had enough support. The Liberals with the help of the Socialists and the Greens can overcome the EPP-ED. We are the third strongest group in the Parliament, so it's enough if I get the support of either the Socialists PSE or from centre-right EPP,[14] and that means I don't have to work more than this, as I don't need an absolute majority of the whole EP. In order to minimize the work [at the six party negotiations], I approached each of the MEPs explaining what the Resolution meant exactly, article by article, and if they didn't like it, we negotiated each of the words. Lívia [Járóka] never participated in these negotiations. The political groups appoint one person each for these inter-Parliamentary negotiations who speaks and negotiate on behalf of the group. However, the EPP-ED never appointed Lívia [Járóka], never in the past four years that we have been here, neither has Els De Groene ever been appointed by the Greens, you know the MEP that Martin Demirovski [Romani activist] is working for. And as for the Socialists, even though Katalin Lévai is the PSE spokesperson on Romani issues, they have never appointed her either. These negotiators – the Socialists, the Greens are always the sending the human rights-relevant people to the Group, and not others who do not know anything about the issue and who are simply just shouting at the end of the votes. If they wanted to vote against the finger-printing resolution, then they were free to do so, because I had enough supporters and that was enough. And the same thing happened with the other eight Romani-related resolutions: I wrote them, my advisor sent them to the committee and so on.

Is it frustrating for you that these are non-binding resolutions?

Yes, of course it is painful and it is frustrating that we're working three to four months on it, we're sweating blood, and then it is only symbolic.

What do you think now, you have four years of experience here in the European Parliament, you have learned a lot, maybe you got frustrated a lot, perhaps cried a lot, maybe you also discovered many new things…. So based on your experiences here, also as you come from Hungary as a Hungarian Romani citizen, as a European citizen also, what would you most like to see happening in the future? What are the most critical things for Roma to become emancipated, to become more accepted?

The law and the law and the law – what the current Council directive is not reflecting. For instance, I have a meeting coming up with public workers, civil servants, government bureaucrats, and 100% of their support would be needed to adopt this horizontal directive, which has been approved, but does not reflect [has not impact] on Roma. I already explained to several Romanian and Hungarian MEPs that they should be sending the Directive back to the Commission to rework everything,[15] and then next week, I will know how to place issues of desegregation into the new directive. If this will not happen, then this will not have a negative effect necessarily, as we will try again, we've got to try again and again. I want to disseminate this concept into human rights reports, fundamental rights report, the Rights of the Child, programme-making, etc.; I want to disseminate this to all areas. Now it's not possible, but the main thing is not to forget this theme: here is the Directive, here is the Directive. Without the Directive, nothing is possible, the EU Roma Policy itself is not important, for me, the Law is more important – focusing on discrimination in housing, health care, education, employment, all spheres of life. The rest we already know how to do.

Notes

1. Held in her offices in Brussels at the European Parliament on 15 September 2008.
2. Juan de dios Ramirez de Heredia (former Socialist MEP from Spain) and Lívia Járóka (2004, centre-right FIDESZ party from Hungary) were the first two MEPs of Romani heritage.
3. See further Keller and Mártonfi (2006). For details of segregation of Romani children in Central and Eastern Europe, read ERRC (2002, 2004).
4. This amount was evidently included in the broader education outlay from the European Structural Fund, it was not specifically earmarked for desegregation *per se*. A European Commission report on the European Social Fund in Hungary (2007–2013) is accessible at http://ec.europa.eu/employment_social/esf/members/hu_en.htm.
5. As a result of Act no. LXI (2003) 'Amendment of Act no. LXXIX of 1993 on Public Education'.
6. The Gandhi Gimnazium in Pécs, southern Hungary, is an institution which provides education at the highest level. It is a pilot project in the field of minority education.
7. The term 'disadvantaged' was created in the Act no. LXXIX on Public Education (1993) because Hungarian data protection measures make sensitive data registration (such as ethnicity) almost impossible. According to this Act, disadvantaged children are those whose parents attended only

elementary school or whose family is eligible for supplementary family allowance or who have special needs.

8. On 2 July, 2008, the Commission published its *Renewed Social Agenda*, which contained 19 initiatives, including a proposal for a Council Directive 'implementing equal treatment irrespective religion, belief, sexual orientation', see further http://ec.europa.eu/prelex/detail_dossier_real.cfm?CL=en&DosId=197196. This Council Directive does not cover ethnicity, see also 'explanatory statement' in an EU Report on the proposal at http://www.europarl.europa.eu/sides/getDoc.do?pubRef=-//EP//TEXT+REPORT+A6–2009-0149+0+DOC+XML+V0//EN&language=EN.

9. Article 13 of the Treaty of the European Union states, 'Without prejudice to the other provisions of this Treaty and within the limits of the powers conferred by it upon the Community, the Council, acting unanimously on a proposal from the Commission and after consulting the European Parliament, may take appropriate action to combat discrimination based on sex, racial or ethnic origin, religion or belief, disability, age or sexual orientation.' The EP was only consulted on this proposal; however, after the ratification of the Lisbon Treaty by all Member States, it will be under a co-decision procedure.

10. In the past few years, several prominent cases against Greece have been brought to the European Court of Human Rights by Greek citizens of Romani origin. See for example, *Bekos and Koutropoulos v. Greece* (application no. 15250/02); the judgment, from 2005, can be viewed at http://www.echr.coe.int/Eng/Press/2005/Dec/ChamberjudgmentBekosandKoutropoulosvGreece131205.htm

11. At this point of time in Hungary, as in the rest of Europe, there was more optimism, possibly also due to an immanent change in Washington DC with the optimism surrounding Obama's Presidential bid. The situation has changed rather dramatically in Hungary, and both fear and tensions are on the rise as a result of the activities of the *Magyar Garda* (Hungarian Guard) and several incidents of murder. See letter from ENAR (European Network Against Racism) to Prime Minister Gyurcsany at: http://cms.horus.be/files/99935/MediaArchive/letter_roma_hungary_final.pdf.

12. Located in Skopje, Macedonia, Shuto Orizari ('Shutka') is the largest predominantly Romani municipality in Europe; it has a population of over 40,000 inhabitants with a city infrastructure largely managed by members of the local Romani community.

13. See further an interview with MEP Járóka about the Italian government policies on finger-printing Roma (Euractiv 2008).

14. The centre-right group in the Parliament, the European People's Party with their partners (EPP-ED) have 288 seats, the Socialists (PSE) have 217, and the ALDE have 100 seats currently.

15. A large number of delegations requested clarifications regarding the proposal's financial aspects and economic impacts. See further: http://europa.eu/rapid/pressReleasesAction.do?reference=PRES/08/271&format=HTML&aged=0&language=EN&guiLanguage=en.

References

Euractiv (2008) 'Roma MEP: Italy's fingerprinting should be seen in wider context', 31 July, accessible at http://www.euractiv.com/en/mobility/roma-mep-italy-fingerprinting-seen-wider-context/article-174700?_print (accessed on 12 April 2009).

ERRC (2002) 'Segregation and desegregation', *Roma Rights*, 3–4.

ERRC (2004) *Stigmata: Segregated Schooling of Roma in Central and Eastern Europe*, Budapest: ERRC.

Keller, J. and Mártonfi, G. (2006) 'Inequalities and special needs in education', *Education in Hungary 2006*, Budapest: National Institute for Public Education, accessible at http://www.oki.hu/oldal.php?tipus=cikk&kod=ed uhun2006–10_inequalities.

7
The Limits of Rights-Based Discourse in Romani Women's Activism: The Gender Dimension in Romani Politics

Angéla Kóczé

Until recently, most political scientists and historians writing about the Romani 'movement' eschewed a consideration of the conjunction of ethnic and gender identity in their analyses, partly as a result of the traditional emphasis on forms of political struggle in which men have taken a leading role. Moreover, recent scholarship on Romani politics or political mobilization tends to be celebratory, and excludes critical consideration of gender as it operates to produce political identity, to ground ideology or to inform leadership structures, goals or dynamics. The lack of gender awareness deprives us of a crucial perspective which could serve to rework key concepts such as power, resistance and identity within this area of engaged scholarship. It also hinders our understanding of how gender systems have been shaped by – and have profoundly shaped – other forms of power in social relations.

One of the most striking features of the contemporary Romani movement is that it aspires to share an important aspect with other anti-racist social movements: the centrality of gender-based activism as a progressive force and gender equality discourse, both of which have become elements of political leverage. In this chapter, I analyse various manifestations of 'Romani women's issues' in European public discourse. In so doing, I interrogate the issue of forced sterilization which has primarily affected Romani women in Europe. Specifically,

I examine how this issue connects with the global women's movement, the impact of the coerced sterilization issue at the transnational level, and how it has gendered the Romani political discourse.

Furthermore, I identify various political discourses and institutions where this issue has manifested itself, and the social and political effects of the coerced sterilization of Romani women. The political recognition of the sterilization of Romani women offers multiple opportunities for activists, and I further interrogate them in this chapter. Coerced sterilization is a question connected intimately with the violation of reproductive rights and effective measures to control birth rates of 'undesirable' communities. I analyse how the issue of sterilization can support the construction of a pan-European Romani political identity, wherein Romani leaders (mostly men) portray Romani women as the symbolic repository of collective identity. I argue that the forced sterilization of Romani women is the most accepted and recognized gender issue by male Romani leaders because it contributes to the construction of their own political identity.

In the second part of this chapter, I examine the intervention of Western liberal feminist discourse on those issues identified as 'Romani women issues', in particular, early marriages. I base these on discussions with Romani women who are involved in international Romani political activism, and who perceive mainstream Western liberal feminist discourse as an imperial 'white' gaze which sees Romani culture as patriarchal and backward/primitive (cf. Oprea 2005b). Thus, white feminists are compelled to intervene and 'save Romani women' (much as their attempts to save other women in the Third World). This mainstream Western liberal discourse within feminism will then be contrasted to the scholarship of critical feminists who demonstrate the intersectionality of ethnicity, gender, class and other vectors of inequality such as age, disability, etc.[1] The real question and challenge for Romani activists is how to avoid the trap of condemning their own 'culture'. One way would be to explain how centuries of oppression by majority societies against Roma have resulted in certain internalized forms of oppression which work against women, such as early marriage. At the same time, it is definitely a struggle for Romani women's voices to be heard in the public sphere, but the fundamental question is: what are the structural forces and realities which have generated this?

Health and gender

Across Europe, available data shows significantly higher rates of illness and mortality amongst Roma than amongst other populations who are their co-nationals.[2] According to the European Commission's (2006: 1) project summary:

> [the] health status of Roma are far below the mainstream society in Europe: the life expectancy rate for Europe's Roma population is approximately 10 years lower than the overall average. The incidence of environment-related illnesses is higher for Roma than for the general population. Lack of vaccination and nutritional deficiencies are detected in the case of children.

Moreover, gender, ethnicity and class[3] belonging have profound impacts on the health status of Romani women.[4] The World Health Organization (WHO 2009) itself states that:

> Across continents and cultures, established gender norms and values mean that women typically control less power and fewer resources than men. Not surprisingly, this often gives men an advantage – in the economic, political, and educational arenas, but also with regard to health and health care.

It is interesting to note the WHO's approach distinguishes women's vulnerable health position from that of men, exposing an asymmetrical power structure at play. Ethnographic studies indicate similar phenomenon in Romani communities, and moreover, the gendered status of woman in various communities makes them more vulnerable and defenceless regarding their health status as compared with Romani men. For example, based on one expert's statements and ethnographic fieldwork, large numbers of Romani women suffer physical or sexual violence committed by an intimate male partner at some point in their life.[5] Some studies in Hungary suggest a trend in the underdeveloped regions of northeast and southern Hungary where Roma are overrepresented, and where every year, adolescent Romani girls are becoming mothers earlier than it was ten years ago (Durst 2007: 74–103; Virág 2003). The high fertility rate is explained not by cultural phenomenon, but rather as an outcome of the severe ethnic and social territorial segregation. There are also particular reproductive health problems, such as sterilization, miscarriages and low birthrates which – amongst Europeans – solely affect Romani women's health status.

In 2003 the European Monitoring Centre on Racism and Xenophobia (EUMC) and the Council of Europe (2003) published one of the first gender-related reports to surface in international debates, and this was on the issue of the vulnerable health status of Romani women. Generally speaking, Romani women suffer from poor access to health care. Several reports show that when Romani women do receive health care, it is usually of poor quality due to discrimination based on their ethnicity, gender and class belonging. Moreover, they are discriminated against based on assumptions that Romani women's reproduction and fertility rate are higher than for non-Romani women.[6] The core problem here is the European perspective of the 'undesirability' of the community – perceived of in less-than-human terms and as a drain on society. On the other hand, we can contrast this to pro-natal government policies in France which encourage French (white) women to have children. In other words, the question is not about high fertility, but of *whose* fertility? If we would talk about white middle-class women's fertility, a rise would be praised within European societies.

However, to date, there is no adequate policy attention given to Romani women's particular needs and lack of access to health care at the national level. There is not even a constructive discussion about demographic changes in the Romani population. If there is a concern on this in some quarters, it is regrettably coming from extreme right-wing conservative groups, such as the nationalist Hungarian *Jobbik* or the Bulgarian *Ataka* – who play on 'fears' of losing their 'own white nation'. However, if offered the benefit of serious educational investments from early childhood to the university, a youthful and growing Romani population could comprise the future workforce (tax payers) for an aging Europe. Realizing this would require serious structural and policy changes – emerging from paradigm shifts – which might challenge the current neoliberal perspective where welfare systems are diminished and/or privatized.

According to the late Tracy Smith (1997: 183–196), during the 1970s and 1980s, most of the studies used an insensitive empirical approach to Romani women's health which tended to blame Romani 'lifestyles' and culture for health problems, rather than addressing deep-rooted structural inequalities such as poverty and illiteracy which prevent them from receiving adequate health care. These kinds of studies – directly or indirectly – perpetuated the socially inferior, 'undesirable' image of Roma, without offering any substantive analysis of their social and economic exclusion which significant impacts health. Romani women's reproductive rights were severely violated during twentieth century European history based on a belief that the increasing 'undesirable' Romani population poses a threat to society (Trehan and Crowhurst 2006). Therefore, currently reported human rights violations such as the coercive sterilizations of Romani women are grounded in a historical legacy of previous discriminatory policies by the European states.

The Nazi regime viewed Roma as a diseased population which required sterilization in order to prevent the spread of their 'disease' by reproduction; they referred to Romani communities with the term *zigeunerplage* or 'Gypsy plague.' On 14 July 1933, Germany passed a law permitting the forced sterilization of Gypsies [*Zigeuner*] and others considered 'undesirable' (Lewy 2000: 38). In subsequent years, Roma were subjected to forced sterilization, internment, forced labour and eventually extermination at the hands of the Nazi regime and its local allies in Nazi-occupied territories. Even after World War II, discrimination against Romani women continued, as for example sterilization practices in the socialist bloc[7] but also in some of the Western European countries.[8]

Coercive sterilization rose high on the international agenda with the publication of the report *Body and Soul: Forced Sterilization and Other Assaults on Roma Reproductive Freedom in Slovakia* by the Center for Reproductive Rights and the Advisory Centre for Citizenship and Human and Civil Rights in 2003. The report cites 110 cases of forced and coerced sterilization of Romani women and reveals widespread patterns of discrimination in public hospitals, including verbal and physical abuse by medical staff, racially discriminatory standards of care, misinformation in health matters and denials of access to medical records. The report had an extensive influence on Slovak political discourse inside and outside of the country. Amongst many other developments, for example, Slovak authorities have attempted to deflect attention from their responsibilities by disparaging the report and harassing and intimidating Romani women and their advocates.[9] Nevertheless, the report catalysed the discussion on the sterilization of Romani women not just in Slovakia but many other countries as well such as Czech Republic and Hungary.

Thus, the coercive sterilization of Romani women has not been an isolated phenomenon limited to Slovakia alone. The European Roma Rights Centre (ERRC) (2006) also published a report on the discrimination against Roma in public health care with a specific chapter on coercive sterilization. Several lawsuits were undertaken regarding alleged coercive sterilization of Romani women in the former socialist countries including Hungary,[10] Czech Republic and Slovakia.

Women are particularly vulnerable at the time of pregnancy and childbirth. There were several cases illustrated by the ERRC (2006: 41–42) documenting how pregnant Romani women are routinely abused by medical practitioners. For example, a case from the report illustrates:

> [In] Kumanovo, Macedonia, 30-year-old Ms F.A. told the ERRC and partner organizations that four years previously she had had a very hard pregnancy. One night, the pain was severe but no one came to help her. She asked the nurse to give her some medicine to ease her pains but the nurse reportedly said that the woman complained too much. That night F.A. miscarried. (2006: 42)

One of the most disappointing pieces of news on this subject emerged in July 2008 when it was revealed that the Hungarian authorities had not yet responded to the UN's Committee on the Elimination of All Forms of Discrimination against Women (CEDAW). In 2006, the Committee had urged the government to provide appropriate compensation for Ms. A.S. who was sterilized 'without her full and informed consent':

> Ms. A.S. is a Hungarian citizen of Romani origin. On 30 May 2000, a medical examination confirmed that she was pregnant. On 2 January 2001, she felt pains and she lost her amniotic fluid; this was accompanied by heavy bleeding. She was taken to hospital, where she was examined. It was diagnosed that her foetus had died in the womb, that her womb had contracted and that the placenta had broken off. She was told that a caesarean section had to be immediately performed in order to remove the dead foetus.

While on the operating table, she was asked to consent to the caesarean section and she also signed a hand-written statement written by the doctor on the same page: 'Having knowledge of the death of the foetus inside my womb I firmly request "my sterilisation." I do not intend to give birth again, nor do I wish to become pregnant.' After this, the sterilisation was performed. However, Ms A.S. did not know the meaning of the word 'sterilisation'. (Danka 2006: 32)

Furthermore, the report stated:

[S]he was given no information about the nature of sterilisation, its risks and consequences or about other forms of contraception. This was revealed from her testimony and the lack of any related documentation in this regard. She had lost a great deal of blood by the time she reached the hospital and was in a state of shock after learning that her foetus had died in her womb. The hospital records reveal that seventeen minutes passed between the ambulance arriving at the hospital and the completion of both operations. She only learnt that she would not be able to give birth again upon leaving the hospital when she asked the doctor when she could try to have another baby. (Danka 2006: 35)

In 2001, her attorney filed a claim for civil damages against the hospital, and the Hungarian court – in two separate instances – reached the conclusion that sterilizations as such are fully 'reversible operations' and that since Ms. A.S. had provided no proof that she had suffered lasting detriment, she was therefore not entitled to any compensation. According to health experts, as well as the UN's CEDAW, female sterilizations are not fully reversible operations, in other words, there would be little chance that Ms. A.S.'s sterilization could be reversed. The Hungarian Court, in reaching its judgement, simply dismissed the expert evidence by public health scholars and medical professionals.

Having exhausted all available domestic remedies, the ERRC and the Legal Defence Bureau for National and Ethnic Minorities, a domestic Hungarian NGO, filed a joint complaint against Hungary with CEDAW relating to the illegal sterilization. In 2006, the CEDAW concluded that Hungary had violated the Convention on

Elimination of All Forms of Discrimination against Women because of the illegal sterilization of Ms. A.S. The CEDAW conclusion was based upon the ERRC/NEKI arguments that 'sterilization is intended to be irreversible, that the success rate of surgery to reverse sterilization is low and depends on many risks.' Furthermore, the Committee stated that the applicant 'has a right protected by Article 10 (h) of the Convention to specific information on sterilization and alternative procedures for family planning in order to guard against such an intervention being carried out without her having made a fully informed choice.'

In 2008, the ERRC organized a campaign to compensate Romani women who had been sterilized. The spokesperson of the campaign stated that even though in 2006 Hungary violated the Convention, and the CEDAW urged the authorities to take the necessary steps and compensate the victim of illegal sterilization, the government had not done anything to date, not even a public apology towards Ms. A.S.

Meanwhile, Ms. A.S. underwent a divorce from her husband, in large part as a result of her coerced sterilization. She subsequently became seriously depressed, during which time she did not receive appropriate support from any advocacy organizations, not even those who had originally advocated for her rights[11]. She desperately waited for the government's financial compensation but in the last couple of months she would have been happy even with a public apology as well. As it turns out, the Hungarian Ministry of Justice come up with an absurd idea to finance the victim's operation in order to 'reverse' the sterilization. This idea was not publicly announced because the Ministry of Social and Labour Affairs (where the gender department is located) opposed it, and thought that would be an 'unfair compensation'.[12]

This illustrates that even in those instances when the issue of sterilization against Romani women is recognized at the highest institutional levels, the *act of recognition itself* does not necessarily result in justice for Romani communities in Europe, nor for individuals such as Ms. A.S. in this particular case.

Despite the fact that several international conferences, meetings and workshops raised the issue of forced sterilization against Romani women in Europe, neither in Slovakia nor in Hungary the sterilization against Romani women got enough political support from gender advocacy group. As Slovak human rights lawyer Barbora Bukovská notes: 'Slovak feminist organizations were not brave enough to defend Romani women's reproductive rights. They did not articulate this issue as a gender [rights] violation, rather they relegated it to the field of "Roma issue" '.[13]

In Slovakia, emphasizing the sterilization issue was seen as a highly political attack on the Slovak nation. Many Slovaks protested, saying that it was not the right time to raise this issue, and efforts to publicize sterilization abuse were seen as jeopardizing Slovakia's entry into the EU in 2004. According to Bukovská (2006), even some Slovak feminists saw them as 'traitors' to Slovakia. Moreover, some Slovak leaders claimed that the human rights activists advocating on behalf of the Romani women were all foreigners, and thus they did not understand Slovak social reality.[14]

Bukovská also noted that one of the most disturbing denials was exhibited by the Slovak Roman Catholic Church, generally a strong advocate of pro-life positions and pro-natal policies, who, in this instance, were totally silent on the issue. It would have been interesting to see the Church's reaction if sterilization had been performed on ethnic Slovaks in the same manner as with Romani women.

In Hungary, the sterilization of Romani women was similarly constructed in the public discourse as solely a 'Roma issue'. Hungarian feminist organizations were not even involved in the campaign organized by the ERRC in July 2008 for Hungarian Romani women whose reproductive rights had been violated. Moreover, feminist organizations have made no conscious effort to problematize the issue of sterilization as an instance of intersectional violence based on gender, ethnicity and class against Romani women. Rather, they prefer to use exclusionary categories such as either gender or ethnicity, whilst ignoring the intersectional territory requiring more in-depth analysis. Certainly, this could also be a failure on the part of international elite organizations such as the ERRC to reach out to Hungarian feminists and construct the issue of sterilization as an intersectional problem that is a violation with both ethnic and gender components.

Sterilization recognized by Romani men

All the cases illustrated above in human rights reports underline the reality that a specific gender dynamic, combined with deep-rooted poverty and racial discrimination, can have a devastating impact on Romani women's access to health care, and increase their vulnerability to poor mental health and abuse by medical professionals and state authorities.

As suggested earlier, the concept of *intersectionality* as a critical approach within social science analysis continues to be missing from discussions related to Roma (Crenshaw 1994; Anthias 1998; Wekker 2004; Lykke 2003, 2005; McCall 2005; Oprea 2005a, 2005b; Verloo 2006; Yuval-Davis 2006; Walby 2004). In the past few years, there have been some developments regarding intersectional thinking in relation to Romani women, such as at the World Conference against Racism, Racial Discrimination, Xenophobia and Related Forms of Intolerance (WCAR) in Durban, South Africa in 2001. Evidently, this environment encouraged one member of the Romani delegation, Andrea Bučková, the President of the Cultural Association of Roma in Slovakia to speak up and expose an internal gender dynamic:

> Romani [male] leaders only allowed them to discuss one issue – involuntary sterilisation – at the Forum. Seen as an effort to reduce the Romani population and thus as a racist attack, sterilisation of Romani women was presented as a violation of Roma rights and not necessarily women's human rights. In addition, leaders said that violence against women was not a big problem (Mihaiache 2003).

According to the Romani women participants, Bucková's statement was considered to be insolent by many of the male Romani activists. Romani women's sterilization is about Romani women, however, as minority women's bodies are also the site of ethnic cleansing (in wars, through rapes, but in this case through sterilization), it is also an assault on the Romani community as a whole as it effectively destroys future generations (unborn babies).

The issue of sterilization is one of the most extreme examples of gendered racial discrimination where an intersectional approach can be applied. Despite the fact that the male leadership did not fully support Romani women in their attempts to discuss internal oppressions or domestic violence, in an official report from the Conference, the UN recognized the intersectional discrimination of Romani women. The report states:

> As a member of the Romani population, she has few advocates and is the target of constant hostility. She is marginalized within

her community because of her minority status and within her family because of her gender. The same can be said of an aboriginal woman living in Australia, a Dalit woman living in India, a female asylum seeker living in England and so on. These women live at the crossroads of gender and racial discrimination. (UN WCAR 2002)

Thus, the UN report partly responds to the claims of Romani women activists as it recognizes that such women 'live at the crossroads of gender and racial discrimination'. The social, political, even economic responses connected to their disadvantage generates their subject position in their social context.

Many men in the Romani political movement hold positions which share similarities to those male Romani activists who encouraged Romani women to talk exclusively about the sterilization issue at the WCAR in Durban. This resonates with the claims of Yuval-Davis and Anthias (1989) that men's interest is to control women and their sexuality, which is central to the processes of nationalization and ethnicization of groups. If they allow women to talk about the internal gender fragmentation, it could destroy 'Romani political solidarity,' which must be the normative foundation of their own political significance. To condemn sterilization as an extreme form of discrimination is to fit it perfectly into the pan-European contested political identity-building process. This is a classical picture about women in many other national and ethnic processes as a symbolic repository of collective identity. Women bear the burden of being 'mothers of the nation,' as well as being those who reproduce the boundaries of ethnic/national groups, who transmit and cultivate culture and who are the privileged signifiers of national/ethnic difference. Certainly, the sterilization of Romani women threatens the whole Romani population because it limits the reproduction of the disputed Romani political nation. This tension between Romani women and men presumably comes from the fact that all of them who are engaged in the Romani political activism base their tacit agreement and solidarity towards each other on the loyalty to their ethnicity. Ethnicity has been defined as the centre of gravity which dominates Romani-related discourses. According to this perspective then, other critical gender issues such as domestic violence and internal (and internalized) oppressions, thus just dilute the central focus of the movement.

Other readings of sterilization can be that the state/health institutions deprive Romani men from their reproductive power. The state/health institutions render authoritative decisions about future Romani souls. It creates an inevitable competition with Romani men above reproductive competences. In the case of Ms. A.S. for example, when her husband received the news about his wife's sterilization, he became completely depressed and later on, this eventually led to the divorce of the couple. Indeed, this is not particular to Roma *per se*, in many other 'traditional' and oppressed communities; you find men who would divorce their wife under these circumstances (that is, the wife has lost her ability to procreate).

What is noteworthy here is the power differential between a community which has been facing hostility for centuries (Roma), and the outside world and its oppressive imagery of them. In an oppressed group such as the Roma – who have been racialized and minoritized through social and political negotiations – there is a high probability that those who are oppressed will become new oppressors in a different domain of social life. These forces of centuries of oppression(s) which are carried within the collective memories of a community can thus turn against themselves and the outside world, or against those in the community who are most vulnerable. Hence various types of violence and discrimination against Romani women are not cultural phenomena *per se*, rather they should be viewed as the outcomes of manifestations of various oppressions. While I would not wish to deny individual responsibility and one's volition *to not act* as a violent aggressor, nevertheless, an awareness of the hierarchical social oppression matrix in which Romani males are located is crucial to recognize. The reaction of Romani male leaders to sterilization is a defensive measure to protect their own reproductive power, and from their perspective, by doing so, they do not lose the focus of their political interventions. Ethnicity (and thus racial discrimination) is maintained as the most dominant frame and basis for political claims.

'Saving' Romani women

In the media, apart from sterilization, there are particular gender issues related to Romani women which receive international coverage or even generate political concern, mostly illustrating the 'exotic nature' of Romani culture or serving to depict it as backward, primitive and oppressive. This kind of representation and motive is known from the colonial script of 'saving brown women from brown men'. This construction of brown women suggests that they are simultaneously victims of male oppression and objects of compassion by colonizers. As Loomba (1998: 218) states:

> [F]or both the colonizers and the colonized, women, gender relations as well as patterns of sexuality come to symbolize both such a cultural essence and cultural differences. Veiling, clitoral excision, polygamy, widow immolation, matriliny, or same-sex relations (to take just a few examples) are interpreted as symptoms of the untranslatable cultural essence of particular cultures.

This view purports that coloured women's issues are recognized if they illustrate that their culture is distinct, alien, exotic and oppresses women, thereby confirming the expectations of the white audience (Mohanty 1988). The issues confronting women of colour which are well received by the media include the following: sati, dowry death, veiling and arranged marriage. This mode of representation of women of colour as formulated by many scholars suggests that Third World women offer a discursive 'site' rather than being the subjects of certain cultural-historical debates. Most of the time, issues which capture society's attention clearly legitimize the image of cultural and social backwardness of Third World peoples (Roma included). Discussions of these 'cultural' practices are almost never contextualized, nor is there much reflection on how, why and what did Third World people *react to* in a specific localized social, cultural and political context. Such explanations would offer a different reading of these stories. 'Untranslatable cultural essences' are not a fixed sculptural development; they have been developed in a relational or reactional mode towards their internal and external communities.

Regarding the recognition of Romani women's issues, arranged marriages (with an emphasis on the youth of the bride) has been the most visible 'cultural phenomenon' which continues to receive the widest media attention in Europe. In 2003, in the context of the EU accession process, specifically *Romani* arranged early marriages gained frontline visibility in European politics. Such was the case of Miss Cioaba's wedding, a 12-year-old Romani girl from Romania. The debate emerged within the framework of Romania's preparation for

EU accession. International media depicted the arranged marriage as an oppressive and criminal traditional act by the girl's Romani community (BBC 2003). The debate in the European Parliament was initiated by the British MEP (Member of European Parliament) and the EU's Special Rapporteur for Romania, Baroness Emma Nicholson. She called for police to 'remove Ana-Maria [the Romani girl due to be married] from harm'. The Romanian authorities – with an eye on EU accession in 2007 – mounted an inquiry (Macrae 2004). According to Macrae (2004), a journalist reporting on the story for the British press, 'the effect was to encourage another episode in the vilification of Romani people'. That is one way of seeing it.

In a more nuanced analysis, Oprea (2005a) used the example, and the occasion of the intensely mediatized wedding, to challenge the prevailing images of Romani women in the media and the political discourse that portrays them as culturally and traditionally oppressed by their communities. Oprea's point was 'not to deny that Romani women [were] profoundly oppressed, but to challenge the monofocal conceptualization of 'Romani culture' as being the sole factor affecting their experiences' (2005a: 133–148).[15]

Spivak (1988), a leading feminist literary and post-colonial scholar, in her writing on *sati*, which was a practice in India (until 1829) of widows immolating themselves upon their husbands' funeral pyres.[16] observes that '[T]he masculine imperialist ideological formation that shaped that desire into "the daughter's seduction" is part of the same formation that constructs the monolithic "third world women"' (296). Spivak identifies the colonial conquest as the same mechanism elaborated on in Freudian psychological analysis. This mechanism is characterized by a denial of guilt, scapegoating, the finding of excuses, and projection onto the Other. Instead of facing structural exclusionary forces which interplay with internal (as well as internalized) oppression, it is easier to interpret this as a cultural phenomenon which clearly pivots upon the colonized Other. In Spivak's view, the manifestation of these practices is used as a pretext for 'saving brown women,' and these are colonial desires and imperialistic advances which then become masked as a 'social mission' to intervene.

'Traditional' and 'progressive' Romani women[17] activists hold competing views of Western feminist interventions. The traditionalist in particular sees some emancipatory approaches as 'colonial conquests', One of the more contentious Romani feminist projects was led by Enisa Eminova, an outstanding Romani woman from Macedonia. In 2001, she began to organize workshops for women in her community. She recalls that:

> the group had no agenda, apart from their determination to do more than talk. How about doing something practical to advance the rights of Roma women? ... [O]ne tradition stood out as particularly debasing: a humiliating virginity test on a Roma woman's wedding day.[18]

Later on, she conducted a research project on the virginity cult, and a related campaign was supported by the OSI's (Open Society Institute) Network Women's Program. The project was heavily criticized by some Romani leaders, including traditional Romani women. Some even viewed Eminova as a traitor who was making an outrageous attack on Romani culture. Moreover, some Romani men criticized Western liberal feminism which they viewed as 'invading' the Romani movement by brainwashing potential Romani women leaders.[19] Once again, the fundamental question is how Romani women's activists can talk about these issues – what kind of theoretical framework and argumentation can be used which would not in the same instance condemn Romani culture?

Conclusion: 'Just advocacy'? Human rights advocacy and the fundamental oppression of Romani women

This wording – 'just advocacy' – invokes a double meaning, as first described by Hesford and Kozol (2005: 20):

> It signals 'just' as in justice, but also 'just' as in, is that enough? In other words, it asks, *who does* and *who can* advocate on whose behalf? How do representational strategies function as tools of advocacy? How can we recognize the many acts of violence committed against women and mobilize the power of rights discourses whilst avoiding the re-inscription of Western imperial gazes?

Hesford and Kozol (2005) in the introduction of their book, problematize the contemporary dominating rights-based discourse. They foster further reflection on it and they attempt to expose the possibilities and the limitations of the human rights vernacular. In order to examine the human rights advocacy of Romani women in the last ten to fifteen years, these questions should be asked from the advocates directly, such as the European Roma Rights Center and the European Women Lobby.

The groundbreaking work in 2002 by the Center for Reproductive Rights and *Poradna*, where they exposed the coerced and forced sterilization practices in Slovakia, and also the widespread abuse and discrimination against Romani women in the country's maternity wards, encouraged human rights and policy advocates to speak out about Romani women's sterilization within broader Central European society.

As mentioned above, *Poradna* initiated the research on discrimination against Romani women in the health care system, and involved the New York City-based transnational advocacy organization to provide expertise to bear on this issue in an international arena. *Poradna*'s claims to authority, agency, and authenticity on behalf of Slovak Romani women thus rested on a very specific and localized relationship to oppression embedded within human rights discursive practice. The call to acknowledge and redress human rights violations involves the discursive and representational negotiation of many obstacles on the part of the oppressed. The purpose of human rights is not simply moral, but political. As a domestic NGO, *Poradna* therefore had to struggle to retain control of its own agency when transnational organizations become involved in the process.

In negotiating the politics of human rights advocacy, the victims of abuse are assigned one primary form of agency in the international exchange – the right to claim the authority to define authentic experience and produce representations of that experience at the local level. Within this discursive relationship, the 'call for help' is authorized by the victim, but the nature and the scope of protective intervention is determined by more powerful actors – whether those organizations are international human rights organizations or transnational feminist advocacy organizations.

Nevertheless, international feminist activism can also backfire in unexpected ways, particularly when the narrative of 'saviour' and 'victim' overshadow the need for accurate and up-to-date information. For instance, in the case of many African women, female genital mutilation does not necessarily 'head the list of wrongs – heat and dust storms, general bad health care, and overall poverty threaten the women of Africa, but these are not as easily nor as powerfully presented as female genital mutilation' (Gunning 1998: 203–224). The case of Romani women is thus quite similar to that of African women's situation in many aspects.

Moreover, in addressing systemic parallels, it is important to note the influence of contemporary neoliberal policies upon the present situation of Romani women's health throughout Europe.[20] Indeed, there is little discussion in either post-socialist countries, nor in more advanced western European countries, about how welfare reform policies may negatively impact Romani women's status. There is not even a critical feminist ideological framework which would address Romani women's inferior position and the systemic social, political and economic injustices which serve to perpetuate it.

The complexities surrounding transnational feminist involvement emphasize the degree to which such work is inescapably political because protection of the 'victim' necessarily invokes some kind of authoritative intervention by the 'saviour' that redistributes or (re)inscribes power within the context of oppression. The politics of advocacy complicates the ability of local/indigenous advocates to retain their authority and agency beyond the authority of specific 'authentic' experience when they pursue social justice within existing constructs of human rights advocacy and transnational feminist collaboration (Hesford and Kozol 2005). Within my own work with various human rights NGOs, I witness frequently how Romani advocates and non-Romani advocates struggle with this power asymmetry at the local level, and this applies well beyond the simple binary notion of transnational advocate versus local advocate, as embedded *within* the local context is also a struggle for authenticity.

As stated earlier, the call to acknowledge and redress of human rights violations by human rights advocates in the field of 'Roma rights' involves a discursive and representational negotiation of many obstacles on the part of the oppressed. Usually, the oppressed group in question has very little influence on the trajectory of the legal discourse, and instead of embodying the role of active subject, members of the group become passive objects in human rights advocacy projects (Trehan and Kóczé 2009). From this crucial perspective, legal discourses used by human rights advocates have thus been rendered powerless in post-socialist Europe, powerless to fundamentally challenge and alter the position of embedded social, economic and political deprivation of 'second-class' Romani citizens.

Notes

1. Intersectional approaches assist in developing a language which serves to underline the diversity of Romani women, who are not a homogenous group.
2. Recent studies on the health status of Roma include: Delphio Consulting (2004); European Commission (2006); Ringold et al. (2003).
3. See Emigh et al. (2001); Ladányi (1996).
4. According to the UNDP (2002), 4–5 million people in the Central and Eastern European region endure living conditions close to those of sub-Saharan Africa in terms of illiteracy, infant mortality and malnutrition.
5. There is a reference to domestic violence in 'On the Situation of Romani Women in the Republic of Macedonia' (October-November 2005). In advance of the January 2006 review of Macedonia's compliance with the UN's CEDAW, the Roma Centre of Skopje (RCS), the ERRC and the OSI's Roma Women's Initiative (RWI), with technical and financial assistance from UNIFEM's Bratislava office, submitted a parallel report to CEDAW highlighting the key human rights issues facing Romani women in Macedonia. See full text at: http://www.soros.org/initiatives/women/articles_publications/publications/macedonia_20051101/nwp_20060303.pdf.
6. Various sources refer to the complex health problems and discrimination faced by Romani women in public health institutions (EUMC/Council of Europe 2003; UNDP 2006, pp. 92–93.
7. On sterilization policies of the socialist countries, see Helsinki Watch/Human Rights Watch 1993; McCagg 1991 and Ulc 1991.
8. Lewy (2000: 39) notes that 'In Sweden, large-scale sterilizations were carried out on those accused of leading an 'asocial way of life' well into the post-World War period', According to the World Council of Churches, in Norway, '[Romani] children were taken from their parents, women suffered from forced sterilization, people were named "insane" so that society could get rid of "troublemakers"'.
9. There is a summary of the government of Slovakia's response to 'Body and Soul: Forced Sterilization and Other Assaults on Roma Reproductive Freedom in Slovakia', see: http://www.reproductiverights.org/pdf/report_slovakiafollowup_0603.pdf.
10. According to ERRC's statement at the OSCE's (Organization for Security and Co-operation in Europe) Human Dimension Implementation Meeting in October 2006 in Warsaw, there was 'an important breakthrough at international level, in August 2006, the UN's CEDAW condemned Hungary for violating the Convention on the Elimination of All Forms of Discrimination against Women in connection with the

sterilization of a Romani woman without her consent in January 2001. Ms. S. had been admitted to hospital following a miscarriage and was sterilized without being provided with information she could understand on the implications of the procedure. The CEDAW ruled that Hungary's failure to provide Ms. S. with due compensation for the act violated international human rights law.' See http://www.errc.org/cikk. php?cikk=2637 (accessed on 7 May 2007).

11. See Bukovská's (2006) excellent piece about the tensions and power imbalances between legal advocates and their clients from vulnerable groups.

12. Author's interview with G.J., a Gender Officer in the Hungarian Ministry of Social and Labour Affairs, Budapest, 12 August 2008.

13. Author's interview with Bukovská, Budapest, 28 June 2008.

14. By 'foreign,' they were referring to the New York-based Center for Reproductive Rights, which, jointly with *Poradna*, published the pathbreaking advocacy report.

15. Moreover, it is important to consider historical forces external to a community that impinge upon (and even distort) cultural practices within an oppressed community. See for example Oprea's insight about the connection between the institution of Romani slavery in Moldavia and Wallachia and early marriage practices amongst Roma today (Oprea 2005b).

16. See also Oldenburg (1994).

17. Note that these terms are themselves contested, and certainly, many Romani women have characteristics regarded as both 'traditional' and 'emancipated'.

18. Accessible at http://advocacynet.org/resource/492.

19. Author's interview with S.J. on 28 July 2006.

20. For a perspective on the issue of social welfare reforms in Slovakia and their impact on Romani communities, see Marušak and Singer in this volume.

References

Anthias, F. (1998) 'Evaluating 'diaspora': beyond ethnicity', *Sociology*, 32(3): 557–580.

BBC News (2003) 'Gypsy child couple separated', 2 October 2003, http://news.bbc.co.uk/2/hi/europe/3159818.stm (Accessed 5 May 2007).

Bukovská, B. (2006) *'Dignitati memores, as optima intenti…?* Some reflections on human dimension of human rights work', conference paper, *Human Rights and Public Interest Law Fellows Retreat*, 26–29 January 2006, Cairo, Egypt.

Center for Reproductive Rights and the Advisory Centre for Citizenship and Human and Civil Rights, 'Body and soul: forced sterilization and other assaults on Roma reproductive freedom in Slovakia', http://www.reproductiverights.org/pub_bo_slovakia.html#report (Accessed 12 May 2007).

Crenshaw, K. (1994) 'Intersectionality and identity politics: learning from violence against women of colour' in Fineman, M.A. and Mykitiuk, R. (eds) *The Public Nature of Private Violence*. New York: Routledge.

Danka, A. (2006) 'In the name of reproductive rights: litigating before the UN Committee on the Elimination of Discrimination against Women', *Roma Rights Quarterly*, 4: 31–37.

Delphio Consulting (2004) *Cigányok Magyarországon – szociálisgazdasági helyzet, egészségi állapot, szociális és egészségügyi szolgáltatásokhoz való hozzáférés*, Budapest.

Durst, J. (2007), 'Több a kára, mint a haszna: születésszabályozás a "gettóban"', *Demográfia*, 50. évf. 1. Szám: 74–103.

Emigh, R.J., Fodor, E. and Szelenyi, I. (2001) 'The racialization and feminization of poverty', in Emigh, R.J. and Szelenyi, I. (eds) *Poverty, Ethnicity, and Gender in Eastern Europe during the Market Transition*, Westport: Praeger.

EUMC and Council of Europe (2003) *Breaking the Barriers – Romani Women and Access to Public Health Care*, Luxembourg: Office for Official Publications of the European Communities.

European Commission (2006) 'Reduction of health inequalities in the Roma community', see project summary at: http://ec.europa.eu/health/ph_projects/2004/action3/action3_2004_01_en.htm (Accessed on 22 December 2008).

European Roma Rights Center (2006), *Ambulance Not on the Way: The Disgrace of Health Care for Roma in Europe*, Budapest, ERRC: 41–42.

Gunning, I. R. (1998) 'Cutting through the obfuscation: female genital surgeries in neoimperial culture' in Shohat, E. (ed.) *Taking Visions: Multicultural Feminism in a Transnational Age*, New York: MIT Press.

Helsinki Watch and Human Rights Watch (1993) *Struggling for Ethnic Identity: The Gypsies of Hungary*, New York: Human Rights Watch.

Hesford, W.S. and Kozol, W. (eds) (2005) *Just Advocacy? Women's Human Rights, Transnational Feminisms, and the Politics of Representation*, New Brunswick, NJ: Rutgers University Press.

Ladányi J. (1996) 'Romák Közép-Kelet-Európában', *Társadalmi Szemle*, 4: 32.

Lewy, G. (2000) *The Nazi Persecution of the Gypsies*, Oxford: Oxford UP.

Loomba, A. (1998) *Colonialism/Postcolonialism*, London: Routledge.

Lykke, N. (2003) 'Intersektionalitet – ett använbart begrepp för genusforskningen', *Kvinnovetenskaplig tidskrift*, 1: 47–55.

Lykke, N. (2005) 'Nya perspektiv på intersektionalitet. Problem och möjligheter' [Intersectionality Revisited: Problems and Potentials], *Kvinnovetenskaplig tidskrift*, 2–3: 7–17.

Macrae, C. (2004) 'Gypsies defy calls to ban child brides', *The Observer*, 30 May 2004:, http://observer.guardian.co.uk/international/story/0,6903,1227799,00.html.

McCagg, W.D. (1991) 'Gypsy policy in socialist Hungary and Czechoslovakia, 1945–1989', *Nationalities Papers*, 19(3): 313–36.

MIhalache, I. (2003) 'Romani Women's Participation in Public Life', Roma Rights, 4/2003: Political Rights, accessible at http://www.errc.org/rr_nr4_2003/womens2.shtml

Mohanty, C. (1988) 'Under Western Eyes: Feminist Scholarship and Colonial Discourses', *Feminist Review*, 30: 61-88.

Oldenburg, V.T. (1994) 'The Roop Kanwar case: feminist responses' in Hawley, J.S. (ed.) *Sati, The Blessing and the Curse: The Burning of Wives in India*, Oxford: Oxford University Press.

Oprea, A. (2005a) 'The arranged marriage of Ana Maria Cioba, intra-community oppression and Romani feminist ideals: transcending the "primitive culture" argument', *European Journal of Women's Studies* 12(2): 133–148.

Oprea, A. (2005b) 'Child marriage a cultural problem, educational access a race issue? Deconstructing uni-dimensional understanding of Romani oppression', *Roma Rights* on theme of 'Rights and Traditions', 2, Budapest: ERRC.

Ringold, D, Orenstein, M.A., and Wilkens, E. (2003) *Roma in an Expanding Europe: Breaking the Poverty Cycle*, Washington, D.C.: World Bank.

Smith, T. (1997) 'Racist encounters: Romani "Gypsy" women and mainstream health services', *The European Journal of Women's Studies*, 4(2): 183–196.

Spivak, G.C. (1998) 'Can the subaltern speak?' in Nelson, C. and Grossberg, L. (eds) *Marxism and the Interpretation of Culture*, Urbana: University of Illinois Press.

Trehan, N. and Crowhurst, I. (2006) 'Minority groups and reproductive rights: coerced sterilisation and female genital mutilation in Europe', Widdows, H., Alkorta-Idiakez, I., Emaldi-Cirion, A. (eds) *Women's Reproductive Rights*, London: Palgrave.

Trehan, N. and A. Kóczé (2009) 'Racism, (neo)colonialism, and social justice: the struggle for the soul of the Romani movement in post-socialist Europe', in Huggan, G. and Law, I. (eds) *Racism Postcolonialism Europe*, Liverpool: Liverpool University Press.

Ulc, O. (1991) 'Integration of Gypsies' in Czechoslovakia', *Ethnic Groups*, 9(2): 107–17.

UNDP (2002) *Avoiding the Dependency Trap: Roma in Central and Eastern Europe*, Bratislava: UNDP.

UNDP (2006) *At Risk: Roma and the Displaced in Southeast Europe*, Bratislava: UNDP.

UN WCAR (2002) *At the Crossroads of Gender and Racial Discrimination*, http://www.un.org/WCAR/e-kit/gender.htm.

Verloo, M. (2006) 'Multiple Inequalities, Intersectionality and the European Union', *European Journal of Women's Studies*, 13 (3): 211-228.

Virág, T. (2006) 'A gettósodó térség', *Szociológiai Szemle*, 2006: 60-67.

Walby, S. (2004) 'The European Union and gender equality: emergent varieties of gender regime', *Social Politics*, 11(1): 4–29.

Wekker, G. (2004) 'Still crazy after all those years…: feminism for the New Millennium', *European Journal of Women's Studies*, 4(11): 487–500.

WHO (2009) 'Why gender and women's health?', http://www.who.int/gender/genderandwomen/en/ (Accessed March 2009).

Yuval-Davis, N. (2006) 'Intersectionality and feminist politics', *European Journal of Women's Studies*, 13(3): 193–209.

Yuval-Davis, N. and Anthias, F. (1989) (eds), *Women–Nation–State*, London: Macmillan.

Part Two

Domestic Perspectives

8
The Romani Movement in Romania: Institutionalization and (De)mobilization

Iulius Rostas

Introduction

The chapter explores the ways in which Roma participate in public life in Romania, the EU country with the largest number of Roma,[1] which is characterized by an apparently permissive minority participation system[2] and visible advocacy organizations at the national and international level. In spite of these positive developments, Roma in Romania have not managed to send more than one representative to the Parliament or to achieve the kind of political influence that the Hungarian minority in Romania has achieved. This chapter seeks to assess the degree of institutionalization of Romani organizations and the way they operate and to analyse the causes for the weak mobilization of Roma.

How can one explain the limited capacity of Roma organizations to mobilize Roma? There are two key observations to start with. First, in spite of the openness of the Romanian legal system for minority participation, there are structural causes within Romani non-governmental organizations (NGOs) that negatively affect their capacity to mobilize Roma.

The second observation is that the strategy chosen by Romani organizations – improving the situation of Roma based on a liberal human rights approach – lacks the capacity to mobilize Roma (cf. the chapter regarding Kosovo). Even though human rights discourses are valid when used to describe the situation of Roma, a strategy based on a liberal human rights discourse cannot build a community, be it political or civic, in which its members take part actively in the *res publica*. This strategy contradicts the representation function assumed by Roma NGOs (cf. Nirenberg's chapter). A human rights approach prefigures a patron-client relationship. The organization, the leader and/or the advocate of human rights for Roma has an asymmetrical relationship with the victims of human rights abuse. There is no equality and reciprocity involved in this relationship. It is a vertical relationship, not a horizontal one. It does not lead to the formation of those skills, practices and norms – such as trust, capacity to access and use public institutions, communication skills, engagement with public institutions (including speaking on behalf of the victim), equality, etc. – that stimulate co-operation and reciprocity, which are all basic ingredients for representing the genuine interests of Roma.

Conceptual framework

To date, there is no political party of Roma in Romania registered as such. Thus, all organizations – formal or informal – are circumscribed to the concept of civil society. The concept of civil society can be defined as 'the realm of organized social life that is open, voluntary, self-generating, at least partially self-supporting, autonomous from the state, and bound by a legal order or set of shared rules' (Diamond 1999: 221). The concept of civil society generally presupposes that individuals are acting collectively in the public sphere and that it is different from the private sphere, the space of individual and family life, or those groups concerned with themselves, from the economic sphere, the space for profit-making of companies, and from the political sphere, where there is competition amongst organized actors to gain control over the state or at least some positions within the state administration (Smolar 2002: 48–62).

It is difficult to separate Romani civil society from the mainstream civil society, but one can define it as comprising of those groups that have as their objective the representation of Romani interests in the public sphere. In this sense, Romani civil society is different from the Romani movement because it includes the supportive organizations which share the goals of Roma organizations but do not declare themselves as being one of them. This distinction between the movement and civil society reverses the one made by Vermeersch (2006: 9–10), who defines the Romani movement as 'the totality of activities carried out in the context of defending and cultivating a shared Romani identity' which includes the supporting organizations. In my view, the Roma civil society includes the movement, as well as organizations supporting the interests of the Roma in public sphere, including media and public opinion. The Romani movement strives to perform the functions of a social movement as described by Cohen and Arato (1992) who suggest '[s]ocial movements struggle over the power to define norms and collective identities' (1992: 405). It is evident that those organizations concerned with the situation of Roma without declaring themselves as Romani organizations are not explicitly focused on defining Romani identity. Alexander (2006) sees social movements as part of civil society and underlines the need for a new concept of civil society as a civil sphere, 'a world of values and institutions that generates the capacity for social criticism and democratic integration at the same time' (2006: 4).

In practice, amongst registered NGOs, it is possible to make a distinction between those that have political aims and the so-called civic ones which are putatively non-partisan. Some commentators suggest that Roma NGOs that have civic aims are better organized, more professional and more influential than those with explicit political aims (Miscoiu 2006).[3] Rughinis (2005) explains the difference between the two types of organizations by looking at how the system of political gains works, thereby signalling an inherent conflict of interest between civic and political organizations. For explicitly political organizations, the gains consist in obtaining the votes of the citizens in a zero-sum game. Since they are competing over the same set of votes, one competitor wins a vote, whilst the other loses it. On the other hand, civic organizations might cooperate amongst themselves because the gains for them consist in getting funding from donors, and cooperation could be an asset.

Legal framework for minority participation

In early 1990, as part of the general post-Ceausescu societal euphoria with politics, Roma set up several political parties, and the fact that only 251 members were required to register a political party added further impetus to this phenomenon. The 1924 law regulating the establishment of associations and foundations was reinstated and several Romani NGOs were registered all over the country. Only seven members were necessary to establish an NGO. The most influential NGO to emerge was the Democratic Union of Roma from Romania (DURR) which was set up in February 1990, and as a result of successful advocacy on the part of its leadership, also came to be represented within the provisional legislative forum of the country – the National Unity Provisional Council (*Consiliul Provizoriu de Uniune Nationala*). Decree 14/1990 regulating the election of the Parliament's lower and upper chambers stipulated that organizations representing national minorities can run in elections as candidates put forward by political parties on their select lists, and moreover, if they do not receive the number of votes required to obtain a seat in the Assembly of Deputies, have the right to representation by one deputy in the Assembly. This principle was included in the 1991 Constitution and in subsequent electoral laws.

In spite of the fact that there was no electoral threshold in the May 1990 elections,[4] and that the electoral system was a proportional list-based one, no Romani political party or NGO that participated in the elections received enough votes for a mandate of Deputy. The reserved seat for the Romani minority was awarded to DURR, the organization that received the highest number of votes. In the 1992 elections, the electoral threshold of 3% set by Law 68/1992 proved to be too steep a bar for Romani organizations to meet and by 2000, the threshold was raised to 5%. In the 1992 parliamentary elections, the reserved seat for the Roma minority was awarded to *Partida Romilor* (PR), which has received the highest number of votes amongst Romani organizations in all subsequent parliamentary elections. The end of Romani political parties came in 1996, when Law 27/1996 required all political parties to register within six months with the condition that they have at least 10,000 founding members, domiciled in at least 15 of the 41 Romanian counties, but no less than 300 in each county. As not one Romani political party has ever met these conditions, they have effectively disappeared.

In 1993, the Council for National Minorities (CNM) was established by the minority organizations represented in the Parliament. Under the law, they are entitled to a Government subsidy for administrative costs, meetings, hiring consultants, publications etc. In the case of

PR, the Government subsidy in the past five years (2003–2008) has been over two million euros per year.

The close relations between PR and the ruling Social Democratic Party coupled with key changes in the electoral laws both for local authorities and for the Parliament resulted in a situation where the rules changed in favour of the organization already represented in Parliament. Thus, the other organizations that intended to register for elections were required to present lists of members with at least 15% of the number of citizens that declared themselves as belonging to that national minority at the last census or, in cases where the population of the minority is higher than 25,000 persons, the organization should present a list of at least 25,000 members domiciled in at least 15 counties and Bucharest, with no less than 300 members in each of these counties. These stipulations clearly impede the competition amongst Romani organizations and destroy local level democratic representation for all minorities, particularly as we bear in mind that they have to be nationally representative to register candidates for even just one county!

Civil society

Institutionalization

Active participation of individuals in collective actions is the basis of a consolidated democracy. As noted above, instead of developing political tools to achieve their aims, Romani activists preferred to use civil society as a strategy to influence political decisions to achieve social change and mobilization of Romani communities, and thus established NGOs to influence politics. One objective of this chapter is to evaluate the impact of this strategy and to identify ways to move forward. I argue that Romani organizations have failed to generate public trust and to build those skills and norms necessary for the democratic process.

Schmitter (1997), analysing the roles civil society can play in democratic consolidation, points out that there are significant differences between civil societies and their impact on democratic consolidation depending on the intensity, distribution and the type of civil society. Starting from his observation that the dilemma of democratic consolidation is the building of institutions by politicians through consensus that are supported by the citizenry, we have to look at the institutions created by Romani leaders and the support these institutions attract from the diverse Romani communities themselves.

Diamond (1999) provides a relevant framework for analysing civil society, citing five characteristics that strongly correlate with the quality of associational life and the capacity of civil society to generate social trust and a democratic political culture: self-government, goals and methods, organizational institutionalization, pluralism and density (1999: 227–250). Applying this framework to the associational life of Roma in Romania helps us to gain a better understanding of the obstacles to mobilizing Roma.

The overwhelming majority of Romani NGOs lack transparency. Except for four NGOs – Romani Criss, Impreuna Agency, Ruhama Foundation and the Center Amare Romentza – no Romani organization has made public its sources of funding, annual reports, structure nor members of its board. The organizational chart and internal regulations of these organizations – crucial to understanding how decisions are made and how sanctions are awarded – are not available to the public. With the exception of Romani Criss, Impreuna Agency and the Alliance for Roma Unity, no other organization has had a change in leadership since its establishment. Even in these three cases, the new leaders were not elected but rather appointed as successors by their predecessors. The organizational structure is highly hierarchical, dominated by an authoritarian leader as is the case with PR.[5] Scandals and suspicions regarding especially the funding have been, and continue to be, sources of tensions and lack of trust between the organization and its members, as well as between the organization and the public at large, including Roma, whom these organizations claim to represent. Such suspicions are generated also by the leadership of some organizations, PR being very vocal against other organizations, accusing them of mismanagement of funds and stealing. Amongst Roma, the level of trust in NGOs is generally very low, a common opinion being that these organizations benefit out of Roma's difficult situation. According to research conducted by the US-based National Democratic Institute (NDI – affiliated with the Democratic Party), only 2% of Roma have ever approached an NGO and only 3% of Roma have participated in an activity of a civic group or a protest (NDI 2006). The lack of confidence in NGOs was revealed by the results of the 2007 Barometer of

Roma Inclusion, along with another key dilemma of Roma organizations: the problem of not being well known amongst Romani communities themselves. The most visible organization – PR – continues to remain unknown to 30% of Roma even after more than 15 years of activity and significant funding from the government to support its projects (Voicu 2007: 27–28).

The internal democracy of these organizations is reflected in the norms and culture that they are promoting amongst their members and to the outside world. It might be that an organization is efficient in promoting the interests of a group, monitors the activities of authorities efficiently and/or fulfils other democratic functions *without* being democratic in self-governing. It seems that most Romani organizations fit this description.

The quality of democracy depends on the existence of maximalist and uncompromising interest groups or those that are willing to use undemocratic methods to achieve undemocratic aims. Romani organizations do not have a maximalist approach. They cannot be considered an irredentist movement that affects the stability of the democratic system. There were instances when some marginal leaders tried to be in the public eye or to negotiate having a maximalist platform, as in the case of a self-declared 'State of Roma' near Targu Jiu in southwestern Romania (CIDCM 2005).[6]

Romani organizations have shown limited capacity for coalition-building amongst themselves as well as with other organizations. Nearly all attempts to establish networks of Romani organizations have failed to achieve greater influence in promoting the general interests of Roma. In spite of the fact that problems faced by Roma cover all the major human rights problems in the region, Romani NGOs have not found significant allies to advance their interests. One notable exception has been the campaign for amending the anti-discrimination law, for which Romani Criss cooperated successfully with other non-Romani NGOs and jointly proposed amendments that were later adopted by the Parliament.

Since early 1990, a large number of organizations, both Romani and non-Romani, have been established for the financial gains available under Romanian law: tax-free status for second-hand cars and imported goods, for example. In these circumstances, it is not surprising that many organizations represent in practice the interest of a small group or a family. Very few organizations have a board. Usually they are dependent on a leader that has an authoritarian leadership style, who sets the objectives and the agenda without deliberation. Dissent is considered an attack and it is punished. There are no clear procedures, foreseeable and repeatedly enforceable, to solve internal disputes. Communication amongst members regarding the mission, objectives, projects and methods is lacking. Deliberative processes are disregarded, whilst the approach for initiatives is generally top-down (cf. Nirenberg's chapter). All these aspects reflect the limited autonomy of organizations, which curbs their organizational efficiency as a whole and contributes to the narrowing of their potential social base. Thus, it is possible that the everyday activities of an organization are contrary to the mission that the organization was established for in the first place.

No better indicator of the limited autonomy of Romani organizations exists than the dependence on donor funding. Most of these organizations lack the capacity to attract resources for implementing their projects and achieving their objectives. The resources available at the community level are ignored most of the time. The majority of those organizations that manage to receive funding for their projects are generally dependent on a single donor. Few organizations manage to diversify their sources of funding, and thus, in this way, limit their dependence on donors. There is no organization self-financed to a degree which would ensure a high degree of autonomy. Even if donors do not set the agenda of a grantee organization, they can still suggest and set priorities and develop a patron–client relationship, and thus influence the agenda of these organizations (Trehan 2001). Indeed, these organizations are more accountable to their donors than to the group whose interest they claim to represent. As long as they operate on a project-by-project basis without having an endowment as a base, and are unable to define their priorities first and then to attract resources for implementing those priorities, Romani organizations will continue to have limited autonomy.

Regarding the complexity of Romani organizations, only those with electoral aims have developed a structure with territorial subunits – PR and the Alliance for Roma Unity. PR was set up in 1990 as *Societatea Romilor din Bucuresti* (Roma Society from Bucharest) by Ion Onoriu, Gheorghe Raducanu, Ivan Gheorghe, Vasile Ionescu, Ion Dumitru Bidia and others, but was taken over by a group led by Nicolae Paun, Gheorghe Raducanu and Ivan Gheorghe and changed its name in 1991. Although PR is not an officially registered political party, in its functioning, it acts like a 'quasi-political party'. Having the financial support of the Government, PR managed to develop a complex structure with subunits at county and local levels covering 30 of Romania's 41 counties. In spite of this established structure which might have served as a large support base, PR did not managed to mobilize Roma in a significant number for civic actions or for voting, with the result that the number of its obtained votes has declined over the last three rounds of elections.[7] The high degree of dependency on the leader, the lack of transparency, the selection of personnel for different positions according to their attachment and obedience to the leader, the influence of gangs or families at the county and local level and the lack of qualified cadre able to work efficiently within the bureaucratic system are some of the most important elements that have limited the capacity of PR in defining and representing the general interests of Roma.

The Alliance for Roma Unity (ARU) was established in 1996 as a political alternative to PR. It was a strong contender to PR in the 1996 parliamentary elections when it ran in a coalition with another organization under the name of *Unirea Romilor*. Unirea Romilor was set up earlier by Gheorghe Raducanu, the Roma MP from PR after he fell into disfavour with the leader of the organization. ARU and Unirea Romilor managed to get 71,020 votes for the Chamber of Deputies while PR received 82,195 votes. In the 2000 parliamentary elections ARU failed to register candidates due to some internal fights among factions. One of its leaders, Gheorghe Raducanu, decided to run for PR and thus left the organization at the last minute, taking with him some official documents that made it impossible to register alternative candidates. ARU's support decreased significantly in the 2004 parliamentary, and it received only 15,041 votes. The coherence of the organization is weak, as the mobilization of its members and subunits occurs primarily during electoral campaigns. It changed its leadership once, but notably, this was not through an open and democratic competition.

The Christian Center of Roma is led by the self-proclaimed 'king' Florin Cioaba who is also a local leader of a neoprotestant church. As one analyst put it, the Center's 'legitimacy is maintained by a mixture elements [issuing] from the nomad or the "sedentary nomad" tradition and the religious elements, such as the obeisance to the pastor' (Miscoiu 2006).[8] It attracts support from traditional communities and some religious communities, usually Pentecostals that acknowledge the authority of the pastor Florin Cioaba. The Center participated in negotiations amongst Romani organizations prior to the 2000 parliamentary elections to present a common list of minority candidates (Project on Ethnic Relations 2000). Although the negotiation failed, the Center managed to register candidates for the elections. However, it received only 12,171 votes in spite of the support received from the Community of Roma Ethnicity from Romania (CRER) led by a traditional Roma leader, Ion Dumitru Bidia.

The CRER participated in the 1996 parliamentary elections and received 5,227 votes. It is an organization based on family ties and has no formal structures. Its leader, Ion Dumitru Bidia, has made some unsubstantiated statements in the past, as a way to penetrate the media. For example, in a statement from 16 January 1995, CRER announced that Roma would start a civil war in order to defend themselves against the violence perpetrated against them by non-Roma (CIDCM 2005). In the 2000 elections CRER did not register any candidates and in the 2004 election, it failed to meet the requirements of the new electoral law and thus could not register candidates, even though it had intended to have a candidate for Presidency.[9]

The Roma Civic Alliance from Romania (RCAR), a network of NGOs acting mostly at local level, was set up in the spring of 2006 after two years of discussions. One of the reasons for setting up this network was the hegemonic tendencies of PR and the authoritarian attempt of the government to block any form of criticism. RCAR has territorial subunits but analysing its activity to date it is clear that its coherence is low. Currently, it has a board consisting of three persons, leaders of member organizations. Its main focus was the central government as it assumed the role of monitoring government policies towards Roma. After a successful launch of the organization, the enthusiasm of other NGOs to join this legally registered network decreased as it took a while to clarify its mission and role, and the pressure from PR and the government eased significantly following the change in government in December 2004. Some Romani activists perceived RCAR as a political alternative to PR or as an elite club they wanted to join. During the annual meeting in 2007, when for the first time a Roma organization presented and debated its activity report, the organization made clear that it will not run in elections. Since then, a change in leadership through an open competition took place and the members of the board were elected by its members. In spite of its potential and its qualified human resources, RCAR failed to increase its number of members and its visibility decreased.

The Roma Center for Social Intervention and Studies (Romani Criss) and Impreuna Agency have developed networks of organizations to implement their projects. Romani Criss is a leading Roma rights monitoring and advocacy NGOs based in Bucharest and was founded in 1993 by a consortium. Its coordinator was Nicolae Gheorghe, one of the best known and most influential Romani activists in Europe.[10] Romani Criss has focused its activities on human rights monitoring but has also developed innovative projects in areas like education and health. It serves as a model for a number of NGOs established by activists that have worked with them in the past. Many of these NGOs are currently part of the networks of human rights monitors contracted by Romani Criss all over the country. It has a board, but the names have not been made public on the website. Romani Criss managed to change its leadership three times since its establishment, though the new leaders were appointed and not elected by its members. Nevertheless, Romani Criss is one of the most well-known Romani NGOs in Europe.

Impreuna Agency was set up in 1999 with the aim of contributing to the development of Romani communities and cooperating with other actors involved in implementing projects targeting Roma. It has also successfully undergone a change in leadership to date. Impreuna Agency developed a network of experts and NGOs acting at the community level in the places where it had implemented projects covering development of human resources, education, health, culture, housing and research. Impreuna Agency cooperated with a number of state institutions, NGOs, local authorities and universities. The networks developed by Impreuna Agency and Romani Criss depend on their founders to a large degree. The fact that both organizations have contractual relationships with the members of their network makes a difference in the objectives they pursue. It is difficult to assess the commitment of the members to the objectives of either organization outside of the contractual relationship. Financial resources obtained through network membership help local organizations to survive.

Other Roma organizations that have had some success in gaining visibility are the Bucharest-based Roma Center Amare Romentza, the Ruhama Foundation, based in Oradea, western Romania and Aven Amentza. Amare Romentza focused its activities on intercultural education and promoting Roma identity in the public sphere including within the educational system. Ruhama Foundation is a service provider established in 1996 that targets vulnerable groups, including Roma. In the last four years, Ruhama has become more involved with Roma communities and attracted the public attention while representing the victims of police abuse in a Roma community near Oradea. Aven Amentza, led by Vasile Ionescu, was a visible organization until he left Romania in 2005. The organization tried to be a promoter of Roma identity in the public sphere. It published two periodicals: *Aven Amentza*, published with the support of the Ministry of Culture, where Vasile Ionescu had a position of advisor, and *Romathan*. Both publications ceased to exist after several issues. *Aven Amentza* also had a publishing house where an important collection of titles on Romani history, the Holocaust, literature, etc. were printed.

Some Romani organizations have become highly bureaucratic and professionalized. They hire full-time technocrats to focus on specific fields. This indicates the degree of institutionalization, a process which tends to limits the dynamics and flexibility of civil society. Focusing on the post-socialist countries of Eastern Europe in particular, this process is referred to as 'NGOization' by one scholar, who notes 'the transformation of social movements into organisations and the increasing dominance of "modern" NGOs which emphasise issue-specific interventions and pragmatic strategies with a strong employment focus, rather than the establishment of a new democratic counter-culture' (Stubbs 2007). In other words, NGOs have become a specific sector that offers employment and career opportunities for a new generation.

All of the above mentioned organizations became more professionalized through their experiences with implementing projects and reporting procedures. Thus, they have gained a dominant position within the Roma civil society. The EU enlargement process has led to an acceleration of this process. Those organizations focused on project implementation will have to deal with the requirements of the European bureaucracy to maintain their positions, as partners of state institutions or as direct applicants for tenders in different EU programmes. Thus, the spontaneity to react to diverse stimuli – a basic characteristic of civil society – will continue to decline.

No organization can claim it represents all Roma interests even if PR, due to the institutional arrangements for national minority protection, claims that it is the sole representative organization of Roma. Roma are a very diverse group, stratified according to multiple cleavages – degree of assimilation, spoken language, kin relationships (*neamuri*), occupations and geographical dispersion – so that such a claim is futile. Pluralism is a pre-condition for a democratic society. The high number of Roma organizations is normal and beneficial. But are there limits to such numbers? The fragmenting of Roma civil society leads to a low efficiency in representing the interests of the Roma. This low efficiency is due to extreme pluralism where a large number of organizations fight amongst themselves to represent the same interests of Roma.

Organizational density is an indicator of a solid civic community. A high number of organizations with diverse specific interests at the level of community can generate a democratic culture through cooperation, reciprocity and trust. It can lead to the development of specific agendas representing diverse interests and offer a higher number of opportunities to individual to have multiple affiliations. In the case of Roma, the number of effective grassroots organizations is low, as is their membership (National Democratic Institute 2006). Many communities lack any form of organization. Even when such organizations exist, they do not clearly define the interests they claim to represent and the membership is exclusive.[11] Moreover, the relationships among organizations that operate in the same community are strongly competitive and multiple affiliations are out of question. In most of the cases the competition is generated by the fight for accessing limited resources and influencing the authorities, each organization claiming that it has a monopoly over the representation of Roma.

Modus operandi

The Romani movement has managed to influence policies of different cabinets toward Roma and to limit the power of the state. It has contributed to the establishment of structures dealing with Roma issues within the public administration, to the adoption of the government strategies for Roma, to monitoring and influencing some of the local and central authorities' activities and to blocking initiatives that were contrary to the interests of the Roma. However, the Romani movement has been reactive to critical events, rather being than a movement which is able to influence government agendas directly through innovative proposals. In other words, it did not manage to set the political agenda for Roma. Priorities have been defined by other actors. The achieved successes were due mostly to circumstantial factors.

Roma participation in *res publica* should not be left only to the political parties, whether they be ethnic ones or mainstream. Civil society plays an important role in supplementing the role of political parties, particularly as political organizations of Roma have not managed to attract a sufficient number of votes to become a player in the political arena. The highest number of votes that Roma organizations received was in the 1996 election, and since then the number of votes has declined. The number of elected Roma representatives at the local level is low in comparison to the number of Roma even if one considers the official figure of 535,000, according to the 2002 national census. In the overwhelming majority of cases, Roma play a marginal role in local politics. Usually the pressure on local authorities seeks to obtain the fair distribution of social assistance benefits. Even the most outrageous abuses by local authorities do not mobilize local community to act collectively to defend their interests. Usually, there is a need for those organizations acting at a regional and national level to intervene and put pressure on local authorities by mediating the case and sending petitions to central authorities.

Roma organizations did not manage to put 'Roma problematique' on the agenda of the political parties or make it a topic for debate during the electoral campaign. Only the Social Democratic Party (PSD) has a section in its party platform on the social inclusion of Roma, and it is also the only party which has had a Romani MP on its party list be elected (elected in 2000, he was not re-elected in 2004).[12] For the November 2008 parliamentary elections, the National Liberal Party announced that two Roma would run for Parliamentary seats. In turn, the Social Democratic Party responded by announcing that it would field two Romani candidates on its party list as well. In addition to the representative of the minority organization (only PR registered to run for offices in these elections), two other Roma ran, representing two extremist parties: the New Generation Party and *Romania Mare* Party. These were the first elections in which a total of seven Romani candidates ran for offices on behalf of different political organizations. The representative of the minority organization, Nicolae Paun, received a place in the Parliament due to constitutional provisions. A second Romani candidate representing PSD, Madalin Voicu, managed to receive a mandate after a redistribution of votes at national level. No other candidate came close to winning a mandate in the Parliament, even though some of them made a positive appearance in the campaign. These candidates were selected by the parties due to their connections and relatively good public image as Romani activists, not because of their support from Romani NGOs or their proven capacity to mobilize Roma in the past.[13]

These facts indicate that Romani organizations are not perceived by political parties as being able to mobilize a significant number of citizens. To date, no protests or meetings organized by Romani organizations have ever mobilized over a thousand participants. Even ARU, which managed to collect 25,000 signatures in order to register in the 2004 elections, cannot be considered a mass organization since it received less votes than the number of members declared. PR, despite receiving consistent financial support from the government and the large number of posts its members hold within Romanian public administration, has not managed to develop subunits in all of the country's counties, having branches in only 31 counties or about 75% of the country. Other organizations with electoral goals mobilize their militants only during electoral campaign season, with the number of those who are active on a permanent basis being very low.

The number of active members of Romani organizations varies between one – many organizations being in fact one-man shows – and in the tens. Romani NGOs with civic goals, in spite of their low number of adherents, do gain the support of some committed and highly educated and qualified activists. In fact, they were not interested in attracting new members but rather in getting those highly qualified activists as employees, consultants, volunteers or supporters. They are focused on producing qualified Roma and to developing their human resource potential, with most of the Roma that are holding positions in the state administration being in the past connected to such NGOs.

One common feature of Romani organizations is the way in which they perceive resources. Resource evaluation is done almost always in financial terms. In fact, the most important resource is at the community level: citizens that can be mobilized to act collectively for a public interest. Their number, skills and the quality of involvement should be the measure of success for these organizations in achieving their goals rather than the financial resources attracted from donors or from the government. Moreover, involvement in NGOs broadens individuals' vision and interests, and changes their knowledge and the way they relate to the political system, with its political culture becoming a participative one, thus increasing the potential for community members to get involved in political activities. Thus, civil society contributes to the development of local democracy and decreases the community's dependency on clientelism and the intervention of external actors.

Roma organizations did not have educating citizens about democracy as a priority. Only in the last years have Roma organizations become interested in monitoring elections, in developing education projects on electoral process and voting, or in distributing information regarding access to social services. Initiatives that have proven helpful in promoting civic education amongst marginalized and oppressed communities in different parts of the world, such as street law initiatives and the development of paralegal networks, have not been successfully developed by Romani organizations.

The influence that civil society in the former communist countries, including Romani civil society, has achieved is largely the result of external factors which act as independent variables, rather than dependent variables such as the capacity to influence decision-makers and mobilize citizens (Vermeersch 2006: 184–213). These external factors were connected to the foreign affairs priorities of the Central and Eastern European countries – such as the membership to the Council of Europe, NATO and the European Union – as well as to the activities of some transnational networks like Human Rights Watch, International Helsinki Federation for Human Rights, Amnesty International and others (Jenne 2000: 189–191).

Romani organizations were the agents of ethnic identity formation and reproduction. With the emergence of the nation-state, identity is formed and reproduced on a large scale by state institutions, mainly the educational system and army. In the case of Roma, without a kin-state, this function was assumed by Romani organizations. One important advantage in the case of Romani identity is that it is fluid; it is open to criticism and debate, and is able to accept and incorporate different views and interpretations on events, relations and characters. The disadvantage is that, Roma organizations being relatively weak, the formation and reproduction of Romani ethnic identity might be so fluid that it is difficult to promote a coherent ethnic consciousness amongst Roma.

But the most important role played by Roma civil society has been that of ensuring channels for articulating, aggregating and representing the interests of Roma. This is one of the basic functions of political parties but they do not have a monopoly over it. In fact, this function of civil society is very important when the interests of some significant groups are not represented by political parties due to the electoral system or other causes. Mainstream political parties were not interested in tackling the *Roma problematique* as they were afraid that this would lead to a diminishing of their electoral support. The electoral threshold to get into Parliament and the bureaucratic regulations which condition local democracy on the existence of a significant national representation have lead to a predominance of this characteristic of civil society amongst Romani organizations. Another cause of the preponderance of this function was the lack of direct support from the donors of Roma political participation. Unlike other national minorities from the region which were supported by the kin-state, Roma did not receive support to develop organizational infrastructures and qualified cadres to be able to compete efficiently with other political groups. Donors were mostly interested in an associational approach based on projects that responded to some critical issues within the community.

Mobilization

To the question of how one can explain why Roma are voting in such small numbers for organizations that purport to represent their interests, generally the classical answer is that the programmes of these organizations do not take into consideration the real needs of the communities and that their agendas do not match the needs of citizens. However, this answer reduces the political and electoral process only to the rational component of the political behaviour of individuals.

Another common question which is posed is: how do you increase the involvement of Roma in politics and thus generate political participation on a broader scale? This question is put to both Roma and to non-Roma politicians. The usual answer from politicians is either that Roma are not interested in politics, that they do not matter as an electorate or that when electoral competition is very tight, their votes can be bought. Other questions that invariably arise about Roma and politics in Romania are: should Roma set up their own ethnic political party or should they join mainstream parties? Why have Roma been unable to set up a successful political party to date? Is such a party relevant for their situation, and why have no Romani organizations managed a mass mobilization of Roma even once? Why is the level of trust in state institutions and in Romani politicians so low amongst the Romani masses?

The answers to these questions are complex and one has to examine the different levels of social life; for example, how are the political attitudes of Roma formed? What are the political values that guide Roma? How is the public interest of Roma aggregated and represented? How are they participating, who sets the political agenda, etc.? But it is also important to look at some historical circumstances. While this chapter provides some answers, there is a critical need for further comprehensive research on these topics.

Community

In general, Roma have a parochial political culture (Almond and Verba 1963). Information of high interest to Romani communities is often related to social problems they face and interaction with the political system is at the local level. Knowledge about political life, institutions and the relations between different components of the political system is extremely limited (Voicu 2007).

Roma's engagement with public institutions and trust in public authorities is extremely low. Roma believe that these institutions constitute a tool for social control of their minority communities. The usually hostile attitude of these institutions towards Roma reflects the hostile attitude of the general public towards Roma. Being often victims of police abuse and the denial of basic rights, as well as lacking any support from local authorities, Roma tend not to participate in the public life of their local community.

One continuing expression of the low level of trust in and engagement with public institutions in Romania is the fact that Roma are not represented at the local level, even when they do represent a significant percentage of the local population. Roma do not usually run for local public office, although most of the problems they face can be solved at the local level. Even those few that manage to be elected fail to develop a trust relationship with their constituency, being often unprepared for that position, and as a result, usually do not get re-elected. This derives from the perception Roma have that even if their representatives are elected to public office, their everyday problems do not get solved. The low institutional performance and the general perception that public officials retain a power relation to their electorate reduce the level of trust towards public authorities and the possibility for Roma to be elected and re-elected.

Generally, trust in public institutions is determined by the existence and quality of the co-operation between members of specific communities and these institutions. The solidarity within local communities has been declining during transition – both formally and informally – within the post-communist Romanian society as a whole. Voluntary participation in community affairs has also been decreasing. Individuals primarily focus on personal short-term interests with a disregard to the long-term benefits of community co-operation as a whole. Roma, a group that has been worst hit by the hardship of transition from communism and shows a higher level of poverty compared to the rest of society, apply the same rationale for social behaviour and aim to maximize personal gains over collective interests.

Most commonly, Roma are referred to in terms of poverty and poverty reduction discourse. Social exclusion and extreme poverty constitute a serious drain of community resources. Nevertheless, there are Roma who do not necessarily fall into the category of the poor and their communities retain considerable human, financial and symbolic resources. These communities' interests are usually disregarded as most organizations that aim to mobilize Roma fail to consider the actual stratification of Roma communities. For example, there are Roma that have achieved social status through education, music, sports etc. They are not the target for mobilization for Romani organizations, though they do represent role models for society and could contribute significantly to the mobilization of Roma on a mass scale. Perhaps as a result of stereotyping, Roma are depicted in general terms as facing extreme poverty, huge unemployment, lack of education etc. It is clear that Roma who are successful in their careers do not fall in this category, and do not identify themselves with other Roma as they face different sets of problems.

In analysing the electoral mobilization of Roma in Hungary, the Czech Republic and Slovakia, Vermeersch (2006) identifies another factor: the intensity of electoral competition when mainstream parties are playing a decisive role in the electoral process. Irrespective of the chosen strategy for representation – either ethnic or mainstream parties – it is problematic to define the limits of the community for Roma. Thus far, the limit has generally been determined by the level of social exclusion and extreme poverty.

The mobilization of those Roma that have managed to lift themselves out of poverty and exclusion will need to take into account the challenges of this definition. Roma activists will need to construct a new identity of 'Roma' without the stigma attached currently to Romani ethnicity. Many Roma that are not poor and managed to climb the social ladder do not openly acknowledge their ethnicity and even deny it because of the negative perception in society of being a 'Gypsy'. Many of them do not speak Romani, do not identify themselves with the mainstream media depictions and stigmatization of Roma and do not follow the actions of Roma 'leaders'. These Roma are usually assimilated to a significant extent and retain a fear of losing their social status and current benefits in case they were to assume their identity publicly. Roma activists, in addition to constructing a new public identity for Roma, will also need to offer symbolic benefits for those assimilated Roma that will associate themselves with the movement.

Roma generally lack civic traditions and were never part of the political community due to past systemic exclusion, extreme oppression, slavery, assimilative attempts and extermination. Thus they have never been part of the social contract. Their exclusion and slavery status was reflected in everyday language. The slave was not treated as a human being, and this treatment continued after their liberation. Even today, Romanian folklore contains sayings that underline the non-human nature of 'the Gypsy'.[14] Indeed, the majority of descriptions of Roma in Romanian folklore contain zoological associations. Hence, throughout the centuries, Roma have developed various survival strategies which are often in conflict with current democratic and legal norms. Relations and co-operation with non-Roma focus mainly on maximizing immediate gains and profits, and are normally tinged with a lack of trust.

Today, civil society organizations play an important role in the continued alienation and widening distrust between Roma and public institutions. This is primarily the result of the existence of NGOs with obscure, non-transparent and/or poorly applied organizational norms and regulations which lower the level of trust both amongst the members of respective organizations and the public at large. As a result, these organizations fail to enlarge their social basis, to generate public trust and to promote a democratic and participative political culture based on cooperation and reciprocity.

Leaders and leadership style

The civil society is the medium where much of the necessary knowledge and skills for Roma leaders are developed. It has an important role in defining the *Roma problematique* and in promoting social and political values of the community. Civil society constitutes a de facto 'laboratory' for the political process, and the increased political participation of Roma through civil society organizations rather than political parties confirms this argument. Taking this into account, Roma civil society has an important role in forming and promoting attitudes, rules and practices for transparent political and civil participation of Roma in public sphere. These attitudes and practices could be later institutionalized within the community itself. The development of an effective and vigorous Roma civil society could compensate for the lack of civic traditions amongst Roma, but this process is rather long and tenuous.

The participation of Romani representatives in public life solely via civil society organizations prefigures thier general lack of accountability. This is explained by the fact that Romani civil society leaders and their respective organizations are not subject to the test of free elections or other accountability measures, as are political parties and public officials. Thus, they do not usually consider it necessary to respond to the needs and expectations of the community. These leaders instead tend to develop strongly hierarchical structures as a way to increase their power. The lack of accountability towards the public results in a lack of transparency, which leads to distrust. The appointment of family members or close friends to high positions within the organization develops a leadership 'clique' which then creates full dependency of the organization on that leader and/or clique. This modus operandi and the resulting distrust contradict the original goals and objectives of the organization and debilitate effective cooperation among the members within the organization and with external partners. As a result, the organization cannot enlarge its social basis and loses credibility and support from Romani community. Eventually, the organization focuses solely on its competitiveness vis-à-vis other Romani organizations, with Romani leaders thus playing an important role in extreme fragmentation of Romani civil society.

At the same time, Romani NGO leaders, without a clear mandate from the community to represent them, are nonetheless treated by governmental institutions as legitimate representatives of Roma. This leads to dependency of Roma communities on these leaders for access to public services and constitutes a source for corrupt practices that discourages effective participation. The source of these leaders' power is their official recognition by the government. In turn, Romani leaders depend on this recognition and thus tend to be perceived by the community as state agents rather than as representing common interests of Roma. This, in itself, leads to the inability of leaders to mobilize the Roma.

Another source of power for some Romani activists is their ability to successfully navigate the bureaucratic system of state administration. This capacity is used to legitimize the power they exhibit. But this capacity does not provide for mobilization of significant number of Roma, which would enable the activists to negotiate on behalf of Roma on equal footing with governmental and non-governmental actors.

Strategies

Romani civil society has focused its strategy on a human rights discourse, which internationally had the merit of putting the Roma issue on the agendas of various international organizations and individual governments. In this way, a thin strata of English-speaking Romani activists became the spokespersons for the whole community, lacking a mandate from their people and lacking a social base for those claims (Trehan 2001). This is one of the reasons why there is such a gap between the claims of Romani activists and advocates at the international level and the discourse of Romani activists at the local level.

This approach has its disadvantages for civic movement and citizen mobilization. First, it cannot mobilize the Roma because it is mainly reactive and does not connect human rights with issues of Romani identity (cf. Gheorghe and Acton 2001: 65–67). Second, human rights organizations do not normally develop horizontal relationships with their constituencies and other organizations, and this leads to the formation of vertical power relationships. Thus, human rights groups focusing on Roma do not necessarily promote the development of a civic community with a high level of cooperation and trust among its members (Putnam 1993: 102–133).

Expressing the interests of Roma exclusively as human rights claims neglects the importance of engaging in the political debate at the local and national level. While human rights claims are moral and legitimate, Romani activists did not take into account the competition with other groups in society for setting the political agenda and gaining access to power and resources. The Roma focused their attention on the state rather than trying to negotiate their interests with other political actors. It is also true that they could not negotiate their interests because human rights are not negotiable due to their universal character. One cannot claim that a community needs more right to life or more right to a fair trial but one can claim a better and/or equal implementation of the right to life or the right to a fair trial for a community (Kennedy 2004: 3–35).

Another important factor that has influenced Romani civil society and perpetuated the lack of political culture based on consensus and trust amongst Roma was the position of donors. The competition for donor funding and support led to a limited cooperation among Roma organizations and to a donor-driven rather than community-driven political agenda. They were perceived by the community as competing for donors' favours, rather than acting on behalf of the community. Priorities were not set by Roma or their organizations and this resulted in full accountability to donors at the expense of the Roma communities (Trehan 2001).

Conclusions

In this chapter, I suggested that the degree of institutionalization of Romani organizations is relatively low, thereby contributing to a low level of public trust amongst those they claim to represent. In fact, this lack of public trust is a major obstacle in mobilizing Roma on a large scale. Romani organizations should find solutions to increase their transparency and become self-sustainable to a higher degree. A first step could be to set up boards of directors that could oversee the application of rules and procedures.

It is a challenge to develop a membership-based organization able to attract the masses and to use community resources as a primary reservoir, thus contributing to the genuine spread of a self-help civic spirit as an alternative to 'NGOization'. Setting up an organization seeking actively to increase the number of its members and to involve them in collective actions could be seen as alternatives to the growing process of professionalization and bureaucratization of Romani NGOs, especially those that have accumulated expertise in project implementation. Such organizations concerned with the situation of Roma do not seek large public support for their activities. On the contrary, a mass-based organization would focus primarily on placing issues of collective interest for Roma onto the public agenda.

The development of some networks for self-help might be a direction for action for Romani leaders and organizations. The role of such networks should be to generate trust, cooperation and reciprocity amongst individuals and to be a channel for expressing the collective interests of the individuals, which is much stronger than individual action alone. Increasing the number of informal action groups for the benefit of community members would also bring spontaneity to civil society. There is a need to develop programmes at the level of community civic education such as street law initiatives and community paralegal networks as a way to increase the social capital of Roma.

With respect to the Romani movement, changes in leadership and leadership style, increased cooperation and a consensus-building approach amongst leaders and developing relations with political parties, other NGOs and trade unions are all developments that would increase the public trust in Romani leaders and would increase their ability to set the political agenda.

But above all, Roma should get involved in politics. Problems faced by Roma are political in nature, and in order to deal with them, there is a need for a consistent budgetary allocation from the state. At the end of the day, Roma will have better lives only when they are strong enough to have a say in politics. Social change is not God-given but man-made.

Notes

1. According to the 2002 national census in Romania, the population of Romani citizens stands at 535,000. However, it is commonly understood that the census has particular limitations and does not accurately reflect the real number of Roma. Credible research estimates the number to be between 1.5 and 2.5 million out of a total population of 22 million people in Romania.

2. The term 'permissive' describes a minority protection system which, despite a liberal appearance, is designed to control and manipulate national minorities. Between 1990 and 1993, a post-Ceausescu authoritarian regime sought to mobilize all national minorities against the powerful Hungarian minority by offering them certain benefits – parliamentary representation, the right to run for office in local and parliamentary elections without being officially registered as political parties, consistent government subsidies, etc., and all these measures appear to be part of a liberal minorities agenda. Another reason for the adoption of these measures was the Council of Europe accession process. As observed in this chapter, once Romania's integration into Euro-Atlantic structures became immanent, the system of minority protection became increasingly restrictive. On national minority protection issues, see to Weber (1998) and Oprescu (2005).

3. While the analysis made by Miscoiu (2006) is interesting, there are some factual errors: there are no political parties of Roma in Romania at present. To avoid any misinterpretations, the name of *Partida Romilor* has been kept in Romanian, rather than translating it as 'Roma Party'.

4. In the 1990 elections, political parties and other political groups, including minority NGOs, were not required to obtain a specific proportion of votes to gain entry into Parliament. This aspect changed in the 1992 elections when the electoral threshold was set at 3% requiring all parties to receive at least 3% of the votes at the *national level* in order to gain Parliamentary seats. Thus, even candidates who gained sufficient votes at the district level were effectively prohibited from the Parliament if they could not reach the 3% threshold at the national level.

5. These dynamics are not limited to Romani-run NGOs *per se*, but are prevalent amongst NGOs in the region as a whole.

6. See the chronology of significant events for Roma in Romania at the Center for International Development and Conflict Management (CIDCM) website, 'Minorities at Risk' project. According to the Center, citing *Agence France Presse*, from 6 March 1997, 'The self-proclaimed emperor of the world's Gypsies, Iulian Radulescu, announced on Thursday the creation of the first gypsy [*sic*] state in Tirgu-Jiu, in southwest Romania.'

7. In the 1992 parliamentary elections, *Partida Romilor* received 52,704 votes. In 1996 it attracted 82,195. In 2000, the number decreased to 71,786 and in 2004 to 56,076. And this is despite the fact that the Romani electorate is expanding!

8. I disagree with Miscoiu (2006) that the Center is a religious party of Roma.

9. Until 2004, the parliamentary elections and presidential elections took place at the same time. The candidate that CRER announced for the President of Romania was Viorel Bumbu, a traditional community leader from Transylvania. However, the last minute changes in the electoral laws made it impossible for CRER to collect the required number of signatures. No Romani individual has run for President of the country yet.

10. Gheorghe is a sociologist and was associated with the Sociology Institute of the Romanian Academy of Sciences. He was also the Senior Advisor to the OSCE's (Organization for Security and Co-operation in Europe) Office of Roma/Sinti Affairs until 2007, and a founder of Romani Criss.

11. For example, the European Roma Grassroots Organization, in spite of its name, is not a grassroots organization, being based in Bucharest and taking part in different activities at national and international level with little connection to local Roma communities.

12. Madalin Voicu, the son of the world famous Romanian Roma violin player Ion Voicu, former MP 1996–2000 representing Roma minority *Partida Romilor*, was elected as MP for the Social Democratic Party. He was always close to Social Democratic Party (SDP) since he was very well connected with the former communist nomenklatura.

13. Gruia Bumbu, the President of the National Agency for Roma, and Dana Varga, personal adviser to the Prime Minister, were announced by National Liberal Party as candidates. Madalin Voicu and Costel Bercus, President of the Board of the Roma Education Fund and former Director of Romani Criss, were announced by Social Democrats as their candidates. Tudor Gheorghe represented Romania Mare Party and Daniel Onoriu was on the list of New Generation Party candidates.

14. 'A Gypsy is not a human being even on Easter day' (*Tiganul nu e om nici in ziua de Paste*) or 'Neither is osier [wicker] a tree, nor is the Gypsy a human being' (*Nici rachita nu e pom, nici tiganu nu e om*).

References

Alexander, C.J. (2006) *The Civil Sphere*, Oxford: Oxford University Press.

Almond, G. and Verba, S. (1963) *The Civic Culture: Political Attitudes and Democracy in Five Nations*, Princeton: Princeton University Press.

CIDCM (2005) 'Minorities at Risk' project, Center for International Development and Conflict Management, http://www.cidcm.umd.edu/mar/ (Accessed 25 September 2007).

Cohen, J. and Arato, A. (1992) *Civil Society and Political Theory*, Boston: MIT Press.

Diamond, L. (1999) *Developing Democracy towards Consolidation*, Baltimore and London: The Johns Hopkins University Press.

Gheorghe, N. and Acton, T. (2001) 'Citizens of the world and nowhere: minority, ethnic and human rights for Roma during the last hurrah of the nation-state' in W. Guy (ed.) *Between Past and Future: The Roma of Central and Eastern Europe*, Hatfield: University of Hertfordshire Press.

Jenne, E. (2000) 'The Roma of Central and Eastern Europe: constructing a stateless nation' in Stein, P.J. (ed.) *The Politics of National Minority Participation in Post-Communist Europe: State Building, Democracy and Ethnic Mobilization*, New York: M.E. Sharp.

Kennedy, D. (2004) *The Dark Side of Virtue: Reassessing International Humanitarianism*, Princeton: Princeton University Press.

Miscoiu, S. (2006) 'Is there a model for the political representation of the Romanian Roma?', *Sfera Politicii*, 123–124:78–89.

National Democratic Institute for International Affairs (2006) *Studiu privind Participarea Politica a Romilor din Romania*, opinion poll conducted by Center for Urban and Regional Sociology, Bucharest, August 2006.

Oprescu, D. (2005) *Un Pas Gresit in Directia cea Buna: Mminoritatile Nationale din Romania*, 1990–2005, Bucharest: University of Bucharest Press.

Project on Ethnic Relations (2000) *Roma and Elections in Romania*, Targu Mures, http://www.per-usa.org/1997–2007/romania.htm

Putnam, R. (1993, tr. 2001) *Cum Functioneaza Democratia: Traditiile Civice in Italia Moderna* (original title *Making Democracy Work: Civic Traditions in Modern Italy*), Iasi: Editura Polirom.

Rughinis, C. (2005) 'Organizatii rome cu profil electoral' in Baltasiu, R., Dobrica, P. and Jderu, G. (eds) *Reprezentari si Reprezentativitate. Perspective asupra Comunitatii Roma*, Bucharest: Editura Omega Ideal.

Schmitter, P. (1997) 'Civil society: East and West' in Diamond, L., Plattner, M., Chu, Y., and Tien, H. (eds) *Consolidating Third Wave Democracies: Themes and Perspectives*, Baltimore: Johns Hopkins UP.

Smolar, A. (2002) 'Civil society after Communism' in Diamond, L. and Plattner, M. (eds) *Democracy after Communism*, Baltimore and London: the Johns Hopkins UP.

Stubbs, P. (2007) 'Aspects of community development in contemporary Croatia: globalisation, neo-liberalisation and NGO-isation' in Dominelli, L. (ed.) *Revitalising Communities in a Globalising World*, Aldershot: Ashgate Press.

Trehan, N. (2001) 'In the name of the Roma' in W. Guy (ed.) *Between Past and Future: the Roma of Central and Eastern Europe*, Hatfield: University of Hertfordshire Press.

Vermeersch, P. (2006) *The Romani Movement: Minority Politics & Ethnic Mobilization in Contemporary Central Europe*, New York & Oxford: Berghahn Books.

Voicu, O. (2007) *State of Mind, Institutions, Political Options of the Roma in Romania*, in Roma Inclusion Barometer, Open Society Foundation Romania, http://www.osf.ro/en/publicatii.php?cat=16

Weber, R. (1998) 'The protection of national minorities in Romania: a matter of political will and wisdom' in Kranz, J. and Küpper, K. (eds) *Law and Practice of Central European Countries in the Field of National Minorities Protection After 1989*, Warsaw: Center for International Relations.

9
Social Unrest in Slovakia 2004: Romani Reaction to Neoliberal 'Reforms'

Martin Marušák and Leo Singer

> Parents don't let their children go to school because they can't afford to pay the bus fare. The ones with decent shoes walk to school. Although hungry, children are sent to school because their parents don't want to lose family benefit. I witnessed how a 7-year-old girl collapsed from hunger [...] no after-school activities are possible. Children are hungry [...] these are families with three or four children, and they do not even belong to the most 'backward' families.
>
> Nataša Bažová, Romani teaching assistant,
> *Roma Press Agency* (2004)

Our chapter draws attention to the events of the winter of 2003/2004 in Slovakia when a wave of social unrest circulated in the Romani communities within the country. It was a reaction to the cuts in social benefits provision by the then prevailingly neoliberal government. The government's response – dramatic in its scope for a post-socialist 'democratic' regime in Europe – was to mobilize the army for the first time since the revolution in November 1989. We consider these events as the first grassroots mobilization of Roma against the effects of free market capitalism and neoliberal 'reforms' in Slovakia. Romani people living in segregated communities are the most excluded population group in Slovakia and their struggle shares both ethnic and social components. Therefore, we would wish that the events of the Slovakian 'winter of discontent' are not lost.

To the contrary, it is hoped that our exploratory contribution here would inspire further research on these events.

What really happened? As each narrative of social mobilization is necessarily value-laden and subject to the author's political beliefs, our explanatory framework is informed by the work of scholars and activists engaged in new social movements' struggles against neo-liberalism and commodification of life, be it the Zapatista uprising in 1994, the French movement against public sector reforms in 1995, Seattle in 1999 or the peasants' movements against enclosures of land and natural resources. However, as the character and scale of the Slovak events cannot be compared to any of the internationally known struggles, one must be careful about setting them into the broader context and defining them as a particular form of a collective behaviour. We will discuss this issue at the end.

Background information

The number of Roma inhabitants in Slovakia is estimated at 320,000–380,000 (7% of the total population), most of them living in eastern and central Slovakia. Out of the total Romani population, approximately one half are socially excluded. Their housing can be divided into three types (Ministry of Housing and Regional Development 2004):

1. urban and municipal concentrations;
2. housing located at the edges of towns or villages;
3. settlements which are spatially segregated from towns or villages.

There are 620 more or less segregated settlements in the country. According to the socio-demographic mapping exercise conducted in 2004, of these settlements, 149 are completely geographically segregated from the majority. Thirty-nine per cent of the settlements have a water pipeline, 89% of the settlements have electricity and 39% have a water pipeline; only 15% of them dispense of gas heating and 13% have sewerage facilities. However, the research identified 46 settlements without any infrastructure and accessible roads. One third of all dwellings in these localities are illegal (built without permission), and most of them are simple shacks of the worst kind (Office of the Plenipotentiary for Roma Communities/OPRC 2004). In this chapter, we refer to this part of the Roma population as 'the marginalized Roma population' or 'the marginalized Roma communities'. Unsurprisingly, given such a high level of social exclusion, the average life expectancy amongst Roma is 12 to 15 years shorter than the majority's (OPRC 2004).

The educational system itself further reproduces Romani exclusion. Independent studies suggest that as many as 80% of children tracked in special schools in Slovakia are Roma. These schools are generally for children with mental disabilities or special needs, and therefore, Romani children receive a substandard education and have very limited opportunities for employment and further education (Amnesty International 2008).

From 2004 to 2005, the United Nations Development Programme conducted research on Romani unemployment which took into account both the recorded employment and unemployment rates, and the International Labour Force Survey measure which takes account of casual work in the grey economy. Unemployment rates for Roma in 2004–2005 were 72.0% (men) and 51.5% (women), while employment rates were 10.5% (men) and 4.6% (women). In contrast, the unemployment rates for non-Roma were 24.4% for men and 24.5% for women, while employment rates were 51.7% for men and 41.2% for women respectively (Filadelfiová, Gerbery and Škobla 2007). This gross disparity in unemployment rates is indicative of discrimination in the labour market.

The reform of the welfare provision

The rise of neoliberal policies in Slovakia can be traced back to the period 1998–2002. The first reforms had been implemented by the mixed government coalition of centre-right parties and a left social-democratic party. In the area of labour market reforms, the new policies resulted in a phasing out of early retirement and a reduction of social assistance benefits. In 2001, about 50% of the 324,000 recipients of social assistance benefits in Slovakia (whose household income fell below the minimum subsistence level) were classified as being in this position for 'subjective' reasons. Their level of social assistance was halved (Jurajda and Mathernová 2004). Paradoxically, through the pressure of the Democratic Left Party, the power of the Labour Code had not been weakened but, for a short period of time, strengthened in 2001.

However, after the 2002 general elections, a second government of Prime Minister Dzurinda came to power, this time composed of purely right-of-centre parties. Free market reforms were carried out simultaneously in all important areas of life: labour market, pensions, social benefits, taxes, public finances, health care and transport. Slovakia deserved the name 'laboratory of reforms'. In the area of higher education, the Ministry attempted to introduce tuition fees, a new student loan system and increased competition among universities. This educational reform was blocked in part by an active university students' mobilization in 2004.

The public bus transport company was decentralized into smaller regional companies that were sold separately, after the government's decision from 1999. Parallel to the process of deregulation, bus passengers experienced systematic *adjustments* of fares – an increase of 30% in 1999, and of 28% in 2000, along with a decline in the scope of transport services. The public transport reform had significant impacts on social exclusion of Roma in Slovakia. The poorest communities are scattered across eastern and central Slovakia and are usually quite far from towns with employment opportunities and service provision. Černušáková (2007), who conducted research on the affordability of public transport based on a model situation of a Romani family with four children in a county of central Slovakia, found that public transport costs represented 39% of their income. She thus concluded that for low-income Romani families in Slovakia, transport is even less affordable than for very low-income groups in Third World countries.

Let us now focus on the legislative production of the Ministry of Labour and Social Affairs as these developments were key contributors to the sharpening of the precarious social conditions for Roma and the eventual outbreak of protests. The reforms covered the following areas: (1) social benefits such as child allowances and support for those below the minimal subsistence level of income, (2) a new Labour Code reducing labour costs for the employers and introducing flexible work, (3) reform of the civil service and (4) an introduction of a new, semi-private pension system (Jurajda and Mathernová 2004). The valorization mechanism, regularly increasing the level of minimum subsistence as a function of rising living costs, was abolished. Incremental minimum wage increases also underwent a freeze.

Impact of the cuts in social benefits on poor families

Dral (2006), in his insightful analysis on the discourse of the Slovak welfare policy reform, claims that it was based on the instrumentalization of the embedded ethno-cultural stereotype of 'Roma laziness'. He demonstrates how the presumption of 'Roma laziness' manifests itself differently in three distinct discourses which shaped the production and implementation of the welfare reform: research, policy and media. On the level of social research, the presumption was present at first only subtly as part of the 'dependency culture' argument, and moreover, was balanced with structural explanations of poverty. But within an increasingly 'free market' political climate, it grew further as 'Roma culture' acquired the status of a variable explaining the persistence of Roma poverty in Slovakia.

On the welfare policy level, the traditional stereotype of 'Roma laziness' was translated into 'various measures sought to enhance activation and motivation and fight the supposed abuse of the social system' (Dral 2006: 44). The explanatory report accompanying the Act on Assistance in Material Need claimed that the receipt of social benefits resulted in a lack of motivation for especially those individuals 'who lack deep-rooted working habits, have generally lower standards of living and more numerous families as is common in the society' (Explanatory Report to the Act No. 599/2003 Coll.). These attributes – veiled euphemisms for Romani citizens – implicitly point to how Roma are perceived by the majority: 'Legislators' implications corresponded with the popular belief that Roma extensively abuse the social system by refusing to work and having a lot of children in order to be entitled for higher benefits' (Dral 2006).

The link between the implementation of the government reforms (2002–2006), and the outbreak of social unrest in southern and eastern Slovak villages in 2004, became manifest through the implementation of the above mentioned Act on Assistance in Material Need. Situations of 'material need' apply to those individuals whose income is below the subsistence minimum determined by the government. This involves people with part-time jobs, precarious workers, long-term unemployed people, etc. The Act adopted in 2003 became valid in February 2004 and brought radical cuts in the receipt of social benefits. Among the population groups hardest hit by these cuts, the Roma were the largest due to the larger-than-average size of their families and their concentration in regions with high structural unemployment.

At the moment therefore, when Roma families received the official notices informing them about the impending cuts in social benefits – in February 2004 – mass protests were sparked. We have illustrated the sharp fall in family incomes for benefit claimants and further details in the Annex to this chapter. In order to quickly grasp the impact of this drop in income, let us imagine a sample family 'in material need' composed of two adults and four children. In 2002, before the reform, this family received social benefits worth a minimum £163.73 and maximum £207.63 a month (these are GBP equivalents of the Slovak crown [at 2004 exchange rates], and vary according to several factors, see the Annex). In February 2004, after the economic reforms, this family's combined social support was one of the following variants (see Tables 9.3–9.6 in the Annex for detailed figures on social benefits allowances):

1. Families received a minimum of £91.69 a month including child allowance.
2. If they met certain criteria, they might have received a housing benefit too, so their income would climb to £114.24 a month.
3. If the family was fortunate enough to get the activation work benefit too,[1] their combined income might reach £148.14 a month.

However, if we calculate this family's income based on the scenario that the reform *had not been* implemented – and thus the benefits remained at the same level prior to the 'reforms, only increasing by the inflation index of 16.2% – the total income of this family in 2004 would have been in the range of a minimum of £190.25 up to maximum £241.27. The fall in income thus presents 22% up to 53%. A more detailed explanation and evidence is provided in the Annex.

Furthermore, if we assume that this family of six people lived in a tiny 2-room flat, and if the rent of £87.75 (see the Table 9.1) is subtracted, how much remains for the family to live on?

1. A family with a minimum benefit has to cope with £3.94 a month (£0.13 a day).
2. A family with a medium benefit is left with £26.49 a month (£0.88 a day).
3. A family where the parents managed to get the activation benefit is left with £60.39 a month (£2.01 a day).

Table 9.1 Costs of some basic goods and facilities in 2004

Goods/facilities	Price in £
Bread, 1 kg	0.37
Butter, 250 g	0.64
Milk, 1 l	0.29
Pants	8.47
A bus ride, 34 km	0.64
A train ride, 266 km	6.17
Household electricity (50 KWh)	5.24
Household gas (1m3)	0.25
Cold water (1m3)	0.64
A doctor's appointment	0.34
A medical receipt	0.34
Single bus fare in an average town	0.14
1 room flat, a monthly rent	44.92
2 room flat, a monthly rent	87.75

In reality, there were few families in the third scenario. If we look at Table 9.1, one realizes that the families from group 1 or 2 could not sustain themselves unless they sold their flats and either found a shelter with their relatives, migrated abroad or moved to live in shacks in segregated Romani settlements.

In March the same year, almost simultaneously after a significant portion of income was taken away from the poor families, the government provided a massive subsidy to a private company. It was for the KIA corporation to build a car plant and the funding presented 8.8 billion Slovak crowns (£150 million). On top of that the government committed itself to finish a highway, investing additional 22 billion crowns (£370 million) (*Pravda*, 6 March 2004). KIA was not the only multinational beneficiary of the Dzurinda government and these facts provide an additional rationale for characterizing the government as a neoliberal one.

The outbreak of the February events

The first mass assemblies and demonstrations began in Poprad, Pavlovce nad Uhom, Kráľovský Chlmec, Trebišov and Čaklov in the beginning of February. On 11 February, the first organized looting of a supermarket occurred in the town Levoča, where reportedly 80 persons were

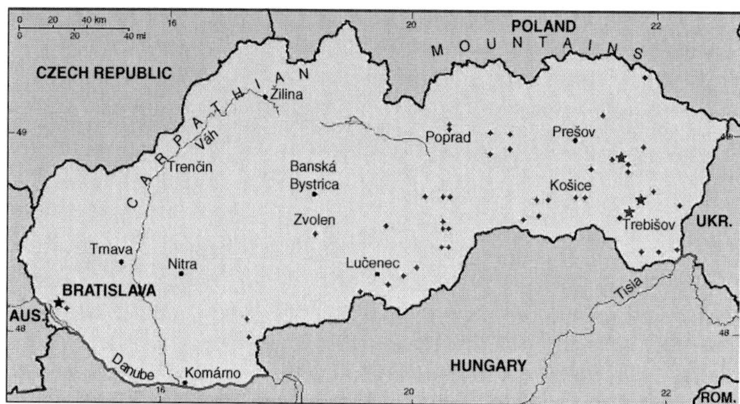

Map 9.1   Map of Slovakia: Diamonds indicate sites of protests in Romani communities; the Stars are villages and towns where clashes with police were recorded (i.e. Trebišov, Čaklov and Trhovište)

involved. During February and March, protests spread to at least 42 towns and villages, mainly in eastern and southeastern Slovakia (see map above). These demonstrations took various forms: rallies, petitions, letter campaigns targeting the members of government, appeals to the European Court of Human Rights, marches, organized lootings of shops and, in a few cases, serious clashes with police. Organized mass looting occurred in the following towns and villages: Levoča, Drahňov, Čierna nad Tisou, Trhovište, Hucín, Rimavská Sobota, Sačurov, Zemplín, Čaklov, Kameňany and Rovinka.[2]

Protesting Roma were openly criticizing the government's social reforms. At one demonstration, slogans on placards read 'We have enough capitalism.' Some of the common solutions to the crisis demanded by the assemblies and petitions were (Verheije 2004):

- private firms should be supported to employ Roma;
- part of the work offered by the local council should lead to extra skills for the people involved, training of working habits etc.;
- support to Roma pupils in the higher education.

The authors are not aware of the source of these demands, however their moderate tone suggests that they were formulated by Romani NGO leaders rather than being the products of mass assemblies. As one leader is himself an employer (Ladislav Fizik), it may suggest a direct material interest in getting these changes through.

Although detailed research of the roots of the unrest remains to be conducted, within the media discourse itself, three basic types of causal explanations for the unrest were given. The first one identified the role of Romani usurers/creditors as the source. According to this view, these creditors were unhappy that their clients' incomes dropped sharply as this meant they would not be able to meet their debt payments. Thus, the usurers were allegedly manipulating events behind the scene by instigating discontent and encouraging violence in order to block the new legislation and benefit cuts.

A second, perhaps less common explanation, attributes the core responsibility for the protests to the Romani leaders from various NGOs. However, our information does not support this claim. The majority of Romani NGO leaders were rather ambivalent towards grass-roots radical actions with changing/fluid positions, and it is debatable whether they had any real influence on the course of events.

A third plausible explanation within the media came with a moderate criticism of the government. Accordingly, the government underesti-mated its communication with the marginalized groups of the popu-lation who were targeted by the social benefits reform. Nonetheless, this opinion itself avoided any criticism of the reforms as such.

In our view, elements of all three phenomena probably played some part in the unfolding of these events. But what these interpretations share in common is that they focus on the secondary effects rather than *primary causes* of the social unrest. As mentioned at the begin-ning of this chapter, a genuine and deep inquiry into the causes of a social unrest or social movement must deal with the core issues of long-term deprivation and poverty, denial of rights and access to resources or systematic discrimination against a minority based on identity or class criteria.

Conflicts with police

There were several documented clashes with police which became violent. The most significant confrontation happened in the town Trebišov on 23 February 2004, when police attacked an unauthor-ized Roma demonstration. They succeeded in forcing the pro-testers out of the town centre using tear gas and water cannons, in freezing temperatures. Romani people defended themselves by throwing stones and bottles on the police. Early the next morning, around 240 policemen subsequently attacked the settlement where the protesters were thought to live. The police conducted house-to-house searches, beating and arresting people. The whole affair took 12 hours, and they enclosed the whole estate for a couple of days. Two weeks later, one of the Roma men who was present at the clashes – Radoslav Puky – was found dead in a water ditch. The Slovak police denied responsibility, but Puky's relatives claimed that he had disappeared after being chased by the policemen. A demand of several human rights organizations to conduct a second forensic examination of his body was refused (*Pravda*, 9 March 2004; *RPA*, 9 March 2004).

An ERRC (European Roma Rights Centre) (2004) delegation went to visit the place a few days later. After interviewing the Romani witnesses they wrote a detailed account of the events. They gathered that the police unit entered Romani homes indiscriminately, without showing any form of warrant or other authorization, often violently kicking in doors. They struck with truncheons and also kicked a large number of Romani, both in houses and outside. They also beat and verbally abused Romani women, minors and people with physical and mental disabilities. Electric cattle prods were used on the head, arms, chest and legs of a number of people.

According to the Head of Police, Mr. Mlynarik, 26 or 27 Roma were detained during the raid and remained in detention for more than 24 hours. According to Roma who had been detained and subsequently released, more than 40 persons had been seen in police detention, and nearly all of them had been physically abused while in custody. In particular, males had been ordered to strip to the waist, face a wall with their hands pressed against the wall, and had been struck repeatedly in the midriff by police officers with truncheons. In addition, officers had jumped on their lower legs/calves with their boots. In addition to a number of adult males who alleged that police had physically abused them during the raid on February 24 (and who were in many cases able to show fresh visible linear bruises apparently caused by police truncheons), the ERRC also interviewed five minors aged 14–17, one of them pregnant, who described to the investigators how they had been kicked, beaten with truncheons or electric prods (ERRC 2004).

In the evening of 24 February 2004, the Slovak government held an emergency meeting. The result was the largest mobilization of the police and army since the revolution against the one-party system in 1989. Two thousand policemen and 650 army soldiers were mobilized in all. Vladimir Palko, the Minister of Interior said, in reference to the Trebisov clashes, that 'water cannons were used yesterday for the first time since the Revolution of 1989' (ERRC 2004). As part of the general hysteria of those days, the neighbouring Czech Republic increased patrols along the common border during the protests. Czech Interior Minister Stanislav Gross said new rules would come into effect after 1 May 2004 (the date of the EU accession) to make it more difficult for Slovaks to cross the border, and vice versa (Tancerová 2004).

The last known use of force was reported from the village of Bystrany on 19 March 2004. A spontaneous rally of about 500 people was dispersed by the police and an army unit used a helicopter to monitor the situation from above. They pushed the crowd away from the village into the segregated Romani settlement, effectively neutralizing the demonstration.

At the initial stages of the protests, members of the non-Romani majority population also participated. They signed petitions and attended demonstrations, although not in high numbers. In the later stage of the protests, they stopped their involvement, despite being encouraged to continue by the Romani participants. The reasons why this happened are varied in nature: 'criminalization' of the protests by the media, the police and army mobilization, the absence of coordination amongst Romani leaders, etc. Moreover, Romani politicians were unsuccessful in their bid to gain support of the trade unions. Alexander Patkolo, the leader of the Roma Initiative of Slovakia tried to negotiate with representatives of the Confederation of Trade Unions but was rejected because the Roma were not collective members of the confederation (*RPA*, 20 February 2004).

The role of the Romani leadership

Local protests were largely spontaneous. For Romani people living in isolated settlements or urban ghettos, direct communication is an important part of daily community life. Thus, when the community received the first official notice of the reduced benefits, they took spontaneous action immediately. This was not the first time that anger ensued after having received cuts to their meagre allowances. Arguments and tensions between Roma and government workers responsible for benefits disbursement were numerous in previous years, and police presence at post offices (where benefits are distributed) was common. But this time around Roma were evidently not scared, and thus could not be deterred.

Thus, we can surmise that neither Romani NGOs nor political parties initiated these riots, but rather they were propelled into the movement by its own dynamics. While none of the Romani organizations approved of the way the government reacted to the situation and used violence to repress the protests, neither were they able to come to a clear agreement on their approach to the reform as such.

Nevertheless, several organizations and leaders supported the reforms, though they were critical of some aspects such as implementation being too fast or the lack of information about the new policies delivered by the government to the excluded communities. Ladislav Richter and Tibor Loran, leaders of the Council of NGOs of Roma communities, publicly stated that the Council would 'cool down the heads of people in the most militant settlements' (*Romano Nevo Lil/RNL*, 7 March 2004b). They said they had prepared three local activation works projects capable of employing 5000 unemployed people (*RNL*, 1 March 2004a). Amongst others who supported the reforms whilst criticizing its timing or the low level of awareness among Roma, were *Rómska občianska iniciatíva* (Romani Citizen's Initiative) and Klara Orgovanova, the government's Plenipotentiary for Romani Communities.

The opposing point of view – a general rejection of the neoliberal reforms – was presented by organizations such as the Roma Parliament (by Ladislav Fizik) and the Roma Civic Initiative (Ladislav Cervenak). A rather stronger refusal was articulated by Alexander Patkolo from the Roma Initiative of Slovakia who criticized the government's measures to rectify the critical social situation of poor Romani families as insufficient, and stated that they were 'just another patch dealing with the effects and not the roots of the problems' (*RPA*, 26 February 2004).[3]

Nonetheless, Romani leaders were unable to demonstrate effective leadership during the social protests as they lacked both *clarity of intentions*, and perhaps the most critical ingredient for success, *cooperation and determination*. For example, the Roma Council addressed a list of demands to the government in February and at the same time in the same document (issued in the middle of the struggle), its co-signatories attacked the Roma Parliament for its opposition to the reform (*RNL*, 23 February 2004). Vermeersch (2006: 148), pointing to the disagreements amongst the Romani organizations, describes how Romani leaders 'were manoeuvring in the narrow space between, on the one hand, criticizing the government and, on the other, avoiding being seen as defending illegal moneylenders and stimulating welfare dependency'.

Some voices questioned the democratic accountability of Romani political representation. For instance, Stefan Kalias of the cultural association *Roma Vychod* challenged the Romani leaders whose common practice – before important political events – was to selectively invite only a handful of other leaders from other organizations. Thus, 'there was no chair left' for many grassroots leaders from local communities, effectively excluding a large section of the community voice (*RPA*, 1 April 2004).

On 21 February 2004, the Roma Parliament organized a large gathering of well over 150 Romani leaders and activists in Zvolen. Several of them had never attended a meeting of the Roma Parliament before, and furthermore, 'all participants came there with a big hope in their hearts to create concrete steps in solving the bad social situation of Roma which culminated in stealing and protests' (Verheije 2004). A strike committee was elected to co-ordinate the protests and a general strike. This committee wrote an 'Appeal to the inhabitants of the Slovak Republic who are in need'. With this appeal, citizens were asked to openly show their dissatisfaction with the new laws on 25 February. Protesters were encouraged not to ask for more money, but for work. 'Labour, Equality and Bread' and 'Work, Work, Work' where chosen as leading slogans for the demonstrations. The protest was to be held peacefully and was seen to be legal (Verheije 2004).

The determination of poor Roma and the state's brutal clamp down lead to an ambivalent standpoint on the part of some of the leaders of Romani organizations. The national protest planned for 25 February was cancelled as there were fears of further radicaliation of the situation (*RNL*, 2 March 2004; *RPA*, 25 February 2004). On the other hand, a few days later, on 28 February, the Roma Parliament called for blockades of border crossings and highways, for a release of all detained Roma, and for international protests in front of Slovak embassies around the world. Slovakia's leading opposition politician Robert Fico (the current prime minister of Slovakia) warned of an 'Argentinean scenario'.[4]

The heavily armed presence of the Slovak police acted as an efficient deterrent and the radicalism of the protestors gradually faded away. At the same time, the media and politicians succeeded in isolating the protests, selling them to the public as an 'ethnic thing' that the majority had not supported. The Interior Minister and General Prosecutor threatened to initiate a criminal investigation against the Romani leaders for their calls to block the highways and border crossings (*Pravda*, 2 March 2004). These threats made an impact too and the radical action were called off by the Roma leaders (*RNL*, 1 March 2004b; *Korzar*, 5 March 2004).

What did Roma people gain from the struggle? The aftermath

According to the police sources, over 200 Roma people were arrested during the 'riots', among them 111 women; eventually, 42 were convicted (*Pravda*, 1 March 2004). But although it was the Roma who bore the brunt of resistance and repression, we want to emphasize that the governmental concessions, listed below, were beneficial for all poor and excluded people in Slovakia, both Roma and non-Romani citizens of Slovakia. They have been preserved in subsequent years too:

- the activation benefits were increased from 1000 SKK (16.95 GBP) to 1500 SKK (25.42 GBP);
- the government provided subsidies for organizations or enterprises that created more than 100 new jobs;
- funded placement opportunities for everybody until 25 years of age (in the original version the period was just two years after leaving school, which for majority of youth is at the age of 18 or earlier);
- increased funding for enterprises and organizations employing disabled workers;
- scholarships for students from poor families studying at high schools or colleges;
- subsidies to schools for pupils' tools and meals so that poor children could afford to eat.

The activation works scheme was a key instrument of the government's commitment to 'make work pay', as its pithy slogan advertised. Each claimant who signed on the activation works scheme was obliged to work at least 10 hours a week. All the 'jobs' were unskilled labour such as maintenance of public spaces in towns and villages or work for non-profits. The official aim of the scheme is to renew working habits amongst the long-term unemployed, and thereby offer them a chance to enter the labour market. Although the programme was financed by the European Social Fund, it strongly resembles the tough 'workfare' policy programmes of the United States (Dral 2006). Even if we forget the implicit assumption of this measure that it is the unemployed who are to blame for their poverty, the question still remains: what were the unemployed people 'activated' for? At that time, the supply of jobs had been several multiples less than the number of unemployed and the situation has not changed in recent years (Oravec and Bošelová 2006).[5]

After the wave of protests the government was forced to find financial resources and allocate more funding to the local governments in the areas which combined the highest unemployment with the recent history of Roma social unrest. The local authorities in these areas were in turn were able to provide new 'employment' for some of the long-term unemployed people, both Roma and non-Roma. In March 2004, the Minister of Employment, Ludovit Kanik, claimed that the government had provided 40,000 new 'activation jobs'. But at the same time, there were 270,000 long-term unemployed people in the country.

Table 9.2 focuses on the possibilities individuals had to sign on to this programme if resident in a small town or village in eastern Slovakia.

A few facts are important here:

- Most of the new 'jobs' were short-term (for a few months) or part-time.
- All these jobs were for unskilled and manual workers.
- In some of the villages mentioned above all claimants were Roma people.

These figures show that masses of Roma people were literally 'hungry for jobs' and clearly refute the widespread traditional stereotype about 'the lazy Gypsies' (cf. Dral 2006).

Table 9.2   Activation work – the difference between demand and supply

Village/Town	Number of long-term unemployed demanding jobs (mostly Roma people)	Number of persons accepted for council 'activation' jobs after the unrest
Varhanovce	260	90
Jasov	545	45
Liptovsky Mikulas	300	45
Humenne	6,969	914
Strane pod Tatrami	343	130
Tornala	2,200	285
Svinica	135	53
Durkov	320	50
Pavlovce nad Uhom	1,100	150

Source: Based on figures reported in *RPA* and *RNL* in March 2004.

Social unrest or social movement?

Finally, one may ask how to best define this kind of relatively short-lived mobilization, which swept over south and east Slovakian towns and villages in the beginning of 2004. The perspective with which we understand what happened comes, as we stated in the beginning of this chapter, from the recent global wave of grassroots social movements against the effects of neoliberal globalization. However, whether the Slovakian case meets the parameters of a real social movement is questionable. Social movements theorists provide many definitions (Della Porta and Diani 1998; Crossley 2002; Diani and McAdam 2003). Blumer's definition (1974: 4–5) is one of the broadest and can serve as a 'checking prism' to look at the Roma mobilization in 2004:

> Social movements can be viewed as collective enterprises seeking to establish a new order of life. They have their inception in a condition of unrest and derive their motive power on one hand from dissatisfaction with the current form of life, and on the other hand, from wishes and hopes for a new system of living.

This definition implies a kind of positive vision ('a new order of life') shared by members of the movement. At the present stage of our research, we are unable to confirm if that was the case among participants and leaders of the Romani mobilization in 2004. Rather, we can clearly identify a more simple kind of collective behaviour which according to Blumer (1974) can be qualified as 'social unrest'. We find all his three types of collective agents playing their roles in the described events: crowd, mass and a public. A social unrest is an earlier stage of organizing and out of situations of social unrest, real social movements tend to emerge.

But regardless of how these particular events are defined, we have to agree with the standpoint of *Romano Nevo Lil*. According to this key Romani newspaper in Slovakia, the events in 2004 were the first autonomous Romani mobilization in modern Slovak history (*RNL*, 7 March 2004b, c). The demands they raised to the government were challenges which constituted a direct resistance to the neoliberal policies based on market reform principles, and were ultimately in favour of *all* unemployed Slovak citizens.

Annex

Tables 9.3–9.6 illustrate the findings of our research. Each table highlights differences in the receipt between a single parent family and family with both parents, and with varying number of children. The amount of money allocated to different kinds of claimants is dependant on their specific situations too, for example, how an individual lost their last job, if the claimant lived in their own accommodation, or if they participated in certain workfare activities, etc.

The tables illustrate the difference and the fall in incomes after the reform. However, in most cases, the real gap is even greater once we realize that only a small percentage of claimants actually received the activation benefits (see Table 9.6) included in the total family incomes. Therefore, if we want to see the real fall in income in the early 2004, we have to subtract the amount of the activation benefits (for the year 2004) and add up the inflation index 16.2% (the year 2002). Then we get the amount hypothetically allowing the same living standard in 2004 as in 2002. In this case, the fall of income for large families (mainly Roma) rises by up to 50%!

Table 9.3   Social benefits before the reform

Persons	Number of children	Social benefits (in GBP) – year 2002				
		Child allowance	Social benefits (min.)	Total	Social benefits (max.)	Total
Single	0	0.00	33.31	33.31	59.15	59.15
+	1	14.07	46.02	60.08	71.86	85.93
	2	25.59	61.27	86.86	112.71	112.71
	4	52.54	87.88	140.42	166.27	166.27
	6	81.36	112.63	193.98	138.47	219.83
	9	122.03	152.29	274.32	178.14	300.17
Couple	0	0.00	56.61	56.61	100.51	100.51
+	1	14.07	69.32	83.39	113.22	127.29
	2	25.59	84.58	110.17	128.47	154.07
	4	52.54	111.19	163.73	155.08	207.63
	6	81.36	135.93	217.29	179.83	261.19
	9	122.03	175.59	297.63	219.49	341.53

Table 9.4   Social benefits after the reform – beginning 2004

Persons	Number of children	Social benefits (in GBP) – year 2004				
		Child allowance	Social benefits (min.)	Total	Social benefits (max.)	Total
Single	0	0.00	25.42	25.42	55.59	55.59
+	1	8.47	37.46	45.93	76.95	85.42
	2	16.95	37.46	54.41	76.95	93.90
	4	33.90	39.15	73.05	78.64	112.54
	6	50.85	57.80	108.64	97.29	148.14
	9	76.27	60.34	136.61	99.83	176.10
Couple	0	0.00	44.58	44.58	101.02	101.02
+	1	8.47	56.10	64.58	112.54	121.02
	2	16.95	56.10	73.05	112.54	129.49
	4	33.90	57.80	91.69	114.24	148.14
	6	50.85	76.44	127.29	132.88	183.73
	9	76.27	78.98	155.25	135.42	211.69

Table 9.5 Social benefits – before and after

Persons	Number of children	Social benefits – the difference after the reform							
		2004 minus 2002				2004 minus 2003			
		Difference in social benefits (min.)	%	Difference in social benefits (max.)	%	Difference in social benefits (min.)	%	Difference in social benefits (max.)	%
Single	0	−7.88	−24	−3.56	−6	0.85	3	6.44	13
+	1	−14.15	−24	−0.51	−1	−5.76	−11	9.15	12
	2	−32.46	−37	−18.81	−17	−24.41	−31	−9.49	−9
	4	−67.37	−48	−53.73	−32	−60.00	−45	−45.08	−29
	6	−85.34	−44	−71.69	−33	−78.64	−42	−63.73	−30
	9	−137.71	−50	−124.07	−41	−132.03	−49	−117.12	−40
Couple	0	−12.03	−21	0.51	1	−4.58	−9	2.71	3
+	1	−18.81	−23	−6.27	−5	−11.69	−15	−4.41	−4
	2	−37.12	−34	−24.58	−16	−30.34	−29	−23.05	−15
	4	−72.03	−44	−59.49	−29	−65.93	−42	−58.64	−28
	6	−90.00	−41	−77.46	−30	−84.58	−40	−75.59	−29
	9	−142.37	−48	−129.83	−38	−137.97	−47	−88.31	−29

Table 9.6 Social benefits – the real difference without activation benefit and including the inflation index

Persons	Number of children	Social benefits – the real difference without activation benefit and including the inflation index (2004 minus 2002)							
		Real social benefits 2002 (min.)	Real social benefits 2004 (min.)	Difference (min.)	%	Real social benefits 2002 (max)	Real social benefits 2004 (max.)	Difference (max.)	%
Single	0	38.69	25.42	−13.27	−34	68.73	38.64	−30.08	−44
+	1	69.81	45.93	−23.88	−34	99.85	68.47	−31.37	−31
	2	100.93	54.41	−46.53	−46	130.97	76.95	−54.02	−41
	4	163.17	73.05	−90.12	−55	193.20	95.59	−97.61	−51
	6	225.41	108.64	−116.76	−52	255.44	131.19	−124.25	−49
	9	318.76	136.61	−182.15	−57	348.80	159.15	−189.64	−54
Couple	0	65.78	44.58	−21.20	−32	116.80	67.12	−49.68	−43
+	1	96.90	64.58	−32.32	−33	147.92	87.12	−60.80	−41
	2	128.02	73.05	−54.97	−43	179.03	95.59	−83.44	−47
	4	190.25	91.69	−98.56	−52	241.27	114.24	−127.03	−53
	6	252.49	127.29	−125.20	−50	303.49	149.83	−153.66	−51
	9	345.85	155.25	−190.59	−55	396.85	177.80	−219.05	−55

Notes

1. The conditional requirement for the receipt of the activation benefit was the individual's participation in the activation works scheme. For more on the scheme, see section titled 'What did Roma people gain from the struggle? The aftermath' in this chapter.
2. Here is the list of all towns and villages where media reported some forms of protest happened (most of them non-violent): Poprad, Pavlovce nad Uhom, Král'ovský Chlmec, Košice, Trebišov, Hraňa, Nižný Žipov, Vranov nad Topl'ou, Michalovce, Šarovce, Šalov, Fil'akovo, Zvolen, Jasov, Humenné, Levoča, Spišské Podhradie, Kecerovce, Tornal'a, Revúca, Gemerská Ves, Hodejov, Rimavská Sobota, Revúca, Kokava nad Rimavicou, Lomnička, Holíč, Blatná, Slavošovce, Roštár, Zamutov, Trenč, Moldava nad Bodvou, Giraltovce, Medzilaborce, Spišská Nová Ves, Čaklov, Turňa nad Bodvou, Bystrany, Novačany, Ďurkov.
3. Another critical voice came from human rights advocates. The International Helsinki Federation and the Slovak Helsinki Committee defined parts of the new law as discriminatory because it denied financial assistance specifically to large families which in fact meant mainly Roma families.
4. In December 2001, Argentineans revolted en masse against the loss of their savings and against restrictive policies of the neoliberal government. The scale of popular organizing was huge and creative politics had been tested by the new social movements. Similar to Slovakia later, the events had started with the organized lootings of supermarkets under real-time media coverage which served as an inspiration for other people watching the news.
5. Another, more sceptical analysis of the 'activation' policy is provided by Tancerová (2004).

References

The Act on Assistance in Material Need, Government of Slovakia (No. 599/ 2003 Coll.)

Amnesty International (2008) *A Tale of Two Schools: Segregating Roma into Special Education in Slovakia*, London: Amnesty International Publications.

Blumer, H. (1974) 'Social movements' in Denisoff, R.S. (ed.) *The Sociology of Dissent*, New York: Harcourt Brace Jovanovich.

Crossley, N. (2002) *Making Sense of Social Movements*, Buckingham: Open University Press.

Černušáková, B. (2007) *Mobility Denied: The Impacts of Privatisation on the Social Rights of Roma in Slovakia*, London: London School of Economics MA Thesis.

Della Porta, D. and Diani, M. (2006) *Social Movements: An Introduction*, Oxford: Blackwell Publishing.

Diani, M. and McAdam, D. (2003) *Social Movements and Networks: Relational Approaches to Collective Action*, Oxford: Oxford UP.

Dral, P. (2006) *Ethnicized Laziness: Roma in the Slovak Social Policy Discourse*, Budapest: Central European University MA Thesis.

ERRC (2004a) *Extreme Rights Deprivation among Roma in Slovakia Leads to Unrest*, Accessed 3 September 2008 from: http://www.errc.org/cikk. php?cikk=1884.

Filadelfiová, J., Gerbery D.J. and Škobla, D. (2007) *Report on the Living Conditions of Roma in Slovakia*, Bratislava: UNDP.

Jurajda, S. and, Mathernova, K. (2005) *How to Overhaul the Labour Market: Political Economy of Recent Czech and Slovak Reforms*, background paper for the World Development Report. Accessed 10 November 2008 from: http:// siteresources.worldbank.org/INTWDR2005/Resources/BP_Overhaul_ LaborMarket_Czech_Slovak_Reforms.pdf.

Ministry of Housing and Regional Development (2004) *Dlhodobá koncepcia bývania pre marginalizované skupiny obyvateľstva a model jej financovania* (Long-term Housing Policy for Marginalized Groups of the Population and its Financing Model). Accessed 22 August 2008 from: http://www.build. gov.sk/mvrrsr/index.php?id=17&cat=266&comment=2317.

Office of the Plenipotentiary for Roma Communities *Strednodobá koncepcia rozvoja rómskej národnostnej menšiny v Slovenskej republike 2008 – 2013*. Accessed 15 November 2008 from: http://romovia.vlada.gov.sk/1799/ vladne-materialy.php.

Office of the Plenipotentiary for Roma Communities *List faktov* (2004). Accessed 15 November 2008 from: http://romovia.vlada.gov.sk/3554/list-faktov.php.

The Office of the Government of the Slovak Republic *Správa vlády SR o ekonomických dopadoch prijatých ekonomicko-sociálnych zákonov na mladé rodiny, dôchodcov – nové znenie, materiál z rokovania vlády SR 25.2.2004, UV-4511/2002* (Governmental Report on the economic impact of the economic and social Acts on young families and pensioners, discussed on 25 February 2004). Accessed 15 November 2008 from: http://www. government.gov.sk.

Oravec, L. and Bošelová, Z. (2006) 'Activation policy in Slovakia: another failing experiment?' *Roma Rights Quarterly* 1, European Roma Rights Centre (ERRC). Accessed 10 December 2008 from: http://www.errc.org/ cikk.php?cikk=2537

Tancerová, B. (2004) 'Looting subsides, tensions remain', *Transitions Online*, 24 February – 1 March.

Verheije, M. (2004) *Labour, equality and bread: Case Study in Slovakia*, Bratislava Netherlands: SPOLU International Foundation. Accessible online at http://www.spolu.nl/index.html?http://www.spolu.nl/m3c5_ casestudy_sk.html

Vermeersch, P. (2006) *The Romani Movement: Minority Politics and Ethnic Mobilization in Contemporary Central Europe*, Oxford and New York: Berghahn.

Media sources

Korzár, 5 March 2004, 'Parlament Rómov odvolal blokádu dialʼnic a hraničných priechodov' (The Romani Parliament called off the blockade of highways and border crossings).

Pravda, 1 March 2004, 'Vláda Rómom neustúpi, tí chcú blokova diaľnice' (The Government will make no concessions to Roma, they want to block the highways).

Pravda, 2 March 2004, 'Niektorých rómskych lídrov začnú vyšetrovať (Some Romani leaders will be investigated).

Pravda, 6 March 2004, 'Dve miliardy pre Kiu nájde vláda v apríli' (The Government will find the 2 billion for KIA in April).

Pravda, 9 March 2004, 'Hľadaný Róm Puky sa utopil' (The lost Roma Puky got drowned).

Pravda, 13 March 2004, 'Poslanci opravovali sociálne zákony' (The MPs were correcting the welfare laws).

Roma Press Agency, 20 February 2004, 'Podľa Patkolóa KOZ využíva Rómov na svoje ciele' (According to Patkolo KOZ has misused Roma for its own goals).

Roma Press Agency, 25 February 2004, 'Aj napriek zrušeniu protestného zhromaždenia hliadkuje na Luníku IX asi 50 policajtov' (50 policemen patrol in Lunik IX even after the protests had been cancelled).

Roma Press Agency, 26 February 2004, 'Opatrenia vlády SR považuje Patkólo za nedostatočné' (Patkolo considers the governmental measures as insufficient).

Roma Press Agency, 9 March 2004, 'Medzinárodné organizácie pracujú na tom, aby sa u nebohého Pukyho previedla druhá pitva' (International organizations seek for another forensic expertise of the dead Puky).

Roma Press Agency, 1 April 2004, 'Rómski lídri v najdôležitejšom okamihu, podľa niektorých aktivistov, sklamali' (According to some activists Romani leaders failed in the crucial moment).

Romano Nevo Lil, 23 February 2004, 'Vyhlásenie Rady Rómov Slovenska' (Declaration of the Romani Council of Slovakia).

Romano Nevol Lil, 1 March 2004a, 'Rada rómskych mimovládiek žiada Rómov z osád, aby nepáchali trestnú činnost' (The Council of Romani NGOs appeals to the Roma people in the settlements not to engage in criminal activity).

Romano Nevol Lil, 1 March 2004b, 'RIS vyzýva rómskych predstaviteľov na upustenie od radikálnych krokov' (RIS appeals to Romani representatives to renounce radical actions).

Romano Nevo Lil, 2 March 2004, 'Občianske zhromaždenia a protesty' (Civic gatherings and protests).

Romano Nevo Lil, 5 March 2004, 'Uznesenie parlamentu Rómov zo zasadnutia krízovej skupiny' (Decision of the Romani Parliament at the crisis group's meeting).

Romano Nevol Lil, 7 March 2004a, 'Nový mýtus o Rómov a nová historická skúsenos (i potvrdenie stereotypu)' (The new myth about Romani and the new historical experience [and affirmation of the stereotype]).

Romano Nevol Lil, 7 March 2004b, 'Reakcie rómskych a nerómskych MVO a rómskych politických strán' (Reactions of Romani and non-Romani NGOs and Romani political parties).

Romano Nevo Lil, 7 March 2004c, 'Reakcie vlády SR, parlamentných a neparlamentných politických strán' (Reactions of the Government, parliamentary and non-parliamentary political parties).

10
Being Roma Activists in Post-Independence Kosovo

Nando Sigona in conversation with Avdula (Dai) Mustafa and Gazmen Salijevic[1]

Background and context

There are an estimated 35,000 to 40,000 Roma, Ashkali and Egyptians (RAE) currently residing in independent Kosovo. Gjakove/Djakovica, Prizren, Ferizaj/Urosevac, Fushe Kosove/Kosovo Polje, Obiliq/Obilic, Mitrovica/Mitrovice, Peja/Pec and Gracanica host the largest communities, whilst about 100,000 live abroad.[2]

Though emigration from Kosovo started in the late 1970s when many Yugoslav citizens sought better employment and life opportunities abroad, the mass exodus of Roma, Ashkali and Egyptians occurred in the aftermath of the conflicts in 1998 between the Kosovo Liberation Army (KLA) and the Yugoslav army and paramilitaries, and the North Atlantic Treaty Organization (NATO) bombing interventions in early 1999, when hundreds of Kosovans of RAE ethnicity were killed or went missing, houses were burnt down or illegally occupied by returning Albanians, and entire neighbourhoods were swept away.

The chimera of a peaceful and equal multiethnic Kosovo, promoted by EU and US politicians and UN technocrats, clashes with the reality of poverty and social segregation of thousands of Kosovan RAE (Mueller 2008). All available social and economic indicators underline the severely disadvantaged position of RAE in Kosovan society today. The UNDP Human Development Report (2004) reveals that per capita income for the RAE population amounts to about one third of that of the rest of the population, with 36% of the communities living in conditions of extreme poverty (1 USD a day) and almost 60% unemployed. Moreover, if employed, Roma, Ashkali and

Egyptians occupy primarily lower level positions. Of particular concern is the situation in the education sector (UNDP 2006), with the percentage of illiterate persons well above the rest of the population (16%), a situation which has been deteriorating in the last 15 years as a result of political instability and war.

These issues, in particular the lack of job opportunities and poor educational levels, resonated in the interviews carried out with activists, organizations and key informants in Kosovo and abroad during the period of research (March–July 2008) (Sigona 2008a, 2008b). On several occasions, respondents directly related the need to address these issues to the broader goal of achieving trust, reconciliation and security as a prerequisite for successful integration.

In the context of interethnic relations in Kosovo, minorities have been under pressure both from the Serb and Albanian sides to show loyalty and assimilate to the dominant culture. According to Galjus (1999), with respect to Romani identity, it was systematically denied, hidden, forcibly removed and then recalled whenever required by dominant groups for the use of political advantage. However, it must be pointed out that this process did not start with the war: it was rooted in public policy and practice which was embedded within the framework of Kosovan interethnic relations. For Marushiakova and Popov (2001: 469; see also Trubeta 2005), 'tendencies towards religious and ethnic assimilation of the Gypsies by the predominant communities have always existed on the Balkans'.

However, discourses around identity are never easy or clear-cut, and categories are dialectically defined, subject to continuous negotiation and far from being hermetically sealed. For Duijzings, 'because of these historical experiences of conversion and 'mimicry', and the consciousness of mixed and composite origins, there is often a high awareness among Balkan inhabitants that most identities should not be taken for granted' (2000: 5; 1997). Nonetheless, the experience of violence and war has contributed to the polarization of the relationship between the two main ethnic groups, thus leaving the Roma, Ashkali and Egyptians caught in the middle.

In this context, any policy of inclusion targeted exclusively at RAE people, without addressing the well-being and development of society at large, risks to exacerbate conflict. The mainstreaming of RAE issues is essential in order to avoid the false impression that in contemporary Kosovo, RAE are somehow privileged in accessing resources. The highly precarious circumstances of RAE minorities in Kosovo today demonstrates clearly that this is not the case; indeed, quite the opposite. Nonetheless, amongst some ethnic Albanians, the idea of RAE being privileged is rooted, and has become the cause of conflicts and emerging enmities.

The research also demonstrates that the way in which international agencies operate on the ground actually reinforces boundaries – imaginary or real – between groups, rather than promoting solidarity and cross-ethnic bonds. The racialization of the political sphere oversimplifies the political dialectics, marginalizing other forms of political and social affiliations and belonging (cf. Kovats 2001; Guglielmo and Waters 2005; Sigona 2009).

The international community seems to pay little attention to the long-term impacts of its actions. Standard monitoring and evaluation exercises are little more than bureaucratic protocols and are unable – because it is not their task – to call into question the discursive framework which provides the ideological validation to the projects. In this way, the responsibility for the failure of so many projects and initiatives to improve the socio-economic conditions of RAE and to promote peaceful ethnic relations in Kosovo remains without explanation, or it is not attributed exclusively to the lack of will or corruptions of locals – NGOs, civil servants, politicians.

Moreover, if RAE inclusion is perceived solely as an issue for 'internationals', then local authorities, the Kosovo government and political parties can derogate their responsibility towards them, and further propel RAE into the role of scapegoats who become targets of the Albanian majority's frustrations. Operating as mediators and translators (both literally and figuratively) between the international community's discourse and agenda, and local political actors and interests puts RAE activists under tremendous pressure. Blaming international agencies for the harsh living conditions and deprivation they experience, some activists pointed out, is less dangerous and, in the short-term, more effective than opening a political confrontation with Kosovo authorities. However, in the medium to long-term this strategy does not help to improve ethnic relations and solve tensions between Kosovan citizens. For RAE activists therefore, adopting the international community vocabulary (and being able to speak English fluently) does not come without a cost. Moreover, while it enables them to gain access to social and economic resources otherwise out of reach, it also put them in a difficult position towards their own community who cannot access these resources.

The Roma in contemporary Kosovo: interview with Avdula (Dai) Mustafa and Gazmen Salijevic

Let's start with a general question. How has the situation of Roma in Kosovo changed since 1999?

Dai: It has drastically changed. Until 1999, Roma had quite a good position in Kosovo. They were educated and had jobs. But, if you look from the perspective of human rights and freedom of thought, there were quite a few limitations due to the Serbian regime. After 1999, the situation goes vice-versa. You got some spaces for human rights and for raising your voice but then you got all the bad sides. Many people were forced to leave. The majority of Roma intellectuals left. Most Roma lost their jobs. The level of education fell dramatically.

Gazmen: Personally, I feel UNMIK [United Nations Mission in Kosovo] administration should be made accountable for the current situation of the Roma in Kosovo. At first, all their power, energy and money were put on the Albanians. In the last two–three years, all their power and resources have gone to support the Serbs only, excluding the other minorities like Roma, Ashkali and Egyptians. The international communities and UNMIK in particular somehow manipulated us. Those human rights Dai has just mentioned for me are just tools to manipulate people, to discriminate among who is entitled to some rights and who is not. Before the war, the Roma had a better social and political position. Economically, we were stronger than now. In nine years, UNMIK did nothing to improve the situation of Roma. Even recently, at the negotiation for the final status of Kosovo, they just forgot to put the Roma in that game. But, we are part of Kosovo. We are part of the current situation and will be part of the future. So, if you consider us as human beings, then you must put us in the game.

In your opinion, why have the Roma been marginalized in these processes, in particular from the negotiations for the final status?

Dai: The Serbs and the Albanians got privileged because they were making problems. They were making noise. While the Roma were

always quiet. Of course, there are some political activists and representatives who sometimes speak out. But that's not enough; they
must raise their voice, all the population. If somebody is discriminat-
ing [against] you, you should raise you[r] voice and making troubles
in order to solve your problems.

*Can you detect any change in the way the Roma issue was dealt by the
international community in the years of UNMIK rule?*

Dai: I think the situation has stayed more or less the same. Yes, there
were some hesitant attempts to identify and solve our problems. But
everything has been really slow and I am not happy personally with
this. If you ask me why any progress is so slow, I would say because
we lack a real and good leadership representing us in all aspects of
society.

Gazmen: The situation is the same; it hasn't changed really. We have
still more than 100,000 Roma living outside Kosovo. There are no
Romani returnees in larger towns like Pristina and Mitrovica. So
the situation is still like it was in 1999 when most of the Roma left
Kosovo. There were some initiatives by the UN mission or even by
the government, but not very effective and mainly driven by the
funding. Everybody now talks about the 'Roma Decade of Social
Inclusion'. My feeling is that they are using the Roma problems
to do self-promotion and make money 'on behalf' of the Roma.
Internationals didn't work hard enough to improve the Roma situation. We still have Roma without shelter, sleeping under bridges.
We still have missing Roma. There are Roma in the list of missing
people prepared by the International Red Cross. Those people were
kidnapped or killed and no one talks about this. We have neither a
state nor a lobby behind us, but we trusted the internationals when
they came in 1999. We thought: 'They are human rights activists.
They will improve our human rights situation'. For me, the situation
is still the same, even harder now because of the independence; they
are using the Roma just like a tool and in their actions sometimes
you can see they adopt a different approach to the Roma in comparison to the Serbs and the Albanians. As I say to many people:
'Sometimes to be a Romani person means that you need to fight with
somebody who is not Romani to show that you are human being';
because many times in many countries, especially in post-conflict

areas like Kosovo, you need to show that you as a Romani person are equal to everybody else. We cannot forget the massive kicking out of Roma, especially from Pristina where we had more than 15,000 Roma and there has been no return.

Dai: I want to go back to the issue of political representation and of the Roma relying on the international community and individual governments to solve their problems. The process has made me think that you can never trust anyone, and never rely on UNMIK and others to represent Romani issues and to assist us. Because people who have been voted in and elected as representatives know that they must do a good job in order to get another mandate and that if they don't do so, they will fail in the next election. The international mission here is not based on that, many people come and go; and there are new faces each time. They don't care about an electoral mandate and votes. They care only about their organization's agenda and their own jobs. I never expect a real commitment from them to resolve our problems. If that happened, I would call it a miracle but it's not happening, it has never happened, and it will not happen until the Roma push their agenda and really raise their voice through each possible method: elections, media and public demonstrations.

Gazmen: The problem is that, even if you try, they will stop you. If you try to push the process of return, for example, international NGOs who are dealing with return will exclude you saying that this is not your mandate or your field of operation. Several times, Roma NGOs and activists have sent requests and asked for information trying to work for their own community. But they are stopped by international NGOs which see them either as tools or numbers. So, when they organize a public meeting and need a Roma, they promptly invite someone from our community to act as a puppet. But if, for example, we ask for information about returnees, they will never share this with us. The result is that we do not know what is going on, not because we are not willing to know, but because they are not willing to share information with us.

Dai: The problem of RAE in Kosovo is a big challenge. We need to identify and detail issues and address them specifically. The issue of education, for example, deserves great attention and you cannot work and treat education as a part of the return programme. These are two complex and different issues. Return is a huge problem. Previously, there were many Roma living in Pristina, about 15,000, now there are a maximum of 10 families, 40–50 people out of 15,000. This is a big problem also for us as Romani civil society because the majority of these people are living in Western Europe, and we cannot and have no mandate to work on their return because they want to stay there.

Gazmen: Yes, but you can work on their property rights. When we are talking about returns, we need first to move out Albanians who have occupied Romani houses. There are more than 1000 Albanians who occupied Roma properties. I know many Roma, even amongst those living in Western countries who are making claims to the UNMIK Housing and Property Directorate, but with no luck until now.

Regarding the attitude of international organizations towards the Roma, once we went to a meeting at the European Commission's Liaison Office in Pristina, and they held a separate meeting with the representatives of civil society to which we were not invited. I asked why they didn't invite us, why they had organized a separate meeting just with Roma, and all they could say was 'we forgot'. I don't believe it.

Shall we try to reflect a bit more on the issue of political leadership among the Roma. Early on you mentioned the fact that the internationals don't have a democratic mandate and they focus only on what is written in their job description without being accountable to the people they claim to work for. But what about Roma leadership? Can we try to explore a bit more what is the relationship between Roma political parties and Roma civil society?

Dai: I would use the same words to describe the political representation of the Roma, because basically this is quite similar to the internationals. The Roma representative in the Kosovo parliament has a guaranteed seat which gives you some privileges in political representation but it can also cause problems, because if you don't have 'free market' and a competition for selection, then if the worst person applies, the worst gets the job and what can you expect there? So free market? We haven't had it so far, I don't know why; there has only ever been one guy who has been a candidate and he gets the mandate over and over again.

But how has it come to be that the Ashkali got more MPs than the Roma, I mean from the demographic point of view, even now in Kosovo, there are more Roma than Ashkali, aren't there?

Gazmen: You can say they are maybe 50–50, but Ashkali political representatives are better organized and connected to their community. They have better relations with Kosovan civil society. If you look at the last nine years, you can see that Roma civil society organizations are now stronger and have developed their capacity to work and deal with many important issues. The [official] Roma political representative, on the other hand, has a reserved seat in the assembly. In general, I can say that if you are quiet and you do not raise your voice against your enemy, than your enemy will keep you as a friend. Ashkali now have three seats in the Parliament because they are more active and closer to their community than our MP. I compare him to George Bush. You've got the same chance to talk to him as with George Bush. He is never available and has never visited Serbian enclaves. He once visited Mitrovica, just after the March 2004 demonstrations, and once Gracanica in 1999. These are all the visits he has made as far as I know.

Dai: If a political representative performs well, does a good job and keeps good connections with the community, then of course in the next election he will be re-elected. But the Roma MP, as Gazmen mentioned, never visits any settlements, does not pay attention to their needs and never makes any efforts to communicate with them. Evidently, he is not too concerned about being voted in at the next elections because there is a reserved seat waiting for him and no competition within the community.

Why cannot you raise other candidates?

Dai: I hope Gazmen will be in the next election!

Everyone, to some extent, is playing a game and there are different roles that political parties and civil society organizations can play. When the independence of Kosovo was declared in February 2008, the Roma MP gave a public statement declaring the support of his community for independence. What do you make of his decision?

Dai: I believe neutrality does not exist. You have to take a side whether you want to or not, indirectly or directly. The Roma parliamentarian took the decision to declare that Kosovo Roma support the independence of Kosovo. Such a display of loyalty contributes to earning points for the Roma who live with the Albanians. But Kosovo is a mixed community; we also have Roma living with Serbs. It is an obvious question to ask: what will happen to those Roma who live with Serbs in the enclaves or in the north of Kosovo? You get the opposite position, so neutrality does not exist, and I don't even know what my own position is.

One of the key issues that I would like to look at is how do you manage to work in such a complex environment where there are at least three different political situations: the north where the Serbians are more or less still in control, the Serbian enclaves in the South, and the situation of the RAE that live with Albanians. What do you think can be done in order to make life better for RAE communities?

Dai: Roma civil society was always pushing some kind of position which was claiming, sometimes artificially, sometimes not, to be neutral. This means putting forward an agenda focused only on rights, improving life conditions, achieving normal standards of living and those kinds of things. This is not easy because if you live with Albanians, they will be like: 'Ok, come with us and you will get all that you are asking for', and you get the same story from Serbs. But in reality this never happens. What they are after are symbolic fights, like a flag, language, territory, who is going to be boss, etc.

In all these symbolic fights Roma always tend to lose. Given that the general political situation of the country is still unsettled and it is not clear who is in control of what, it must be very difficult for activists to address the Roma issues and disentangle them from the general issues of the country.

Gazmen: All these tensions are making me crazy. You see, the Roma don't take positions regarding what is going on, while the display of loyalty from the Roma parliamentarian pushes them too much towards the Albanian side. Myself, I try not to talk from the perspective of the residents of enclaves. However, having talked to many people living with Albanians, even they are not happy with the declaration of support for independence because their situation is equally unclear and, in general, not very good.

Can you tell me more regarding the situation in the enclaves?

Gazmen: In the enclaves we have three institutions: the Serbian government, the government of Kosovo, and UNMIK with all the international agencies. So if you have a problem you don't know who to address. In the enclaves, the Kosovo government and UNMIK are not really in control and don't have power to improve or change the situation, however, sometimes the Serbs will tell you 'we don't have obligations and power, so go to UNMIK'. Roma are just caught in the middle of all this. During the elections, there are lots of political parties, both Albanian and Serbian, who make a lot of promises that they never fulfil once elected. It is difficult to be Romani in Kosovo, especially now after independence as it's difficult to fight for political representation since raising your voice against people like the Romani MP may at times be dangerous for you. He is so close to the Albanians that it is like 'If you touch the slave, you will have a problem with the king'.

Dai: Roma in general tend to be passive. On the other hand, there are too many symbolic fights going on. Even if you could bring a completely new and changed consciousness to the RAE community and an awareness of their human rights, they would have big difficulties because of these symbolic fights which are just too strong and high.

How do you see the future of Kosovo for the RAE minorities?

Gazmen: I call Kosovo the 'European Jerusalem' because, on one side, the Serbs claim Kosovo is their homeland and the cradle of their civilization; on the other, the Albanians talk instead of Illyria and of being the oldest community in the Balkans. This conflict will exist for another hundred years, only a new generation can maybe improve the situation.

As for the Roma, sometimes I don't believe that Kosovo Roma will have a better future. The situation will grow worse for the Roma, especially in the economic sphere. There are many private companies now and they only employ Albanian workers. I am afraid that soon we will have another exodus of Roma to Serbia or Western countries because of the economic situation. Don't forget that some European Union Member States are ready to forcibly return many RAE. If this happens, we will face a very serious crisis.

I would like to come back to two points you raised earlier and which seem to me crucial for understanding the current situation of the RAE in Kosovo: the human rights agenda and the impact of the market economy. First, regarding the human rights agenda, you pointed out how RAE NGOs somehow tactically embrace the human rights agenda because in a way it is seen as neutral and depoliticized – can you please expand on this? Is it possible to fight for rights without engaging with politics? What is the role of international agencies in all this? Second, Yugoslavia was a highly centralized economy and the state was the largest employer in the country. As a consequence, access to the job market for eth-nic minorities was regulated and became a tool for achieving 'Brotherhood and Unity,' the slogan at the core of Yugoslav ideol-ogy. Nowadays, what is the impact of the market economy on RAE minorities? It seems to me that this is an interesting area to explore: the interaction between human rights discourses and the neoliberal ideology. While at a first look they seem to be incompatible both in theory and in practice, on closer inspec-tion, I think they complement each other in moving social and economic inequalities away from the terrain of politics and social conflict and settling them into the more abstract terrain of rights and legal experts' offices.

Gazmen: I have been a critic of the human rights package for quite some time because I feel it can misrepresent and distort reality. When the internationals came here in 1999 and they started to talk about human rights, we were like in the jungle, we had never heard about them but they were shiny and we said 'Ok, we like them'. This happened especially to the Roma. The NGOs came here and said: 'You have the right to call yourself as you like' and then [some] Roma started to follow them and declared themselves as Ashkali and Egyptians and started to move away from the Roma. That's why I like the Socialist era because it was a time when everyone was equal and had equal rights and you didn't think much about differences. Personally, I think the human rights approach is responsible for the fragmentation and loss of our identity. I feel we are playing with fire. Here we heard about human rights in 1999, but human rights began after the Second World War with the Geneva Conventions and the creation of the European institutions. For us they are something new, and if you have lived in the jungle for 40 years, and now you wear a suit and a tie and fly to New York, you can't survive there because you don't know the rules of the game. There are many Roma activists who are not professionals, who don't know the law and are not educated enough. We just attend some training and that's it. We don't really know how to fight using this tool!

> *What you describe is extremely interesting because it shows how the human rights approach and its crusaders can sometimes end up being disempowering for the people they claim to help. Personally, I think that rather than a 'jungle,' which to me seems to bear a negative connotation (i.e. civilization vs. the wild) – I think we should look at the period before 1999, especially Tito's time, as a period where society was organized around a different political and ideological system of values. The fact that RAE had a better quality of life had nothing to do with the human rights package, which was almost absent from the political vocabulary of that time. Human rights are nowadays a useful instrument and framework of reference for global aid workers who 'impose' it on the communities where they operate. The point for me is to understand to what extent the human rights framework offers adequate solutions and answers to the needs of RAE communities and how RAE activists cope/work with it.*

Dai: I don't share the negative opinion of Gazmen regarding human rights because I believe you can use human rights in many positive ways. But how effective you are depends on how strong you are in your position and how much time and effort you put into your work. However, I agree that human rights in some situations can be also instrumental to create or legitimate conflicts where it is up to the strongest party to impose its 'rights'.

> *It is all about power, discourse and tactics. If you don't have the tools and the power to alter the hegemonic discourse (i.e. humanitarianism*

and what you called the human rights package), you learn how to fight for your interests as a group and as an individual by using the tools available to you within the boundary of the hegemonic discourse. However, it is also important to keep a critical eye and to recognize that the current hegemonic discourse is not eternal and can be changed.

Gazmen: Regarding human rights, the NATO bombed Yugoslavia in 1999 because of the brutal human rights violations against ethnic Albanians. I have asked international experts on human rights a million times why are they not bombing Kosovo *now* given the human rights violations against Roma? For example, everyone knows about the lead poisoning of RAE in IDP camps in North Mitrovica,[3] but Roma still live in those camps like animals, and children die almost every day there. Is this not a human rights catastrophe? No! They are only using human rights for their needs. If they want to talk about human rights, then let's put the rules on the table. Human rights need to be equal for everybody, no matter how powerful or powerless they are.

There are so many people working on the Roma issue in Kosovo. Meetings, roundtable and conferences on this issue are organized almost any other day. My impression is that there are too many actors involved and their mandates and roles are often unclear. Moreover, among international personnel there is a high turnover, with people frequently leaving their job after a few months. I wonder: does this affect the effectiveness of their work? And, as a Roma activist, how do you engage with them?

Dai: There are so many institutions and offices: the UN, the EU, the Kosovo government, the NGOs and the Serbian authorities in North Kosovo. There are just too many actors and decision makers whose position is not very clear to anyone, not even to them. It's happened many times that you create a contact list for one issue and after a while you send out an invitation for a meeting or a report, and receive an automatic reply: 'I am in Afghanistan now, contact this person'. This makes our work difficult.

It is surprising how there is very little thinking about the impact of their working practices on the people which live and work in the country where they operate, especially the local NGOs.

Dai: Many times I feel like a teacher, it's like all these internationals come and work for sometime, graduate and leave, generation after generation.

> *Even if the person is changing position within the same office, it can be very difficult to do the handover and transfer knowledge.*

Dai: It takes six months to learn the work of their predecessor. Then they perform for another six months and move on.

Gazmen: Let me try to answer your question about why there are so many institutions. For me it is a form of money laundering. Apparently there is lot of money coming to Kosovo to solve the problems of minorities but, on closer inspection, this money is never invested directly on RAE, but goes back to individuals and organizations of the donor countries and just the 'leftovers' reach the people in need.

Dai: I hear these kinds of remarks from many Roma, and personally I don't care whether a Romani or a non-Romani gets paid; what I care about is that the person who provides the service must have the knowledge and the mandate to do a good job.

Gazmen: The problem is that international organizations use Romani leaders to keep Roma quiet. They don't like the Roma who speak out. Now in Kosovo we have a generation of RAE activists who can work for the RAE communities. That's why I say internationals need these activists if they want to improve the situation. You need to have young Roma doing the job and not those Roma who can be manipulated by internationals with 1000 Euro salaries.

> *In my field visits, I also met Romani leaders who didn't seem to be doing a good job for their communities.*

Dai: That's why I think that it is crucial for everyone to be accountable, transparent and knowledgeable. We have situations where Roma do not provide a good service to their communities, but there are twice as many more situations where non-Roma do a terrible service to the Roma.

Gazmen: But most of them are doing a good job for their own interests.

Early on you mentioned the money laundering. There is a lot of money coming into Kosovo. It is astonishing to think that in the last ten years something like 70% of the money that came in the country went back to the donor countries through salaries and contracts awarded to firms from those countries. There is a side effect of this mechanism that really worries me. International organizations claim they do a lot of things for the RAE and put significant resources into their programmes. This, as we just said, is only partially true. However, if you talk to people in the street they will tell you that the Roma are privileged and are getting rich with all this money, that they get the best schools etc. etc. This is already causing some jealousy among the Albanian majority and it can ultimately increase ethnic tensions and further marginalize the RAE.

Dai: Something similar has happened in Bulgaria as well with all these integration programmes for Roma. It has created huge jealousies, and the Bulgarians think the Roma are getting everything; in reality, what you say is true and most of the money goes to non-Roma because the non-Roma create the projects and get the posts. You just need to go to visit Romani settlements, view the terrible conditions, the total lack of infrastructure, the kids in the streets and not at school, etc., to understand if these programmes are effective.

Gazmen: The only way out of this is to employ more Roma and to make these projects accountable first of all to the RAE communities. Everybody talks about the Roma, lots of money comes for the Roma but the Roma don't get much out of these investments. Just as Dai said if you visit the Roma *mahallas* [neighbourhoods] you can see the terrible conditions. But when the Serbians and Albanians hear that a Romani education programme is getting 1 million Euros, they think it is us who are stealing the money.

In the last three years in Kosovo the 'integration' of Roma has been high on the political agenda. Personally, when I hear someone talking about integration, I always ask myself of whom are they talking about, and into what do they want him or her to integrate. What are the government and the international agencies talking about when they want to 'integrate' RAE communities in Kosovo?

Dai: Integration to me means dignity, but to the institutions it is just another condition or standard to mark in their list.

What is the future for the RAE in this country? Do you think that the work that they are doing for integration can be productive?

Dai: I am always a kind of self-critical person and I expect more from Roma ourselves. If we analyse the situation in general, if you read the papers, the laws, the constitution, there is some good stuff in it, not everything, but there are still lots of good principles. These can be used, if not today, then in five–seven–ten years down the road, when hopefully the awareness amongst Roma for their rights will be heightened, and they come to the point of asking for those rights and using those chances given in the law. That's why I say I am self-critical and we should be more engaged and more active in these processes.

Gazmen: Integration for me means assimilation; you can't integrate if you are not assimilated. Regarding what internationals with the Kosovo government are doing to integrate Roma, I can freely say that they aren't doing much. I think what the Kosovo government together with the international community should do is first of all is to create a programme to build trust, because people do not trust them. As a Romani person, I believe many other Roma don't trust Albanians and Serbs because of the conflict and post-conflict situation, and I think that they need to build trust in order to build bridges between communities in Kosovo; only then we can begin to talk of integration.

Notes

1. The present conversation was recorded in the office of the Roma and Ashkali Documentation Centre (RADC) in Pristina, Kosovo, 30 June 2008. The transcript was successively edited by the interviewer in cooperation with the interviewees.
2. Around 45,000 to 50,000 Kosovo Roma, Ashkali and Egyptians live in Serbia (23,000 as registered IDP), 35,000 are in Germany with temporary status (*duldung*) and around 10,000 live as refugees in Montenegro, Macedonia and Bosnia and Herzegovina. An unaccounted number lives as refugees, illegal migrants or migrant workers all over Western Europe. As of October 2007, 6,899 Roma, Ashkali and Egyptians returned to Kosovo since January 2000 (UNHCR 2007).
3. Further details about the campaign for an immediate medical evacuation from the camps by Kosovo Medical Emergency Group (KMEG) and Society for Threatened Peoples can be viewed at http://www.toxicwastekills.com.

On 1 April 2009, the Kosovo Ombudsman, Hilmi Jashari, released a report sent to PM Thaci supporting the campaign's claims that the situation in the camps constitutes a medical emergency requiring immediate intervention; the full report can be downloaded at: http://www.ombudspersonkosovo.org/?cid=2,4.

References

Duijzings, G. (1997) 'The making of Egyptians in Kosovo and Macedonia' in Govers, C. and Vermeulen, H. (eds) *The Politics of Ethnic Consciousness*, London: Macmillan.

Duijzings, G. (2000) *Religion and Politics of Identity in Kosovo*, London: C. Hurst & Co.

Galjus, O. (1999) 'Roma of Kosovo: the forgotten victims', *Patrin Web Journal*. Available at: http://www.geocities.com/Paris/5121/patrin.htm.

Guglielmo, R. and Waters, T.W. (2005) 'Migrating towards minority status: shifting European policy towards Roma', *Journal of Common Market Studies*, 43(4): 763–785.

Kovats, M. (2003) 'The politics of Roma identity: between nationalism and destitution', *Open Democracy*. Available at: http://www.opendemocracy.net/people-migrationeurope/article_1399.jsp.

Mariushiakova, E. and Popov, V. (2001) 'New ethnic identities in the Balkans: the case of the Egyptians', *Facta Universitatis: Philosophy and Sociology*, 2(8): 465–477.

Mueller, S. (2008) 'Minority report', *Transitions Online*. Available at: http://www.tol.cz.

Sigona, N. (2008a) 'Integrating minorities in a post-conflict society', working paper. Available at: http://nandosigona.wordpress.com/2008/05/15/integration-integrazione-alcune-riflessioni/.

Sigona, N. (2008b) 'Towards the social inclusion of RAE minorities in Kosovo', working paper. Available at: http://nandosigona.wordpress.com/2008/09/04/towards-the-social-inclusion-of-rae-minorities-in-kosovo/.

Sigona, N. (2009) *I rom nell'Europa neoliberale: antiziganismo, povertà e i limiti dell'etnopolitica*, paper presented at the Department of Social Anthropology, University of Genoa, 29 March 2009. Available at: http://www.osservazione.org/documenti/sigona_genova.pdf.

Trubeta, S. (2005) 'Balkan *Egyptians* and Gypsy/Roma discourse', *Nationalities Papers*, 33(1): 71–95.

UNDP (2004) Kosovo Human Development Report. *The Rise of the Citizen: Challenges and Choices*, New York: UNDP. Available at: http://hdr.undp.org/en/reports/nationalreports/europethecis/kosovo/kosovo_2004_en.pdf

UNDP (2006) *Kosovo Human Development Report 2006. A New Generation for a New Kosovo*, New York: UNDP.

UNHCR (2007) Analysis of the Situation of Internally Displaced Persons from Kosovo in Serbia: Law and Practice, Geneva: UNHCR. Available at: http://www.unhcr.org/refworld/docid/4704bff72.html.

11
Spanish *Gitanos*, Romani Migrants and European Roma Identity: (Re)unification or Self-Affirmation?

Miguel Laparra and Almudena Macías

Introduction

After over five centuries, the presence of the *Gitanos* (Spanish Gypsies) in Spain[1] can only be explained by their extraordinary capacity for survival, both in a physical sense (overcoming persecution and a precarious livelihood), and in an ethnic sense (maintaining their identity). What is most surprising is how little is known about them. A generalized lack of interest by the majority society in conjunction with a defensive strategy practiced by Gitanos themselves, as well as an often misplaced commitment to discretion by public administrations may help to explain this lack of knowledge.[2]

Despite the scarcity of available information and resources, admirable progress has been made by some social researchers in studying this community, usually coupled with activism and social commitment (San Román 1997, 1999; FPT 2005; FSG 2006a,b, 2008). Though fragmented, information is available about the history of the Gitanos in Spain. From an anthropological viewpoint, steps have been taken in recording Romani traditions and cultural elements that differentiate them from the rest of the Spanish population. Nevertheless, there is a serious deficit in sociological data concerning their current situation, the internal diversity in the community, processes of social change, and the tendencies of these changes. Centuries of strong ethnic discrimination, a long history of persecution and rejection, and absolute inequality has placed Gitanos at the bottom of the social hierarchy. A key question to ask is: are the social differences – material and symbolic – being reduced or are they increasing between Gitanos and Spanish society in general?

This chapter describes the situation of the Spanish Gypsy community and analyses this situation from a contemporary European perspective. First, we highlight differences and specificities in comparison with Eastern European Romani communities. Secondly, we investigate the arrival of Romani people from Eastern Europe to Spain, and the relationship between indigenous Gitanos and foreign Roma migrants, problematizing the idea of a common, shared Romani identity. Nevertheless, we conclude that by engaging with the Romani communities in Europe, and exchanging knowledge and good practices with other countries, Spanish Gitanos would enhance the political relevance of Romani issues both domestically and at the European level.

The Spanish Romani community – in a process of transition

Despite an apparent consensus on the size of the Gitano community, estimated at 800,000 people[3] – our first premise is that we do not know exactly how many Gitanos and Roma live in Spain. Since the mid-1970s, a lack of reliable data has resulted in conflicting estimates, though a reasonable one is between 570,000 and 1,100,000 persons (Laparra 2007), making the Romani population in Spain the largest in Western Europe and possibly the second largest in the European Union after Romania (Liégeois and Gheorghe 1995). A recent research has estimated the Gitano community to be 2.1% of the Spanish population (around 970,000 people) (Laparra and Pérez Eransus 2008).

Although there is no clear data to back up this claim, it is generally accepted that the Gitano community has experienced a rapid demographic expansion due to a generally high birth rate. In recent decades however, the birth rate of Spanish Gitanos has progressively decreased and concurrently, life expectancy figures (that is, an increase in members over the age of 65) have risen (Figure 11.1).

Changes in the occupational structure may well become a key element in spurring changes in the balance of power between the

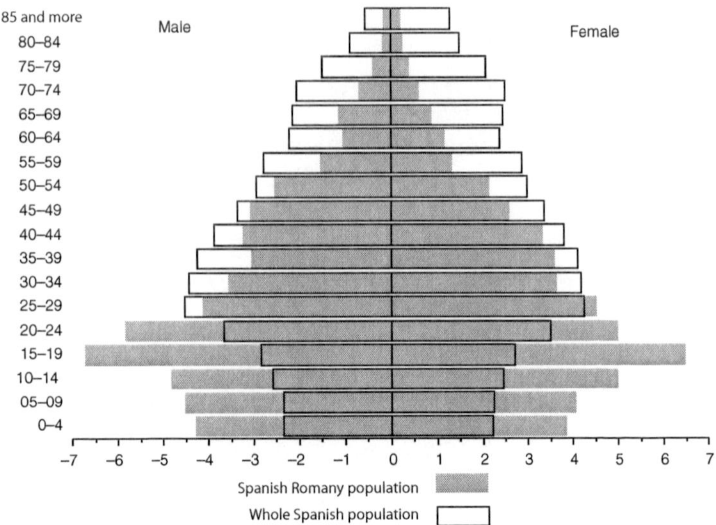

Figure 11.1   Demographic pyramid of the *Gitano* community and the Spanish population (2004).[4]

sexes. Things appear to be changing in this sphere, although the true effects remain unclear, and it is too early to be able to identify any clear tendency.

Flea markets have become an economic lifeline for Gitanos in recent decades. A series of studies made in the region of Galicia concludes that the proportion of Gitanos that are in this kind of work has increased by 24%: from 39% in 1983 to 52% in 1990 and up to 63% in 2000 (CFPEMJ 2002). This data varies considerably amongst regions in Spain, so though a conclusive evaluation cannot be made, there is a noticeable increase in this activity. One outcome is that younger generations may have limited options to thrive in this activity in the future as the market becomes saturated.

Forty-seven per cent of the Gitano active population is in wage-earning employment. Nonetheless, access to labour market is clearly hindered by underemployment and short term contracts, which makes this segment of the community highly vulnerable. Only 7.4% of the working population (16% of wage-earners) has a fixed job. Self-employment or work in the family business (almost half of those at work are in one of these two situations) is often the only hope for subsistence and it does not always satisfy their economic needs or career aspirations.

If we calculate these indicators in terms of full-time equivalents, the employment rate decreases by 20% to an overall 43%, and unemployment is up to 38% (Laparra and del Pozo 2007). Indicators such as these better illustrate the distance between the Gitanos and the rest of the Spanish society (the employment rate was 50% and unemployment rate was 10.4% for the general population at the same time, in 2004).

Twenty-four per cent of occupied persons in the Spanish Gitano community work less than 20 hours per week (40% in the case of those working in family businesses), but four out of ten persons in such situations expresses their desire to work more hours. Hawking and peddling, junk collection and recycling are the main sectors of (under)employment.

High inequality: earnings, health and housing

Though there is little reliable data concerning the economic situation of Spanish Gitanos, Gitanos themselves acknowledge that their livelihood has improved in recent decades (in the region of Galicia for example, the annual nominal increase in income was 6.5% during the 1990s), and it is likely that extreme poverty rates are declining. Nevertheless, within the framework of overall household income growth, it would be safe to say that the relative poverty rate (as a measure of inequality) has remained constant or may even be increasing. In one of the most recent and representative studies of this phenomenon, it was estimated that in 2007, relative poverty[5] was affecting 77% of Gitano households in Spain, with 37.5% of these in extreme poverty[6] (Laparra and Pérez 2008).

Despite the persistent stereotype of Gitanos living off of social services, evidence confirms that the community as a whole receives fewer social benefits than the average Spanish citizen. This is due largely to a far lower number of pensioners and their generally lower monetary amounts since many of their benefits are linked to social assistance/non-contributory pensions. The access to minimum income support schemes run by the autonomous regions of Spain is approximately 10% among Gitanos, and it is probably significantly lower than what should correspond to poverty-stricken Gitano families. In the autonomous regions where such programmes are more far-reaching, the proportion of Gitano households with these benefits is significantly higher as 38% of recipients are Gitanos in Navarre, although the community amounts to 1% of the regional population (Laparra et al. 2003).

Spanish Gitanos have a life expectancy that is eight to nine years less than the national average. From an international comparative perspective, the life expectancy of the Spanish Gitano community is comparable to countries such as Peru, Nicaragua, Egypt, Morocco, Turkey or Cape Verde, as well as falling below figures for Spain in 1975. Taking into consideration the deep changes that have taken place in Spanish society in the past 30 years, it is clear that the Spanish Gitano community is lagging behind.

Child mortality (1.4 times higher than the national average), higher rates of infectious/contagious disease (e.g. nine times more incidence of Hepatitis A), high rates of chronic illness and handicaps, as well as the contraction of illnesses that have been practically eradicated in Spain – such as leprosy – are all clear indicators of morbidity that are directly related to living conditions for Gitanos (FSG 2005).

It is important to note that the generation that was born in the 1940s is now reaching retirement age. They were living for decades under the Francoist regime subject to persecution by the Civil Guard and they survived extremely difficult conditions during most of their life. Only with the advent of democracy, did they begin to benefit from new social policies that did not treat them differently from the majority population. It is hoped that the health of Gitanos, and thus life expectancy, will improve in coming generations, although no timeframe or reliable data is available to quantify anything in this respect.

Housing policies providing dignified homes for Gitano households in recent decades often settled them within a context of spatial segregation.[7] In the late 1980s, only one out of every five Roma families lived in non-problematic neighbourhoods, while the rest resided in public housing developments with a high concentration of social problems (50%) or in marginal neighbourhoods and slums (28%). This distribution has played a major role in the prospects for social integration for Gitano citizens (Pass 1991).

Notably, the housing situation has improved in recent years since the Government's adoption of a 'micro level' approach (case by case, in local housing projects) to its intervention for clearing degraded housing areas. However, in the meantime, the speculation in the real estate market since the mid-1990s and the lack of a comprehensive social housing policy has had a negative effect, increasing other problems such as overcrowding and bad quality housing.

As a result, after half a century of struggling to eradicate slums, Gitano families continue to live in them. There is no doubt that they are a minority within the Gitano population as a whole, but it is also significant that it is practically the only social group that has been unable to fully overcome this marginalized existence: almost all of the slum dwellers in Spain are Gitanos/Roma[8] and this has continuing symbolic effects on the community as a whole.

To summarize, it could be said that although inequality remains high, Gitanos have made noticeable gains as a result of the policies of the Spanish welfare state, particularly in terms of housing, health insurance and welfare benefits.

The educational deficit and ethnic discrimination determine the spread of inequality

It is clear that educational standards have improved remarkably for Gitanos since the 1950s. Most of the youth attend school, something which was not the case for the generation that is now in their 50s. By the 1990s, most Gitanos attended educational institutions (in Navarre, only 13% of Gitanos between the ages of 16 and 24 were not in school in 1997).

In primary schools, there have been significant changes: obligatory attendance for children of seven years of age was 79% in 1994 and up to 94% in 2001; absenteeism (more than three months of absence) has dropped from 43% to 31% during the aforementioned period; performance levels have also improved at this level (up 2% to a total of 22% (Andrés and Fresno 2002).

On the other side, recent reforms in the secondary education system have not been kind to Romani and Gitano children (AECG 1997) and some estimates indicate that two out of three children are not in school between the ages of 13 and 16.[9] If one takes into account the considerable improvements in the educational level of society as a whole, it must be admitted that the situation of the Gitanos has actually worsened in comparative terms with the rest of the society and has become a major setback in their access to the labour market.

The general lack of information related to the long history of Gitanos and their contributions to Spanish society within the school curricula (only 12% have introduced such elements) prove that there is still a distance between the mainstream education system and Gitanos (Fernández Enguita 1999). Two out of three schools have run out of ideas and do not plan any future initiatives for overcoming this gap. Gitanos are one of the most stigmatized and rejected groups in Spanish society about which many stereotypes and prejudices still prevail. According to the latest CIS barometer,[10] the Gitano community is the group which Spanish society is most unfriendly toward. The persistence and reproduction of such racist attitudes – clearly demonstrated in all of the studies performed since the 1970s – is disturbing, especially because in most cases, these value judgments are not based on personal experiences and rest solely on the transmission of stereotypes. There is no precise data describing how such discriminatory attitudes affect specific situations, but there are declarations in reports published by organizations that are involved with this community, in which conduct based on biased attitudes is observed to be habitual, for example, when applying for a job or renting a home.[11]

This deeply rooted and persistent discrimination impacts on several key aspects of the life of Gitano communities; however, it is not recognized as such by broader Spanish society and by many Gitanos themselves.[12] For instance, in the region of La Rioja in 2003, only 11% of them felt that they are not treated fairly or that they are discriminated against (AAVV 2003b). This lack of awareness (or strategic silence) about discrimination may hinder the positive impact of work done to overcome stereotypes and discriminatory practices. Other studies, such as the EDIS/FSG employment study in 2005 revealed that 36% of Gitanos interviewed felt discriminated during their job search and 19% felt it in the workplace. These figures indicate a growing awareness in this sense, and if addressed, it may lead to a better situation in the future.

Anti-discriminatory legislation has not generated a complete resolution to the problem. Indeed, EU directives against discrimination have been transposed into Spanish laws in a way that reduces their operability as a legal instrument against this type of conduct: most reported cases never make it to court (AAVV 2003a; Cachón 2004; FSG 2006a).

A low capacity for collective action

The size of the Gitano population and its territorial dispersion has no doubt posed a challenge to its political capacity for collective action and for influencing decision-making processes. The present institutional model in Spain only acknowledges a political entity if it is associated with a particular territory,[13] and this has rendered it almost impossible for Gitanos to build up their own representative institutions. Moreover, territorial dispersion combined with low voting rates among Gitanos, has limited the possibility of influencing the agenda of mainstream political parties. Recent success in this respect in some Eastern European countries is in contrast with the minimal political power that Gitano citizens hold in their own country[14] (Laparra 2005; cf. Rostas's chapter).

It is not surprising to observe that the rate of citizen participation is lower amongst Gitanos than in the population as a whole: approximately one half of the Gitanos in the region of Catalonia participate in associations. Most of these are ethnic-based organizations run by Gitanos and they rarely participate in non-Romani organizations (FPT 2005). Currently, therefore, the network of Roma associations and federations is an essential mechanism for the political participation of Gitanos and for collective action. Thus, it is necessary to take into account the excessive fragmentation, sinecurial (clientelist) relations, appropriation and informality that can be found in this network, in order to improve the democratic density and quality of these organizations (San Román 1999).

It is worth mentioning that evangelical churches have made great strides in this respect through a process of communitarian densification based on religious practice, organizing new associations and meeting many people. This situation has made it possible for some Gitanos to transcend the restrictions of family ambience, and open the way to transformation through wider networks of interaction, including with non-Roma (Méndez 2002; Cantón 2004). The true effect of this phenomenon remains to be seen and it is too early to declare it as an instrument for the emancipation of the Gitano community. On the contrary, some researchers have reported that the churches aim not only to transform what being a Gitano is about, but also to reinforce the moral barrier between Gitanos and the rest of society (Gay y Blasco 2002).

At an institutional level, the establishment of the Consejo del Pueblo Gitano (The Gypsy People's Council) established in June 2006 may play an important role as a first step towards political recognition for the Gitano community in Spain. The development of this Council will test the capacity of Gitano organizations to channel their demands and aspirations of the people it represents (the Spanish Gitanos).

Gitanos and the arrival of Roma from Eastern Europe

In this context of disadvantage, discrimination and social exclusion of Spanish Gitanos, the eastwards enlargement of the European Union could mean a qualitative change, as the 'Roma issue' gains more and more attention at the European level (OSCE 2000; Revenga and Silva-Jauregui 2002).

According to estimates made by non-governmental organizations and independent researchers, as shown in Table 11.1, the Roma population in the European Union has increased fourfold (the average estimate is six million) following the enlargement. In relative terms, this would account for an increase from 0.45% of EU-15 to 1.24% in EU-27.

Romani communities are present in all of the countries of the European Union and, in fact, are the largest ethnic minority in Europe. This is an important factor that places pressure on European institutions to deal with issues related to Roma (see Will Guy's chapter for a discussion on the EU policy for Romani communities). Research is being promoted that involves the study of the social situation of Romani communities and support has been extended to initiatives put forth by member countries, even prior to their incorporation (PHARE [Poland and Hungary: Assistance for Restructuring their Economies] programme), aimed at improving the living conditions and the guarantees of the civil, political and social rights of Roma in Europe (Fresno and Fernández 2005), all of which has been a significant step in the institutional sense.

However, different 'starting points' should be considered when looking at this process: since the 1980s, Spanish Gitanos have experienced upward social mobility, but the East European Romani communities have been experiencing downward mobility during the same period, as a consequence of the transition to the market economy and the adoption of neoliberal policies. Roma in Eastern Europe with low-skill levels have been left out of the new market 'reform' economies. The social inclusion of Roma was already a priority for communist regimes, and many had joined the mass of proletariat working classes – sometimes at the expense of identity assimilation.

Table 11.1 Impact of the Enlargement on Romani population in the European Union[15]

	Total population	Roma population	Per 100 inhabitants	Distribution of Roma population (%)			
				In EU15	In EU25	In EU27	Total Europe
Spain	40,037,995	750,000	1.87	44.4	24.1	12.5	9.6
EU-15	379,072,361	1,687,875	0.45	100.0	54.3	28.1	21.7
Enlargement in 2004	74,964,533	1,422,250	1.90	–	45.7	23.7	18.3
EU-25	454,036,894	3,110,125	0.68	–	100.0	51.7	40.0
Enlargement in 2007	29,627,082	2,900,000	9.79	–	–	48.3	37.3
EU-27	483,663,976	6,010,125	1.24	–	–	100.0	77.3
Other European countries	307,319,366	1,762,500	0.57	–	–	–	22.7
Total Europe	790,983,342	7,772,625	0.98	–	–	–	100.0

What EU policy promises so far is inclusion based on liberal (or increasingly) neoliberal principles.

By articulating policies against discrimination and social exclusion in conjunction with this eastwards enlargement, the European Union is contributing directly or indirectly to the construction of a pan-European Romani identity, initially at a national level, but also within the scope of Europe[16] (see Kovats 2003). We may be reaching a point in which Roma, the 'largest trans-European minority' (Tubbax 2005) that is geographically and culturally dispersed throughout Europe in a multi-secular diaspora, can now be reunited and recognized as a nation in the midst of a united Europe.[17] This ethnic-based path is in no way risk-free because of the generation of possible exclusionary effects (Trehan 2005).

Romanian Roma migration in the EU

The flow of Roma from Romania to Spain became considerable in 1993; most of the requests for asylum received in Spain were by Romanians from 1994 to 1997, while at the same time measures were being adopted in other Western European countries to restrict migration of Romanians.

On paper, Spain adopted measures in line with other EU members regarding this migratory flow. Restrictive measures and tighter security at border crossings have been the main strategy of Spanish authorities after signing repatriation agreements and modifying its legislation governing asylum and immigration. In 1997, a readmission agreement came into effect between Spain and Romania for the readmission of persons that were found to be in an irregular situation.[18] In January 2002, visa requirements to enter Spain were lifted and migration from Romania became easier. Nevertheless, the number of repatriations also increased significantly (from 1607 in 2001 to 20,089 in 2002).

The actual number of Roma that entered Spain after 1992 varies. Official sources do not provide accurate figures as there is no indication of the ethnic origin of migrants. A number of empirical studies conducted in Spain indicate that the Romanian Roma population could be up to 10% of the total Romanian population in the country, which accounts for approximately 730,000 people.[19] Therefore, we can estimate that Romanian Roma make up around 75,000 people (Macías 2008). Considering that there has not been a significant flow of Roma from other countries, the Romani collective from Romania could make up around 7% of the total Romani population in Spain. However, although the numbers are lower compared to other recent migrant communities, these immigrants are highly visible, as is the case in other European countries (Diminescu 2004).

In Romania, many Roma had experienced a reasonably stable life working in the industrial sector until the factories started closing down in the 1990s. Other Roma had steady jobs in the agricultural and construction sectors. During the transition process, most of them were either forced to make ends meet with temporary jobs at low wages, or were unemployed before they emigrated. In Romania, 80% of the Roma population did not have any qualification, only 16% had some technical qualification and 4% were dedicated to traditional occupations, such as plasterwork, brick production and hawking of wares (Achim 2004).

As a whole, however, it was a family-based migration process. Normally, Romani people do not emigrate alone and instead tend to group together with other members of the family or other families. It must be remembered that the families are large, with a mean size of 6.6 members. Therefore, emigration is an important part of the strategy of the family (Macías 2008).

Nevertheless, the family unit often divides upon emigration. Initially, one of the parents emigrates and later regroups the family when conditions permit. The youngest children are often left in the care of relatives until the migratory strategy of the family has worked itself out. The adolescents stay at home until they finish school and then they are reunited with their families. At present, older members of the family are arriving in Spain to be reunited with their families.

In general, the situation of these families in Spain has been precarious. Most of them lacked residence permits until the EU enlargement in 2007. However, as of January 2007, when Romanian nationals became EU citizens, their right to work in Spain has been governed by several transition arrangements. Although they are allowed to live in Spain, in most cases they cannot be legally hired and are therefore forced to take on informal jobs, since the alternative of self-employment can be difficult. Nevertheless, this new legal and administrative status has fostered the access of Romani families to the labour market and social services.

In some cases, their activity is marginal (but certainly quite visible): begging, selling paper tissues and street newspapers (La Farola, La Calle, etc.), cleaning windshields at traffic lights or scrap collecting/recycling. This group has been the public image of Romani immigrants in Spain and indeed, throughout Europe: a highly stigmatized collective that in the public imaginary is generally associated with mafias, anti-social behaviour and crime. Although many of these same people were involved with the informal economic sector in Romania, it is often true that as a result of emigration, they were forced to get involved in activities that they would not normally associate with in their country of origin. Thus, in this way, emigration can be viewed job-wise as a regression for these migrants. Yet, other families have fared better in some of the sectors of the formal economy: construction (unskilled labour), agriculture and domestic services (house maid and caretakers), although these are often piecemeal by nature, characterized by low pay and job insecurity.

The issue of housing for Romani immigrants in Spain is complex. At the beginning of the migratory flow, many of them lived temporarily in their vans or trailers. Others settled on the street, in parks or empty lots. More recently, however, things have improved. Many of the newcomers already have friends in Spain that assist them in finding a decent place to stay.

Nonetheless, there is practically no contact between Romanian Roma and Spanish Gitano communities. From this practical perspective, their 'reunification' is more rhetoric than reality. This encounter will not likely build up a foundation for fostering an identity as a wider, European 'Romani people', since the Spanish *Gitano* community is not incorporating newly arrived Romani groups from Eastern Europe to any noticeable degree. At least, these are the dynamics currently observed in Spain.

Spanish Gitanos have neither welcomed recent Romani migrants from Eastern Europe, nor offered any aid to them upon their arrival and settling. In Spain, direct solidarity links between Spanish Gitanos and the Eastern European Roma have been scarce, although some Spanish Gitano organizations have campaigned against any kind of racist reactions against them.[20]

In the few contacts that are known to have taken place, marked cultural differences prevailed. The Romani language has not played an important role as a cultural nexus or common identity, since this tongue has been lost by Spanish Gitanos and the dialectical differences in their communication make their idioms mutually unintelligible at a popular level (apart from activists, who have learned the Romani language).

Independent of local Gitanos and from other non-Romani immigrants from Romania, Romanian Roma have established their own associations in Spain. *Gitano* associations, which are numerous, but often with only limited involvement, have not addressed the arrival of Roma from Eastern Europe in any significant manner. In fact, there seems to be a certain degree of specialization (or even separation) of entities, both Romani and non-Romani, in dealing either with Spanish Gitanos or Roma from Eastern Europe. The *Consejo del Pueblo Gitano* (Gypsy People's Council), which was launched by the Spanish Government, has not taken on the role of representing foreign Roma, nor does it appear to be concerned about the social issues of the most marginal Romani communities that have arrived from Eastern Europe. Only a small movement may be observed amongst some activists for showing solidarity with east European Roma, although not very intensively.[21]

In some of the discourse generated by Gitanos, there is even a xenophobic undertone when referring to foreign Roma, not unlike other reactions of Spanish society at large when dealing with this influx of immigrants. From the perspective of Gitanos, the arrival of Eastern Roma, who are often very marginal and heavily stigmatized, can be considered as a threat that can jeopardize the improvements that Gitanos have experienced in regards to living conditions and integration (or acceptance, at least). It could be argued that the Eastern European Roma – Romanians in particular – are tarnishing the 'social image' of Gitanos in Spain. This influx of Eastern Roma may thus exacerbate an increase in discrimination levels against Roma in general. Spanish society already rejects the autochthonous Gitano ethnic minority and, to make matters worse, the newly arrived Eastern Roma are considered to be engaged in criminal activities by the media, spurring racist and xenophobic attitudes in society. It is possible that this image has had a negative effect on the dynamics between Romani communities and groups.

Conclusion

Spanish Gitanos are being confronted with a new scenario resulting from a confluence of social and institutional transformations that have taken place in Spain, along with European Union enlargement, with the consequent 're-encounter,' (whether real or merely symbolic), of different Romani communities.

It is possible that the improvements enjoyed by Spanish Gitanos may be reaching a ceiling, due to a number of factors related to the vicious cycle of social exclusion for centuries that stigmatizes the Spanish Romani minority and makes this group the main object of ethnic discrimination in Spain. On the one hand, the negligible political relevance of the 'Gitano issue' keeps public awareness levels low; whilst on the other hand, the roadblocks for Gitanos at the level of secondary education only serve to prolong and intensify long-term under-employment and poor working conditions that hinder their integration. Furthermore, it is possible that the continuance of a patriarchal tradition blocks the way for Gitana women to have their say in the process of change, while the men appear to be stuck, with no answers within the new context. Perhaps the only way to overcome these barriers is to spur qualitative changes that can lead to a transformation of the inner structure of the Gypsy community (in particular education and employment, as well as gender relations). Such a process can only be undertaken by the Romani community itself.

Nevertheless, there are other scenarios that may nurture social change for the Gitano community. Anti-discriminatory policy and the struggle against social exclusion that is fostered by European institutions are having a positive effect on the Spanish Romani community.[22] The political, economic and social changes in Eastern Europe, as well as EU enlargement, has led to an inflow of marginalized Roma and although this may increase the stigma already suffered by Roma in general, it has also served to clearly identify Romani integration as a priority for social policies at the European level. It has also encouraged the strengthening of organs of social representation, which has opened the road for the political acknowledgement of Roma as a 'people' in various countries in Eastern Europe and even in Spain to a lesser extent. By articulating policies against discrimination and social exclusion in the process of eastwards enlargement, the European Union is contributing – directly or indirectly – to the construction of a possible Romani identity within a European framework. A number of Romani elites in Europe seem to be trying to take advantage of this process by 'Europeanizing' the 'Roma issue' and fostering the Romani identity at a transnational level.[23] This

European network is another possible strategy that several NGOs are attempting to build at the moment.

Within this emerging political framework, the continental migration of Romani groups from Eastern Europe – reactivated today under new historic circumstances, as a part of a broad and ethnically plural migratory flux (Matras 2000) – has shown marked social and cultural differences amongst European Romani communities. In effect, this has led to a 're-encounter' characterized by mutual ignorance, and in which Spanish and foreign Roma tend to simply avoid each other.

It is clear that this symbolic distance is a key obstacle to any strategy that aspires towards a European Romani people that appears to be the intention of certain Romani elites and may even be fostered at an institutional level in Europe. Even if such a political agenda were set for a pan-European Romani community, it is doubtful that *Gitanos* would be keen to play a decisive role or even participate at all, in spite of activities which demonstrate cross-national solidarity.

Independent of any possible political union of the 'Roma nation,' a strategic alliance with East European Roma could be of interest to Spanish Gitanos in order to gain political power within the European Union (and Spanish) institutional frameworks, and to open the road to an exchange of experiences with like-minded people as an aid to social, cultural and economic development, and also to political empowerment.

Notes

1. The term 'gitano' in Spanish has an ambivalent meaning. Amongst the majority population, sometimes it refers to persons with a special talent or grace; more often, however, it refers to a shoddy or unreliable person. Importantly, the Spanish Gypsy community identifies itself as 'Gitanos' with marked pride. There are many associations that use the term 'Gitano' in their title and the word is used broadly by Spanish people and public authorities when referring to programs targeted to this community. We also want to underline the specific cultural and linguistic identity of the Spanish Gypsies. The term 'Roma' is used here, specifically, to refer to Romani migrants from Eastern Europe in Spain and, generically, when referring to the broader academic and political debate on the Romani communities in Europe.
2. Official statistics in Spain do not provide ethnic-specific data on the Gitano population making difficult for social scientists to analyse trends and tendencies.

3. This estimation refers to Gitanos with Spanish nationality, which could include groups of different origin related to different ancient migrations from different parts of Eastern Europe ('Hungaros' and others).
4. Source: By the author (Laparra) and based on data from EDIS ('Población gitana y empleo', Fundación Secretariado Gitano, Madrid, 2006) for the Gitano community and on data from INE [National Institute of Statistics (Spanish: Instituto National de Estadistica)] (Census 2004) for general population figures.
5. Measured as 60% of median available net household income per unit of equivalence.
6. Thirty per cent of median available net household income per unit of equivalence.
7. This is similar to settlement patterns throughout Europe, even in former socialist countries where Roma were most integrated in terms of housing, employment, education, and other social indicators.
8. Most of the low-skilled, irregular immigrants that have arrived in Spain during the last decade have managed to avoid the slums. Only Romani immigrants from Eastern Europe have joined this stigmatized collective of shantytown dwellers.
9. Estimations for Navarre by the Fundación Secretariado Gitano, based on figures of the Government of Navarre.
10. Centro de Investigaciones Sociológicas. Research number 2745: 'Discriminaciones y su percepción' December 2007.
11. See reports on discrimination by Fundación Secretariado Gitano; the latest: 'Discriminación y Comunidad Gitana. Informe Annual 2008'.
12. There is a need for research analysing the reason for this response among the Gitano population.
13. The 'nacionalidad' (nationality) category is acknowledged is historical nations as Catalonia, Basque Country or Galicia, and has served as the base for a significant process of political decentralization during the last three decades. The estimated size of the Gitano community in Spain would situate it as a medium size region, but the political weight of their leaders is far lower than the president of the smallest region.
14. The lack of Roma political institutions (until the recently created Gypsy People's Council with a few competences) and the exclusion of the general political organizations (with only a very few exceptions) shapes the political situation of Spanish Gitanos.
15. Source: By the authors based on the work Liégeois and Gheorghe (1995). For each country, the mean of various estimates for the Romani population made by social organizations was taken.
16. The European Commission itself needs available European organizations or networks as speakers at a European level, not just at national level, to justify any interventions in this respect.
17. Paolo Pietrosanti, who has represented Romani organizations at the UN, declared that 'Romani people are the most *euro-enthusiastic*' (http://www.cafebabel.com,18 April 2005).

18. Agreement between Spain and Romania governing the readmission of persons with irregular status (BOE 5 March 1999: 8859). Accessible at http://www.boe.es/aeboe/consultas/bases_datos/doc.php?coleccion=iberlex&id=1999/05356
19. Official Census, January 2008, National Institute of Statistics (INE).
20. Union Romani has been very active in its press statements and political action on the Italian Romanian Roma crisis.
21. For example a demonstration was organized on 8 August 2008 in Madrid by the Consejo Estatal del Pueblo Gitano against the violence towards Roma in Italy.
22. This is the idea behind the *European Network on Roma Community and Structural Funds*, in which every European country with a significant number of Roma population is present, and which aims to influence on Member States' policies for Roma communities funded by the EU.
23. Juan de Dios de Ramírez Heredia, as the first Romani (Gitano) MEP, could be seen as the start of this process of 'Europeanization' made by Gitanos. In the same way, in the chapter by Simhandl, a possibility is identified of a more active role for Roma in the construction of their identity in the future.

References

AAVV (2003a) *La discriminación racial*, Barcelona: Icaria.

AAVV (2003b) *La población gitana en la Comunidad Autónoma de La Rioja*, Logroño: Consejería de Salud y Servicios Sociales.

Achim, V. (2004) *The Roma in Romanian History*, Budapest: CEU.

AECG, Asociación de Enseñantes con Gitanos (1997) 'La transición de primaria a secundaria', *Boletín del Centro de Documentación de la Asociación de Enseñantes con Gitanos*: 14–15.

Andrés, M.T. and Fresno, J.M. (2002) *Evaluación de la normalización educativa del alumnado gitano en educación primaria*, Madrid: Fundación Secretariado General Gitano.

Cachón, L. (2004) 'España y la directiva 2000/43: de la ocasión perdida a una legislación general sobre la igualdad de trato', *Tiempo de paz*, 73: 13–22.

Cantón, M. (2004) *Gitanos Pentecostales: Una mirada antropológica a la Iglesia de Filadelfia en Andalucía*, Sevilla: Junta de Andalucía, Consejería de Cultura.

CFPEMJ, C. d. F. e. P. d. E., Mujer y Juventud (2002) *A comunidade xitana en Galicia 1990–2000*, Santiago: Xunta de Galicia.

Diminescu, D. (2004) 'La mobilité del jeunes roumains à l'heure de l'elargissement européen', *Hommes & Migrations*, 1251: 42–50.

EDIS/FSG (2005) *El empleo en la población gitana*, Madrid: Fundación Secretariado Gitano.

Fernández Enguita, M. (1999) *Alumnos gitanos en la escuela paya: un estudio étnico sobre las relaciones en el sistema educativo*, Barcelona: Ariel Practicum.

FPT, Fundació Pere Tarrés (2005) *Estudi sobre la població gitana de Catalunya*, Barcelona: Generalitat de Catalunya. Departament de Benestar i Familia.

Fresno, J.M. and Fernández, C. (2005) 'Las políticas europeas a favor de la comunidad gitana: derechos sociales, fondos estructurales e igualdad de trato', *Documentación Social*, 137: 115–128.

FSG, Fundación Secretariado Gitano (2005) *Salud y comunidad gitana*, Madrid: Ministerio de Sanidad y Consumo.

FSG, Fundación Secretariado Gitano (2006a) *Discriminación y Comunidad Gitana. Informe Anual 2006*, Madrid: Fundación Secretariado Gitano.

FSG, Fundación Secretariado Gitano (2006b) *El reconocimiento institucional de la Comunidad Gitana en España*, Madrid: Fundación Secretariado Gitano.

FSG, Fundación Secretariado Gitano (2008) *Discriminación y Comunidad Gitana. Informe Anual 2008*, Madrid: Fundación Secretariado Gitano.

Gay y Blasco, P. (2002) 'Gypsy/Roma diasporas. A comparative perspective', *Social Anthropology*, 10(2): 173–188.

Kovats, M. (2003) 'The politics of Roma identity: between nationalism and destitution', OpenDemocracy.Net, http://www.opendemocracy.net/people-migrationeurope/article_1399.jsp

Laparra, M. (2005) 'La Europa de los gitanos. Identidad, participación y políticas sociales en la Europa ampliada y su incidencia en España', *Documentación Social*, 137: 15–36.

Laparra, M. (2007) (ed.) *Informe sobre la situación social y tendencias de cambio en la población gitana*, Madrid: Ministerio de Trabajo y Asuntos Sociales.

Laparra, M. and del Pozo, J.M. (2007) 'Empleo y ocupación en la comunidad gitana', *Informe sobre la situación social y tendencias de cambio en la población gitana*, Madrid: Ministerio de Trabajo y Asuntos Sociales.

Laparra, M. et al. (2003) *La garantía de ingresos mínimos en Navarra. Un estudio evaluativo de la Renta Básica 1990–2001*, Pamplona, Departamento de Bienestar Social Deporte y Juventud del Gobierno de Navarra.

Laparra, M. and Pérez Eransus, B. (coord.) (2008) 'La exclusión social en España: un espacio diverso y disperso en intensa transformación', *VI Informe Foessa sobre Exclusión y desarrollo social en España 2008*, Madrid: Fundación FOESSA.

Liégeois, J.-P. and Gheorghe, N. (1995) *Roma/Gypsies: a European minority*, London: Minority Rights Group.

Macías, A. (2008) 'La emigración de la minoría étnica gitana de Rumanía hacia España: Factores condicionantes de las migraciones internacionales', PhD thesis, Pamplona: Departamento de Trabajo Social, Universidad Pública de Navarra.

Matras, Y. (2000) 'Romani migrations in the post-conflict era: their historical and political significance', *Cambridge Review of International Affairs*, 13(2): 32–50.

Méndez, C. (2002) 'La mujer gitana entre el catolicismo y el pentecostalismo', *I Tchatchipén*, 37: 30–44.

OSCE (2000) Report on the Condition of the Roma in Europe, Warsaw: OSCE.

Pass, G. (1991) *Mapa de vivienda gitana. Estudio sociológico sobre la comunidad gitana en España*, Madrid: Ministerio de Asuntos Sociales.

Revenga, A., Silva-Jauregui, C. (2002) *Slovak Republic: living standards, employment and labor market study*, Washington: World Bank.

San Román, T. (1997) La diferencia inquietante: viejas y nuevas estrategias culturales de los gitanos, Madrid: Siglo XXI.

San Román, T. (1999) 'El desarrollo de la conciencia política de los gitanos', Revista Gitanos, 36–41.

Trehan, N. (2005) 'Identidad étnica y representación político-institucional de las comunidades romaníes en Europa', *Documentación Social*, 137: 99–114.

Tubbax, C. (2005) 'La plus grande minorité "transeuropéenne"', Accessed at: http://www.cafebabel.com, 18 April 2005.

12
New Labour's Policies and Their Effectiveness for the Provision of Sites for Gypsies and Travellers in England

Jo Richardson and Andrew Ryder

Introduction

> We are determined to address the issues relating to the accommodation and wider needs of Gypsies and Travellers in ways which address both the interests of that community and the settled community generally. In particular … looking also at issues such as social exclusion and community cohesion.
>
> Government Response to the Office of the Deputy Prime Minister Select Committee's Report on Gypsy and Traveller Sites (ODPM 2005: 1)

In January 2005, the Labour Government responded to a Select Committee recommendation to re-introduce a requirement for local authorities to build sites by saying it was 'determined to address the issues'. It did not go as far as to legislate for the building of new Gypsy and Traveller sites, but there have been a number of pieces of legislation and Government guidance which require authorities to assess need and to include sites in local plans, which should, in theory, culminate in the provision of more accommodation for Gypsies and Travellers in England. However, the statement above itself reflects the contradictions in political and everyday discourse surrounding Gypsies and Travellers, suggesting that this is a *binary debate* on the needs of the communities versus the needs of the wider 'settled' population. Approximately two-thirds of the Gypsy and Traveller population of England today live in bricks and mortar accommodation and are thus effectively hidden *within* the wider community. Hence it is not as much a debate about Gypsies and Travellers *versus* the rest of the population, but instead should be a sensible discussion about the differing accommodation needs of a number of wide-ranging communities living in England. The second way in which the Government quotation is contradictory is in the 'determination' or 'commitment' to help meet the needs of Gypsy and Travelling communities, without necessarily providing the (unpopular) legislative force to compel councils to build more sites now.

This chapter explores the effectiveness of new accommodation policies for Gypsies and Travellers that were introduced from 1997 onwards by the New Labour Government, in an attempt to increase social inclusion for these minority groups. We first provide a contextual overview of the situation for Gypsies and Travellers in England. We then examine a number of initiatives introduced which were meant to improve Gypsies' and Travellers' lives, and conclude by discussing whether or not the New Labour Government has been successful in making accommodation provision for these communities.

Gypsy and Traveller – definitions

In legal terms, defining Gypsies and Travellers as a group has been difficult. Whilst we use the umbrella term 'Gypsies and Travellers' here, in so doing, we recognize the imposition of a simplistic exonym on a wide range of distinct communities. Ethnonyms that some community members prefer to use include Roma, Romany, Pavee and Nawken, amongst others. The two largest communities in England are Romani English Gypsies and Irish Travellers; there are also Welsh Gypsies, Scottish Gypsies and recent Romani migrants from the European accession countries amongst others.

Despite the differences in heritage and culture, one of the issues that Gypsies and Travellers have in common is their difficulty in being accepted by broader society and the problems in finding a place to stay and settle. For this reason, we feel that there is enough similarity in issues of social exclusion, and inability to access services to meet even basic human needs, that the umbrella term of 'Gypsies and Travellers' allows generic issues to be discussed in the context of assessing the Government's record on meeting their accommodation needs in England.

The courts have established that Gypsies and Irish Travellers are ethnic groups for the purposes of the Race Relations Act 1976 (as amended by the Race Relations (Amendment) Act 2000) (Commission for Racial Equality v Dutton 1989; O'Leary and others v Punch Retail 2000).

In one particular case, it was found that a person's occupation of their caravan forms part of their ethnic identity (Chapman v United Kingdom 2001). Previously, the focus was on the nomadism of Gypsies and Travellers, as part of any legal definition. However, the Department for Communities and Local Government (DCLG), recognized the difficulties around the concept of 'settled' Travellers; and it included the concept in Circular 1/2006 (ODPM 2006a). This was a marked change to other legal definitions, for example for planning purposes, where nomadism – the very act of travelling – was seen as the *only* defining characteristic of Gypsies and Travellers. Now, with the introduction of the definition following Circular 1/2006, the notion of a 'settled' Gypsy or Traveller was recognized – they became defined by 'being' as well as by 'doing'.[1]

By the end of 2006, Statutory Instrument No. 3190 (2006) was implemented, in order to resolve the definition of Gypsies and Travellers in relation to the duties under the Housing Act 2004 as noted below.

For the purposes of section 225 of the Housing Act 2004 (duties of local housing authorities: accommodation needs of gypsies and travellers [*sic*]) 'gypsies and travellers' [*sic*] means –

a. persons with a cultural tradition of nomadism or of living in a caravan; and
b. all other persons of a nomadic habit of life, whatever their race or origin, including –
   i. such persons who, on grounds only of their own or their family's or dependant's educational or health needs or old age, have ceased to travel temporarily or permanently; and
   ii. members of an organized group of Travelling showpeople or circus people (whether or not travelling together as such).

Context

The Council of Europe estimates that the size of Britain's Gypsy and Traveller population is about 300,000. It is important to note, however, that families either on the road or on sites represent about only one-third of the total population in England since approximately two-thirds of Gypsies and Travellers live in bricks and mortar accommodation (Shelter 2008).

A shortage of official local council sites coupled with restrictions on mobility, have quantifiably negative impacts on the life chances of Gypsies and Travellers. Since the 1994 Criminal Justice and Public Order Act, there has been less toleration of 'unofficial' sites, and as a result, families have either been moved on with more frequency, which has not allowed them the time to access health or education opportunities in an area, or if they have applied as homeless persons, they have been offered bricks and mortar accommodation, not sites. Recent reports and evidence indicate that Gypsies and Travellers are one of the most marginalized groups in society, in terms of health, education and life expectancy (CRE 2006: 13). Gypsies and Travellers continue to face discrimination and harassment in England, despite the positive moves towards a more integrationist approach that affects other Black and Minority Ethnic groups. Richardson (2006a) argues that a process of 'othering' dehumanizes the communities, and is used to legitimize their exclusion and marginalization. Extreme political parties, such as the British National Party, play their part; but so too does the media, the politicians and the general public. The Equality and Human Rights Commission (formerly the CRE) Chair, Trevor Phillips, said at the launch of their Gypsy and Traveller Strategy in October 2003:

> For this group, Great Britain is still like the American Deep South for black people in the 1950's. Extreme levels of public hostility exist in relation to Gypsies and Travellers – fuelled in part by irresponsible media reporting of the kind that would be met with outrage if it was targeted at any other ethnic group. (Crawley 2004: 2)

There are also issues of inequality of health, access to education and employment. Parry et al. (2004: 2) have noted that 'there is now little doubt that health inequality between the observed Gypsy Traveller population in England and their non-Gypsy counterparts is striking, even when compared with other socially deprived or excluded groups and with other ethnic minorities'. This health study, along with other reports, discusses increased infant mortality, lower life expectancy and difficulty in accessing health care. Moreover, it points out that there is a significantly higher chance of long-term illness, and that 'the scale of health inequality between the study population and the UK general population is large. There was more than twice the prevalence of limiting long-term illness and significantly poorer reported health in Gypsy Travellers' (Parry et al. 2004: 65).

Issues around education and the communities are discussed in DCLG's report *Improving Opportunity, Strengthening Society*, which states that 'Gypsy, Roma and Traveller pupils have the lowest attainment levels of any ethnic group' (2005: 15). This low educational attainment clearly has an impact on the ability to access sustainable employment for the future. Again, due to the fact that Gypsies and Travellers are not included in race monitoring, there is no accurate data in this area. The Equality and Human Rights Commission has recently published an extensive literature review detailing Gypsy and Traveller exclusion in the UK (Cemlyn et al. 2009).

A framework for understanding control and marginalization

In order to understand the current system of control and marginalization, it is important to delve into the complex and troubled history that Gypsies and Travellers have faced, and a variety of work examines an English history of Gypsies and Travellers.[2]

Rather than focusing narrowly on practical Government policy and legislation for answers on the treatment of Gypsies and Travellers, it is important to examine *how* they are 'othered' by society and controlled by Governments in England and across Europe, but also to probe the reasons *why* they are marginalized and excluded. Foucault's (1969) explanation of a societal and Governmental 'gaze' reveals how, through discourse and surveillance, communities are controlled and monitored. For example, the negative way in which Gypsies and Travellers are portrayed in some sections of the media, serves as a tool to highlight their 'otherness' and their so-called deviancy from societal norms.

By labelling Gypsies and Travellers as 'other', society is actually making them 'other'; they are constructing their identity as different. Why is this done? It can be a tool to control the person(s) being labelled. It can also be seen as a tool to control society as a whole; for instance, through raising the fear of 'others', the Government could make the population more accepting of political changes. This increased fear can be viewed as a 'moral panic' and it can occur around a fear of any particular vilified group (Cohen 1980). For example, according to prevalent mythology across Europe today, Gypsies are thought steal babies,[3] prominent conservative politician Anne Widdecombe, a Member of Parliament, claims they steal pets, and according to the local people in a planning consultation exercise, they are murderers (Richardson 2006b).

Thus, the role of Gypsies and Travellers as folk devils is played out in Government circles at the level of discourse and policy, and is in addition, reinforced by the media. Moreover, the Government plays a part in this by reacting to media campaigns that attract a popular impetus (as seen in the *Daily Express* 'campaign' against East European Roma in January 2004 (Clark and Greenfields 2006). Rather than the Government and the media having a unilateral relationship, it tends to be a cyclical, mutually re-enforceable one. Misuse of numbers and prejudicial reporting in the press increases fear and conflict in communities in relation to all immigrant groups, but particularly for Roma.

Another relevant concept, explored by Bauman (1989), is the notion of 'proximity' in relation to the construction of folk devils. During the Third Reich, the Nazis removed Jews[4] from the proximity of daily neighbourliness, thereby removing them from the social fabric of German society. Similarly, Roma and Sinti were labelled as 'asocials' by the Nazis and this served to de-humanize them further (Friedlander 1997). As Bauman suggests:

> Being inextricably tied to human proximity, morality seems to conform to the law of optical perspective. It looms large and thick close to the eye. With the growth of distance, responsibility for the other shrivels, moral dimensions of the object blur, till both reach the vanishing point and disappear from view. (1989: 192)

This law of proximity applies to Gypsies and Travellers poignantly. They can be 'moved on', according to the Criminal Justice and Public

Order Act (1994). They are not allowed to settle on certain unauthorized sites and yet there are not enough authorized sites to accommodate them. This bureaucratic conundrum is effective in maintaining a social distance between 'us' and 'them', allowing the wider society to believe they are not like 'us', keeping its conscience clear when Gypsies and Travellers are treated badly either by the public, the press or the Government.

As Shuinear (1997) notes:

> Gaujos[5] need Gypsies to personify their own faults and fears, thus lifting away the burden of them. This need is so overpowering that time after time, in place after place, Gaujos create situations forcing Gypsies to fill this role. It is important to remember that what we're talking about here are not 'alien' faults and problems but Gaujos' own; therefore, the people onto whom these are projected must be clearly distinct from the Gaujo mainstream, but not utterly foreign to it: just as in cinema, the screen must be neither too close nor too distant if the image projected onto it is to remain sharply focused. (27)

Such functionalist theories therefore provide a motive for the control of the group through discourse, and begin to answer the question of why there is a perceived need for the control and 'othering' of minority groups. This 'othering' of Gypsies and Travellers can result in a negative cycle of control and conflict which is a mutually reinforcing problem. Richardson's (2007a) research used a case study approach in outlining examples of how this cycle has been broken and how a positive dialogue can be facilitated. If the fear of the 'other Gypsy and Traveller' can be weakened through inter-community dialogue, then there is potential for less discriminatory discourse by local politicians, media and the public. This might mean fewer objections to proposed authorized sites, and Gypsies and Travellers could be properly housed, thus making them less 'othered', and so the positive cycle could continue.

Recent history of government policy and local authority provision in England

During the post-war period, the strains of Gypsies and Travellers' traditional lifestyles became ever greater as urban development and an ever-growing body of regulations deprived many families of traditional stopping places. Under a Conservative Government in 1960, the Caravan Sites (Control of Development) Act prevented new private sites from being built. The shortage of sites created greater tensions between Gypsy and Travellers and the wider community; and by the mid-1960s these tensions were so acute that policy makers began considering new options. This coincided with a growing campaign for Gypsy and Traveller rights, evidenced in the creation of the Gypsy Council in 1966. In 1968, Harold Wilson's Labour Government introduced the 1968 Caravan Sites Act, which was initiated through a private members bill by Liberal Democrat Eric Lubbock (Lord Avebury). It required local authorities to provide sites for Gypsies in England. Although 324 sites were created in all, many suffered from spatial exclusion and poor facilities. Furthermore, many Councils delayed, minimized or completely avoided the provision of sites and thereby undermined the aim of providing more accommodation for Gypsies and Travellers. By 1972, some local authorities were already exempt from building sites for caravans. This was partially down to the lack of desire of locally elected officials to be associated with what was perceived to be an unpopular cause – more provision for Gypsies and Travellers – and partly down to confusion of responsibilities in the local Government reorganization of this period. This Act required that Counties 'ensure adequate accommodation for all those residing in or resorting to their areas' and that District Councils should design, build and manage sites. The culmination of designation, exemption and then confusing local government reorganization in the early 1970s, meant very little progress was made in the delivery of new sites.

In 1977, the Cripps Report assessed the performance of the 1968 Act and it was seen to be wanting in terms of effectiveness in creating new sites. This perceived ineffectiveness of the legislation to provide sites, paved the way for the Conservatives to introduce further legislation to repeal the 1968 Act. In 1994, the Criminal Justice and Public Order Act repealed many of the duties of the Caravan Sites Act (1968), effectively meaning that the construction of local authority sites came to a standstill. Moreover, local authorities ignored the Circular 1/94 guidance that called upon them to assist Gypsies and Travellers to identify land they could buy themselves and develop as sites. As a result, many families felt forced into a position of setting up 'unauthorized' developments on their own land and then applying for retrospective planning permission. The majority of these applications made by Gypsies and Travellers are refused by councils. However, since the introduction of Circular 1/2006, there has been a rise in the number of planning appeals allowed from 34% to 54% (Lishman and Richardson 2007).

New Labour Government legislation and policy

There is a history of Gypsy and Traveller participation and campaigning. One such recent campaign was to reform the legislation and to provide Gypsies and Travellers with a right to their nomadic lifestyle. Those involved in the drafting of the Traveller Law Reform Bill (2002) believed that the New Labour Government would adopt the Bill. Acton described this umbrella group:

> A rather amazing consolidation of the fragmented Roma/Gypsy/ Traveller organisations and progressive pro Gypsy political lobbies…. This gathered together a momentum for change similar to the last time a popular front of the great and good had pressured a new Labour Government into enabling pro Traveller legislation, the 1968 Caravan Sites Act. (Acton 2005: 29)

Unfortunately, these hopes were dashed when the Bill was not given enough parliamentary time, and it fell. However, campaigners who had supported the Bill were joined by other influential bodies like the CRE (now merged into the Equality and Human Rights Commission) and the Local Government Association and also the ODPM Select Committee in its 2004 report on Gypsy and Traveller sites stated that the Government needed to reintroduce a duty to provide sites. However, the Government shied away from such a course of action stating that such a direct duty did not exist for accommodation for the settled community and it would be wrong to create a special advantage for Gypsies and Travellers. Instead, the Government argued that it was better to mainstream Gypsy and Traveller accommodation with those of the wider community and deliver accommodation through the same mechanisms, namely regional spatial strategies. Thus, when it is a matter of actually providing weight behind a duty to provide accommodation, there is an element of the Government hiding behind a rationale of 'mainstreaming.' In other words, when trying to highlight differences and 'otherness', the political and media discourse is very much on 'them' versus 'us' – however when it comes to actually doing something to help, 'they are no different, why should there be special provision?' This contradictory discourse is hard to reconcile, and one should be critically aware of how this functions to further exclusion.

In 2002, the ODPM published a report, *The Provision and Condition of Traveller Sites in England*, and it has been followed up by a number of reports for the Government (Niner 2002). After some considerable delay, the finalized accommodation policies were launched by the DCLG in February 2006; however, some of the guidance, for instance on the GTAAs, were still in draft form. Since then, finalized procedures on GTAAs, as well as local authority duties, and guidance on site design, have been published by the DCLG.

The Housing Act of 2004 placed a statutory duty on local authorities to assess the accommodation needs of Gypsies and Travellers (Gypsy and Traveller Accommodation Assessment). This needs assessment then feeds into regional spatial strategies and Regional Planning Bodies (RPBs), determining how many pitches are needed within each authority in the region. Whilst there is no direct accountability to Gypsy and Traveller representatives on RPBs, the process of an Examination in Public of draft spatial strategies allows for community representation to comment on draft proposals and the validity of the evidence on which they are based. A new planning Circular 1/06 obliges local authorities to identify land in their Development Plans that is appropriate for sites, which in theory, Gypsies and Travellers would be able to purchase and develop on. As well as new local authority sites, some additional public provision could be created as the Government has now enabled registered social landlords to apply to the Housing Corporation for funds to develop sites. Where local authorities fail to identify land, the Secretary of State has powers of intervention, which includes the right to direct local authorities to do so (ODPM 2006b: 8). The Government reprimanded Brentwood Council in 2006 for not including the needs of this group in their local development plans, as required by the Planning and Compulsory Purchase Act (2004). Indeed, the Secretary of State intervened in the High Court and directed the local authority to include sites in the plans. The Government has since directed other local councils to write development plans to include sites, for example, in Epping Forest District Council in September 2007 (see further below). Local authorities consider such direction a very heavy top-down approach to site provision; but, in the face of strong local resistance to provide sites for Gypsies and Travellers, there is little alternative.

Some suggest that not making provision for sites can be as costly as getting on with provision (Morris and Clements 2002) and there has been examination of how policing policy and wider legislation affects Gypsies and Travellers (Morris 2001; O'Nions 1995; Richardson 2005; James and Richardson 2006). This discourse and debate around 'cost' has been examined in relation to policing and 'clearing up' after Gypsy and Traveller encampments and has largely been a negative debate. However, more recently, local authorities are presenting a 'business case' suggesting that site provision would save councils on the cost of unauthorized sites (Richardson 2007a). One oft-cited example is the savings purportedly made by Bristol council who reduced their budget on unauthorized encampments from £200,000 down to £5000. The Briscoe report also suggested, in referring to cost savings for the whole of the country, that '...there is a prospect that most of the £18m spent on enforcement could be saved [if adequate sites are provided]' (DCLG 2007: 5). Whilst the discourse on 'cost' is still negative in many local newspapers, policy makers and some local politicians are using it as a basis from which to argue for more site provision. The Homes and Communities Agency (HCA) was established at the end of 2008 to oversee a number of housing and development functions, including Gypsy and Traveller sites and the administration of the grant (£97 million announced for 2009–2011).

How effective have New Labour's policies been?

Before moving onto analysis of the effectiveness of the Labour Government's policies for Gypsies and Travellers, it is helpful to think about this within a framework. Ringold et al. (2005) posit a typology which suggests a dichotomy between 'coercive' and 'rights-based' policy approaches towards Gypsy integration in Europe. The recent legislative and policy provision under New Labour cannot easily fit into one typology or another. As suggested earlier, the binary nature of the public policy discourse serves to highlight the divisions and differences between 'them' and 'us', but it also allows the Government to hide behind suggestions that 'they' shouldn't be treated any more favourably than the 'settled community'. A positive appraisal of the Government's record so far may suggest that the approach is moving, albeit slowly, from a coercive policy approach to a rights-based approach.

The Government argues that the amalgamation of the pieces of legislation and guidance effectively amount to a statutory duty as local authorities are obliged to carry out the measures and the Secretary of State has powers of intervention if local authorities err from this obligation. These have already been employed in the case of Brentwood Council and South Gloucester. Under section 15 (4) of the Planning and Compulsory Purchase Act, both councils have been required by the Secretary of State to amend their Local Development Framework and include a Gypsy and Traveller Development Plan Document. Brentwood launched a legal challenge to the directive, but this failed and Brentwood agreed to submit a draft development plan referring to Gypsy and Traveller accommodation needs, but at a later date than that initially proposed in the directive. This was an important test for the new policies and powers of intervention. However, as with the 1968 Act, which gave central Government powers of intervention, such intervention is in part dependent on the political will of the Secretary of State (ODPM Select Committee 2004, para 114). Such political will could be easily compromised by fear of public and media opposition. Indeed, it was a failure to intervene by successive secretaries of state that led to the 1968 Caravan Sites Act having little impact in some areas.

However, others believe that this argument ignores the exceptional level of hostility that exists to the creation of Gypsy and Traveller sites from local communities that can deter local authorities. For example, in 2005/6 two local authorities (Crawley and South Norfolk) dropped plans advocating for site provision because of the huge scale of public opposition, which witnessed public meetings attended by up to 1000 local residents, who had been stirred into a state of frenzy about house prices and anti-social behaviour by some community leaders. To combat such opposition, it was argued that a clear and direct duty is needed to give local authorities the resolve to plough ahead with any plans they may have (CRE 2006: 37).

In Epping Forest, where in the past, British National Party councillors have been elected on a pledge to evict Gypsies and Travellers, conflict emerged over the central Government's direction to include site provision in their development plan documents (Kundnani 2004). In the fall of 2008, the local hostility to more authorized sites in Epping Forest generated heated debates by Parliamentarians. The MP for the area, in a parliamentary debate kept referring to a figure of 96 additional pitches (for the year 2011) when in fact, the need for only 49 pitches had been shown (Hansard 2008a). Another consultation document for this area included a contentious piece of land, reported on the front page of the *Daily Express* (17 November 2008: 1, 5) as being 'a family garden' and 'land adjacent to an elderly couple's home'. This inflation of the figures, and the implication of the need to purchase people's gardens in order to build sites, inflamed public hostilities, and is evidence of the irresponsible approach taken by some local politicians and the media (cf. Hansard 2008b).

However, the legal and planning system may also act as a force of compulsion for local authorities to meet their obligations. Where local authorities fail to meet their responsibilities, it will be a material consideration in the planning process. Planning inspectors should give consideration to this fact in deciding whether to grant a planning application by Gypsies and Travellers. Alternatively, those local authorities that do fulfil Government requirements will find it easier to challenge any unauthorized encampments or developments and invoke enforcement powers (ODPM 2006a: 16).

A challenge for the Government's proposals is a dependency on accurate data gathering to help set targets. The main mechanism for gathering data is the Gypsy and Traveller Accommodation Assessment (GTAA). The Government did issue draft guidance on this, but it was published after some local authorities had already started the research process. The final guidance, issued some time later, also changed the parameters; for example it included the assessment of needs for Showmen – those councils who had already undertaken the assessment before publication of the final guidance had not necessarily included Showmen. Some campaigners expressed fears at the time that some authorities would deliberately minimize the numbers assessed in the survey so as to reduce the number of pitches they would need to find. Generally, there were concerns that either through design, or neglect, there would be an under-assessment of accommodation need. Flaws in methodological process (for example, insufficient consultation with Gypsies and Travellers themselves in some cases) were highlighted as a caution that the final data collected may be inaccurate. However, the DCLG (2007) guidance for regional planning bodies was written to help assess the validity of GTAAs against a range of methodological factors. Nevertheless, even at the stage of discussing incorporation of pitch requirements in the regional plan, there was challenging dialogue between local authorities who did not like the numbers found in their GTAAs.

Discourse centred upon 'need where it arises' *versus* 'need where it should be met' – in other words – those councils who had a large amount of need identified felt that it was not 'fair' that they had to provide for so many, compared with say a neighbouring authority with a smaller requirement. Questions were asked about 'sharing' the burden of accommodation provision. Imagine this debate, in a public examination of a draft regional plan, about any other Black and Minority Ethnic group – certainly, racism is alive and well in the accommodation debate on Gypsies and Travellers. Although there were well-reasoned fears that local authorities would prevaricate over both the completion of GTAAs and the implementation of Circular 1/2006, there has been slow progress made. Despite criticism of some of the GTAA data collection and analysis process, more is now known about the accommodation needs of Gypsies and Travellers, and this data is being incorporated into planning strategies. More planning appeals have been accepted since the Circular, and the length of time given for temporary permissions has been extended. However, there is still little increase in the number of sites actually being built now, and there may be some time to wait before more accommodation is provided, due to prevarication on behalf of some local authorities, and due to objection to new site proposals from councillors, the media and the wider community.

Public hostility may also lead to local authorities identifying land for sites in marginal space where public opposition will be kept to a minimum. One of the sites that Crawley Council identified for a transit site (temporary stay) was next to an airport runway, even though plans to build a warden's house on the site had to be abandoned because of noise pollution.[6] As the CRE has noted such spatial exclusion can lead to '...isolation and inequality in access to services, and perpetuates the sense of Gypsies and Irish Travellers as 'others' (2006: 218).

A further problem in actually delivering sites, particularly through approving planning permission for privately owned sites, may be affordability. Once local authorities identify land for sites in development plan documents, the price may well increase. Thus Gypsies and Travellers may have to pay more than they previously did, for example in cases where they could buy a relatively cheap piece of agricultural land and submit a retrospective planning application. For some families, securing mortgages is problematic. Having, in some cases, no fixed abode or varied patterns of employment will mean mortgage lenders may not look favourably on such potential mortgage seekers. Following the credit crunch and the recession in 2008 in England, this issue of affordability of private provision has been compounded.

There is still a considerable need for public provision especially in urban areas where land prices are prohibitive to private ownership (Avebury 2005). However, there are also the problems of existing local authority sites, which suffer from poor locations, substandard facilities and limited tenancy rights and sense of ownership; all of which impact on perceptions of social inclusion for tenants on such sites, highlighting the structural roots of their social exclusion. Local authorities have been slow to apply for the Government grant scheme for site refurbishment. The LGA has noted the limitations created by the size of the Gypsy refurbishment grant and called for additional revenue funding (LGA 2006: 12). At the end of 2007, the Government announced a grant of £97 million for new site provision and for refurbishment of existing sites in 2008/11; this was in addition to a previous pot of £56m for refurbishment of sites in 2006/8. However, there is some doubt whether funding is sufficient for the huge cost of relocating sites in inner city areas, away from marginalized locations. Thus, for the foreseeable future many Gypsies and Travellers will continue to live under motorway flyovers, next to rubbish dumps and other marginal spaces. There has been little promotion of initiatives to involve tenants more in the management of council sites through the establishment of site forums. Furthermore, the provision of rental sites is being impeded by registered social landlords (RSLs) who appear reluctant to take up the funding to develop and manage sites. However, the Housing Corporation has sought to tackle this reluctance by producing a 'financial toolkit' (Niner and Walker 2008) to demonstrate the 'business case' (Richardson 2007b) for RSLs to build more sites.

Others who continue to suffer include those families who are highly mobile. Although the Government has stipulated that transit provision needs to be considered by local authorities in their accommodation assessments and development plans, public opposition minimizes such provision. Public opposition to new provision of accommodation for Gypsies and Travellers has often been at its most intense over transit sites, which arouse hostility and fear of 'others' from the wider community. Though few have been constructed, an estimated 2,000 to 2,500 transit pitches were estimated to be needed (Niner 2003). Where the Government has developed a specific measure to increase the supply of transit sites, it is linked to enforcement. The Anti Social Behaviour Act (2003) created a provision for increased eviction powers to be utilized where Gypsies and Travellers can be directed to a vacant pitch. The Government had hoped this would motivate local authorities to create transit sites. However, local authorities have been hampered in pursuing these substantial enforcement powers by opposition from local residents, and others, to their transit site plans (see further Richardson 2007a).

Clearly, in spite of the robust nature of some of the Government's accommodation policies and incentives, a common stumbling block for the realization of policies is public hostility. Such hostility can also manifest itself in officer and elected members demonstrating indifference or opposition. The CRE (now merged into EHRC) scrutiny report found evidence of this in some of the frank comments council officials and members made. This report also demonstrated a *reluctance to apply the race equality duty in the amended Race Relations Act to Gypsies and Travellers*, a measure designed to tackle unlawful discrimination and provide equality of treatment (CRE 2006: 68). The commitment and determination of most Traveller Education Services to drive through policies that benefit Gypsies and Travellers is far from evident in other branches of local Government. An Office for Standards in Education (Ofsted) report noted:

> Different agencies acted in a way that was at odds with their own recently published council policies on inclusion and race equality…. A wide gulf still exists between policy and practice in ensuring race equality for all groups, as set out in legislation. (Ofsted 2003: 9)

Government intervention is one factor driving through these policies, but as already indicated, that is in part dependent on the will of secretaries of state to intervene. There are fears that the new Equalities and Human Rights Commission (EHRC), that has replaced the CRE, will be even less effective than its predecessor because of its broader and less focused race role. Furthermore, there is a danger that its powers and equalities duties will be diluted in the forthcoming Single Equalities Act (Ryder and Solly 2007). Raising public awareness and support for new policies could be another means of overcoming the identified hurdles. Part of the Race Equality Duty necessitates local authorities to promote good race relations, thus councils could direct significant resources to the process of public education. However, the biggest determiner of public goodwill (or lack thereof) could well continue to be the press, largely local newspapers and the tabloids. From 2004, the press appeared to launch a sustained media campaign on Gypsies and Travellers, which some felt was both sensationalist and insightful of racism; this reached its zenith with the Sun's notorious 'Stamp on the Camps' articles. For example, on Wednesday 9 March 2005 the Sun's front page headline read 'Sun War on Gipsy [*sic*] Free for All... Meet Your Neighbours Thanks To Prescott'; below this was a picture of a particularly untidy unauthorized encampment. In the wake of this reporting, the EU Commissioner for Human Rights commented on the treatment of Gypsies and Travellers in the UK that:

> to judge by the levels of invective that can regularly be read in the national press, Gypsies would appear to be the last ethnic minority in respect of which openly racist views can still be acceptably expressed. I was truly amazed by some of the headlines, articles and editorials that were shown to me... it is clear that much more serious efforts are required to accommodate their needs and promote greater tolerance towards them than are currently in evidence. (Gil-Robles 2005: 43)

Despite pleas to the Press Complaints Commission, none of the complaints were upheld, as under its code of practice, action can only be taken if named individuals are defamed. The CRE (2006) produced media guidance on reporting Gypsy and Traveller issues, but this has had little noticeable impact over the last decade. Thus, community relations and the treatment of Gypsies and Travellers will continue to be influenced by the press, a matter of concern given that a survey by Stonewall[7] found a direct link between the media and public hostility towards Gypsies and Travellers (Valentine and McDonald 2004). The situation has not improved. On 17 November 2008, the *Daily Express* led with the headline 'Families Must Sell Land for Gypsy Campsites', about the Epping Forest council consultation on provisional sites. The newspaper further quoted the local MP as saying:

> What is the point of all our work to protect people's freedom and to make them feel secure in their own homes when a Labour Government can revert to the worst excesses of Communist dictatorships and compulsorily purchase bits of land next to people's homes? (2008: 1, 5)

Political sentiments such as the above from MPs can only serve to inflame the local debate, and the reporting of the issue by British dailies incites extremely negative feelings towards Gypsies and Travellers.

Nevertheless, there has been an increase in the numbers of caravans on authorized sites since 1997 (see Figure 12.1 below). This may indicate increased provision, but the fact that the count of caravans on unauthorized sites – both private and public – has not decreased, suggests that there is not, as yet, a sufficient net increase in the number pitches available to meet accommodation need. Information on the number of pitches available on council sites is not available as far back as 1997, but there is information on the number of caravans counted on authorized council sites and authorized private sites. For example, in July 1997, there were 5,946 caravans on council sites and 3,776 on private sites – a total of 9,722 caravans. In July, 2007 there were a total of 13,157 caravans on council and private sites, and in January 2008 there were 14,047. Between July 1997 and July 2007, there was a 35% increase in the number of caravans counted on authorized sites – both public and private. This suggests that whilst there are more caravans on authorized sites since 1997, the supply of accommodation is not keeping up with the growth in demand, and thus overcrowding may emerge on sites, hiding the accommodation deficit.

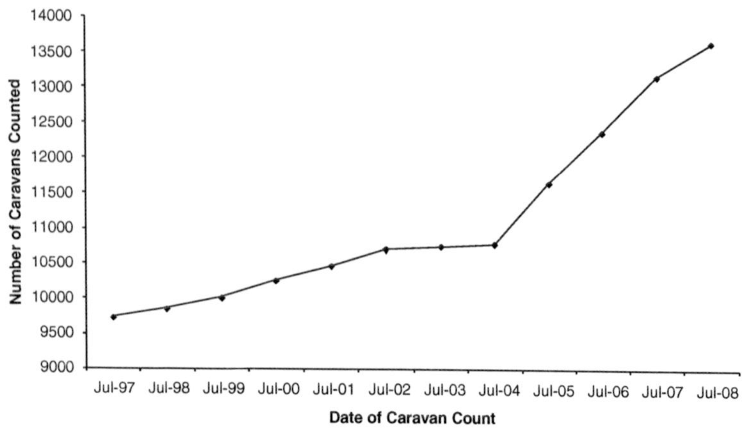

Figure 12.1   Caravans counted on authorized sites – both council and private

Source: Gypsy and Traveller Bi-annual Caravan Counts 1997–2008, DCLG.

'Social inclusion' under New Labour

Though the Labour Government committed itself to tackling the problem of social exclusion[8] in its response to the ODPM Select Committee's Report on Gypsy and Traveller Sites (2005: 1), some claim that the Government has been extremely cautious and slow, as demonstrated by the fact that it did not develop policy responses on this issue until its third term. Labour's package of initiatives regarding Gypsies and Travellers has been enveloped under a 'rights and responsibilities' agenda. Whilst simultaneously introducing policies to address the exclusion suffered by Gypsies and Travellers Labour has also cast attention to the concerns of 'Middle England' preoccupied with notions of Gypsy and Traveller lawlessness and anti-social behaviour. To this end Labour has introduced enforcement initiatives, for example under the Anti-Social Behaviour Act (2003).

At times it would appear that overdue attention has been given to enforcement issues, which in practice has meant enforcement *against* Gypsies and Travellers as opposed to the enforcement of their rights. It is telling that the first major legislative policy intervention on Gypsies and Travellers came in the form of clauses in the Anti-Social Behaviour Act of 2003. This piece of legislation created a provision where increased eviction powers could be utilized where Gypsies and Travellers can be directed to a vacant pitch. One fear though is that these powers could further marginalize Gypsies and Travellers, as, if they refuse to go to the directed pitches, they must leave the confines of a local authority and not return for a three month period; breach of this ruling can lead to large fines and penalties. Thus, a situation could arise where Gypsies and Travellers are loath to follow a direction to occupy a pitch on a substandard and dangerous site and are compelled to leave the authority, only for the same process to be repeated in the neighbouring authority. Hence, Gypsies and Travellers could be subjected to a constant cycle of eviction and any chances of integrating within the wider community and having proper access to services, whilst retaining cultural norms such as living on the road or on sites, could be severely curtailed. This may also create greater pressure on families to abandon more mobile ways of life, and become more sedentary – in other words they are coerced to assimilate to the 'norm' of living in bricks and mortar accommodation, through an enforcement clamp-down on living on the roadside. Other provisions within the Anti-Social Behaviour Act have included the use of Anti-Social Behaviour Orders to prevent Gypsies and Travellers from camping on highway and private land without permission (ODPM 2006b: 23). The Government's preoccupation with enforcement stems from an attempt to address the concerns of a wider society increasingly agitated by sensationalist media reporting.

There is a real danger that local authorities, driven by popular prejudice, are more enthusiastic in taking up enforcement powers than in adopting policies that would tackle the roots of exclusion such as creating extra site provision. The CRE scrutiny report from 2006 hinted at such a development (2006: 51). Likewise, in spite of measures to increase their inclusion, Gypsy and Traveller citizens may also find themselves being targeted with Anti-Social Behaviour Orders, prosecution for non-attendance at school or Parenting Orders, thereby ignoring the fundamental causes of such alienation within the community, which warrant more long-term approaches. Thus greater enforcement, especially if not matched with greater site provision could in tandem with other elements of the 'Respect Agenda' serve to do no more than raise the levels of exclusion for Gypsies and Travellers and bring them into greater conflict with authority and the wider community.

Conclusion

Since 1997, the New Labour Government has introduced a number of pieces of legislation and guidance reflecting the wider 'Rights and Responsibilities' agenda which is pertinent not just to Gypsy and Traveller citizens, but is at the heart of New Labour policy. On the one hand, it entails a requirement to assess needs and include sites in plans; on the other, it increases enforcement powers. The planning process will take a long time to generate more provision, the GTAAs are nearly complete, and some regions have now completed their regional spatial strategy. Ministers, such as Iain Wright of the DCLG, publicly reiterate that there is no need for councils to wait until the end of the planning policy process before they start building the number of pitches needed in their areas, and indeed some Councils are getting on with the provision of new sites. Public opposition – often based on biased media reporting and commonly held myth – does not help to expedite this process. What is more, until the politics can be taken out of the debate on new sites, there will be some politicians who will make capital from the situation, particularly around election time. Direction is needed from the centre, from key Governmental figures, in order to drive the provision of new sites. This was the message of the Briscoe Task Group report (DCLG December 2007), which involved a broad range of stakeholders traditionally not always sympathetic to Gypsies and Travellers, such as the National Farmers Union and Local Government Association. It was also a key finding of the Joseph Rowntree Foundation research (Richardson 2007b).

Although this looks like an improvement on the face of it, the number of caravans counted does not always equate to the number of pitches required. Indeed, sites may be overcrowded because of the lack of appropriate pitches. More research needs to be done by interrogating data on private planning applications, and by aggregating the figures coming out of the GTAAs and the regional spatial strategies, before an assessment can be made on how successful the Labour Government has been in filling the shortfall in accommodation needed for Gypsies and Travellers.

There has been progress, albeit slow, in addressing a variety of issues affecting the health, education and accommodation needs of Gypsies and Travellers in England. The Labour Government has enacted the requirement to assess needs and incorporate findings in local plans – even if it has held back on requiring councils to actually build sites now. For a range of reasons, some local authorities, local politicians and local communities have attempted to stall assessment of need, to endlessly debate the findings, and to then object to any new site proposals put forward. Nevertheless, in some areas, local authorities are quietly getting on with the business of refurbishing existing sites, and successfully getting planning permission for new sites, where a need arises. Although still small, these victories for accommodation provision would be seriously undermined without the commitment of the Government. Gypsy and Traveller activists across England are increasingly having their voices heard in the debate on future site provision, and their messages are being repeated by Ministers like Iain Wright, who seem committed to fulfilling their accommodation needs (Percival 2008).

Such direction and commitment to develop new sites could be at risk if there is a change of Government after the next election, and the Conservatives deliver on a promise indicated by one MP to the Chief Executive of his council.[9] In the letter, the Tory MP states that he had discussions with the Conservative spokesman for Local Government, who assured him that an incoming Conservative Government would seek to remove the necessity to provide sites. Ominously, the MP proceeds to note that it was the last Conservative Government which in 1994 repealed the duties in the 1968 Gypsy Caravans Act. Social inclusion and accommodation entitlements for Gypsies and Travellers may therefore come full circle and there could be little prospect of the acute accommodation shortage and exclusion being alleviated. If a change of UK Government at the next election reverses the commitment to assess accommodation need and to include new sites in regional plans, then this may well strengthen the process of 'othering' of Gypsies and Travellers in the UK, and set a further dangerous precedent in Europe.

The Labour Government has made a commitment to delivering more sites for Gypsies and Travellers, and along with that a hope for better access to education and health, and more social inclusion. There has not been a legal duty implemented for local authorities to build sites now, but there has been a raft of legal measures which should lead towards more site provision. The Government has taken steps to improve accommodation and conditions for Gypsies and

Travellers, and it is now for local authorities, local politicians, policy makers and other agencies to work in local areas and to provide support to those who are trying to drive through the new site provision that is so desperately needed. The Government may not have gone as far as many campaigners would have liked with the legislation – but there is still much to work with, and it is the policy-implementation gap at the local level that now needs to be addressed seriously.

Notes

1. See further Okely (1983), Kenrick and Clark (1999), and Clark and Greenfields (2006) for a discussion of definitions.
2. See Acton (1974, 1994 and 2000), Acton and Mundy (1997), Hancock (2002), Kenrick and Clark (1999), Hawes and Perez (1996), Mayall (1995), Tong (1998) and Clark and Greenfields (2006).
3. The unrest in Italy in 2008 was the result of the moral panic whipped up by the Italian media when a young Romani girl allegedly kidnapped a baby (see Sigona in this collection and COSPE 2008).
4. Note that Roma and Sinti were relegated to settling in outlying areas of German society long before the Nazis came to power.
5. Gaujo (sometimes gorgio and various other spellings) in England refers to non-Gypsy people, invariably so-called members of the settled population.
6. As a result of immense public hostility, this proposal was not passed by the council.
7. A non-governmental organization which campaigns for equal rights in the UK.
8. Madanipour et al. (1998: 22) define social exclusion as 'a multi-dimensional process in which various forms of exclusion are combined: participation in decision making and political processes, access to employment and material resources, and integration into common cultural processes. When combined they create acute forms of exclusion that find a spatial manifestation in particular neighbourhoods'.
9. Revealed in a letter seen by the authors.

References

Acton, T. (1974) *Gypsy Politics and Social Change*, London: Routledge.
Acton, T. (1994) 'Modernisation, moral panics and the Gypsies', *Sociology Review*, 4(1): 24–28.
Acton, T. (2000) (ed.) *Scholarship and the Gypsy Struggle: Commitment in Romani Studies*, Hatfield: University of Hertfordshire Press.
Acton, T. (2005) 'Conflict resolution and criminal justice – sorting out trouble. Can legislation resolve perennial conflicts between Roma/Gypsies/Travellers and "National Majorities"?', *Journal of Legal Pluralism*, 51: 29–49.

Acton, T. and Mundy, G. (eds) (1997) *Romani Culture and Gypsy Identity*, Hatfield: University of Hertfordshire Press.

Avebury, E. (2005) *Hansard*, Lords Debate Column 299, 23 March 2005.

Bauman, Z. (1989) *Modernity and the Holocaust*, Cambridge: Polity Press.

Brown, M. (2008) 'Families must sell land for Gypsy campsites' *The Daily Express*, 17 November: 1, 5.

Cemlyn, S., Greenfields, M., Matthews, Z., Burnett, S. and Whitwell, C. (2009) *Gypsies and Travellers: Simple Solutions for Living Together*, London: Equality and Human Rights Commission.

Clark, C. and Greenfields, M. (2006) *Here to Stay. The Gypsies and Travellers of Britain*, Hatfield: University of Hertfordshire Press.

Cohen, S. (1980) *Folk Devils and Moral Panics: the Creation of the Mods and Rockers*, Oxford: Martin Robertson.

Commission for Racial Equality (2006) *Common Ground: Equality, Good Race Relations and Sites for Gypsies and Irish Travellers*, London: CRE.

COSPE (2008) *Incident Report – Violent Attacks Against Roma in the Ponticelli District of Naples (Italy)*, Brussels: FRA.

Crawley, H. (2004) *Moving Forward, the Provision of Accommodation for Travellers and Gypsies*, London: IPPR.

Cripps, J. (1977) *Accommodation for Gypsies, A Report on the Working of the Caravan Sites Act 1968*, Department of Environment Welsh Office.

Department for Communities and Local Government (2006a) *Draft Guidance for Gypsy and Traveller Accommodation Assessments*, London: DCLG.

Department for Communities and Local Government (2006b) *Guide to Responsibilities and Powers*, London: DCLG.

Department for Communities and Local Government (2007) *The Road Ahead: Final Report of the Independent Task Group on Site Provision and Enforcement for Gypsies and Travellers*, London: CLG.

Foucault, M. (1969) *The Birth of the Clinic: An Archaeology of Medical Perception*, translated by A.M. Sheridan, London: Tavistock Publications.

Friedlander, H. (1997) *The Origins of Nazi Genocide: From Euthanasia to the Final Solution*, Chapel Hill: UNC Press.

Gil-Robles, A. (2005) *Report by Mr Alvaro Gil-Robles, Commissioner for Human Rights, on His Visit to the United Kingdom, 4–12 November 2004*, Strasbourg: Council of Europe.

Hancock, I.F. (1987) *The Pariah Syndrome: An Account of Gypsy Slavery and Persecution*, Ann Arbor: Karoma Publishers.

Hancock, I.F. (2002) *We are the Romani People*, Hatfield: University of Hertfordshire Press.

Hansard (2008a) 22 October 2008, House of Commons Debate Column 126WH.

Hansard (2008b) 18 November 2008, House of Commons Debate Column 117.

Hawes, D. and Perez, B. (1996) *The Gypsy and the State*, 2nd ed., Bristol: Policy Press.

James, Z. and Richardson, J. (2006) 'Controlling accommodation: policing Gypsies and Travellers' in Dearling, A., Newburn, T. and Somerville, P. (eds)

Supporting Safer Communities: Housing, Crime and Neighbourhoods, Coventry: CIH and HSA.

Kenrick, D. and Clark, C. (1999) *Moving On: The Gypsies and Travellers of Britain*, Hatfield: University of Hertfordshire Press.

Kundnani, A. (2004) 'Pressure grows on site after BNP elected', IRR, 24 June, http://www.irr.org.uk/2004/june/ak000012.html.

Lishman, R. and Richardson, J. (2007) *Impact of Circular 1/06: Supply of New Gypsy/Traveller Sites*, Leicester: De Montfort University.

Local Government Association (2006) *Report of the LGA Gypsy and Traveller Task Group*, London: LGA.

Madanipour, A., Cars, G. and Allen, J. (eds) (1998) *Social Exclusion in European Cities: Processes, Experiences, and Responses*, London: Routledge.

Mayall, D. (1995) *English Gypsies and State Policies*, Hatfield: University of Hertfordshire Press.

Morris, R. (2001) 'Gypsies and Travellers: new policies, new approaches', *Police Research and Management*, 5(1): 41–49.

Morris, R. and Clements, L. (2002) *At What Cost? The Economics of Gypsy and Traveller Encampments*, Bristol: Policy Press.

Niner, P. (2002) *The Provision and Condition of Local Authority Gypsy/Traveller Sites in England*, London: ODPM.

Niner, P. (2003) *Local Authority Gypsy/Traveller Sites in England*, London: ODPM.

Niner, P. and Walker, B. (2008) Gypsies and Travellers financial toolkit for RSLs, London: Housing Corporation.

O'Nions, H. (1995) *The Marginalisation of Gypsies*, Leicester: University of Leicester, http://webjcli.ncl.ac.uk/articles3/onions3.html.

ODPM (2004) *Planning for Gypsy and Traveller Sites, Consultation Paper*, London: ODPM.

ODPM (2005) *Government Response to the Select Committee's Report on Gypsy and Traveller Sites*, London: ODPM.

ODPM (2006a) *Circular 01/06 (ODPM): Planning for Gypsy and Traveller Caravan Sites*, London: ODPM.

ODPM (2006b) *Guide to Responsibilities and Powers*, London: ODPM.

Ofsted (2003) *Provision and Support for Traveller Pupils*, London: Ofsted.

Okely, J. (1983) The *Traveller-Gypsies*, Cambridge: Cambridge University Press.

Parry, G., Van Cleemput, P., Peters, J., Moore, J., Walters, S., Thomas, K. and Cooper, C. (2004) *The Health Status of Gypsies & Travellers in England*, Sheffield: University of Sheffield.

Percival, J. (2008) 'Government unveils 40 new Gypsy sites across England', *The Guardian*, 18 December 2008.

Richardson, J. (2005) 'Policing Gypsies and Travellers', Plenary Paper to the *Housing Studies Association Conference*, www.york.ac.uk/inst/chp/hsa/autumn05/papers/Richardson.doc.

Richardson, J. (2006a) *The Gypsy Debate: Can Discourse Control?*, Exeter: Imprint Academic.

Richardson, J. (2006b) 'Talking about Gypsies: the use of discourse as control', *Housing Studies*, 21(1): 77–97.

Richardson, J. (2007a) 'Policing Gypsies and Travellers' in Haye, M.and Acton, T. (eds) *Travellers, Gypsies, Roma: The Demonisation of Difference*, Cambridge: Cambridge Scholars Press.

Richardson, J. (2007b) *Providing Gypsy and Traveller Sites: Contentious Spaces*, Coventry: CIH/JRF.

Ringold, D., Orenstein, M.A. and Wilkens, E. (2005) *Roma in an Expanding Europe: Breaking the Poverty Cycle*, Washington: The World Bank.

Ryder, A. and Solly, R. (2007) 'Gypsies and Travellers and the equalities debate', *Institute for Race Relations*, http://www.irr.org.uk/2007/august/ ha000010.html.

Shelter (2008) *Good Practice Guide: Working with Housed Gypsies and Travellers*, London: Shelter.

Shuinear, S (1997) Why do Gaujos hate Gypsies so much, anyway? In Acton, T. (Ed.) (1997) Gypsy politics and Traveller identity, Hertfordshire: University of Hertfordshire Press.

Tong, D. (1998) (ed.) *Gypsies: An Interdisciplinary Reader*, Hatfield: University of Hertfordshire Press.

UK Home Office (2005) *Improving Opportunity, Strengthening Society*, London: Home Office. Available at http://www.homeoffice.gov.uk/documents/ race_improving_opport.pdf

Valentine, G. and McDonald, I. (2004) *Understanding Prejudice, Attitudes towards Minorities*, London: Stonewall.

13
The 'Problema Nomadi' vis-à-vis the Political Participation of Roma and Sinti at the Local Level in Italy

Nando Sigona

Introduction[1]

The geographical marginalization and social exclusion of Roma and Sinti in Italy is not a recent phenomenon. A number of academic and policy reports over the last decade have stressed the gravity of the situation for Roma and Sinti. According to the European Commission against Racism and Intolerance (ECRI 2002, 2006) the spatial segregation of a large section of this population in so-called 'nomad camps' (*campi nomadi* in Italian) 'appears to reflect a general approach of the Italian authorities which tend to consider Roma as nomads and wanting to live in camps' (ECRI 2002). Similarly, in 1999 the UN Committee on the Elimination of Racial Discrimination (CERD 1999; see also ERRC 2000) declared that 'in addition to a frequent lack of basic facilities, the housing of Roma in such camps leads not only to a physical segregation of the Roma community from Italian society, but a political, economic and cultural isolation as well'.

International public attention on the situation of Roma and Sinti in Italy has increased significantly since November 2007 when the violent murder of an Italian woman by a Romanian Romani immigrant stirred anti-Romani feelings in the country – 'a continuing anti-foreigner outcry unmatched in Italy's recent history' according to Hopper (*The Guardian*, 2 November 2007) – and produced a number of violent attacks on Romani individuals and in nomad camps all over Italy. The government, led by Romano Prodi, responded to the incident and to the public outcry by issuing, as a matter of 'necessity and urgency', a decree (n.181/2007) aimed at facilitating the removal of EU citizens from Italy whenever they were deemed to represent a threat to public and national security. European institutions and NGOs expressed their concern at the risk that the decree would target one ethnic group exclusively – namely Roma from Romania – and would end up legitimizing public anxiety and fear towards migrants coming from new EU Member States (Sigona 2008; Colacicchi 2008; Mai 2009).

A few months later, in the 2008 electoral campaign which led to the victory of the centre-right coalition, the *'problema nomadi'* was high on the political agenda and the main contenders from both sides tried to assert their 'security' credentials by using zero tolerance rhetoric against 'nomads' and 'nomad camps'. For the first time, the electoral manifesto of a mainstream political party, *Partito del Popolo delle Libertà*, refers explicitly to 'combating the illegal nomad settlements and evicting everyone without adequate legal means of support and the right to stay in the country' (see Simoni 2008). Once elected, the new government, acting upon its electoral promise, issued a stream of highly symbolic policy initiatives to address what was powerfully labelled an 'emergency'. Less than a month after the election, the government issued decree n.122/2008 in which it declares the 'state of emergency in relation to the settlements of nomad communities in Campania, Lombardy and Lazio regions' and successively appointed three special commissioners in charge of implementing all the initiatives needed to overcome the 'emergency', starting with 'monitoring authorised camps where nomad communities are settled and identifying illegal settlements' and 'identification and census of people, including minors, and families residing in camps'. These measures raised great concern among European and international human rights monitoring bodies, and a number of delegations and missions such as the European Parliament,[2] the Organization for Security and Cooperation in Europe (OSCE),[3] and the Council of Europe were sent to Italy to assess the situation. International pressure forced the Italian government to make some concessions with regard to its heavy-handed initiatives, yet these alterations appeared to be of a decidedly opportunistic nature and limited in their actual impact (Sigona 2009). On a follow-up mission to Italy in January 2009, Thomas Hammarberg, the Council of Europe's Human Rights Commissioner, declared that 'The situation is unacceptable. Nothing has changed since my last report in July. In fact, living conditions are even worse. So much talk and media attention but nothing happens. This is a display of inept policy' (quoted in *Financial Times*, 27 January 2009).

While, as mentioned earlier, in national politics the 'Gypsy problem' has become a significant issue only in recent months, this chapter demonstrates that, on the contrary, at the local level, 'nomads' and 'nomad camps' have played an important role in electoral contests in the last few years. Moreover, it will explore the nexus, if any, between the high visibility of the 'Gypsy problem' and the invisibility of Roma and Sinti as political subjects.

Based on field research conducted between 2005 and 2006 in four cities (Milan, Bolzano-Bozen, Mantua and Rome), this chapter discusses experiences, possibilities and obstacles to the political participation of Roma and Sinti in Italy at the local level.[4] The analysis of the case studies will be developed along three directions: the role of the 'Gypsy issue' in the political manifestos and electoral campaigns of the main political parties and coalitions; the media coverage of Roma and Sinti issues during the electoral campaign for local elections; and Roma and Sinti views on, and experiences of, political participation within local polities.

In order to investigate these dimensions, a range of qualitative research methods were employed: semi-structured interviews with key informants (local journalists, activists and candidates from Roma and Sinti communities, NGO representatives and local politicians); a systematic review of local press using as key words 'Roma', 'Sinti', 'zingari' and 'nomadi' conducted on two newspapers for each city in the month proceeding the election; and finally a comparative analysis of the contents of electoral manifestos and other electoral material concerning Roma and Sinti.

The selection of the four locations is the result of the combination of a number of criteria: demography of the Roma and Sinti population and diversity of their legal status, variety of political orientations of local authorities, and inclusion of cities where there has been some forms of political participation of the Roma and Sinti.

Even if the main focus of the field research was political participation in local elections, this chapter examines not only Italian Roma and Sinti, and EU Roma citizens, but also non-EU Roma, although the latter have no right to vote in Italy. The rationale for this is twofold: firstly, as it was immediately clear from reading local press and electoral material, most of the time, newspapers and political parties do not distinguish between Italian and non-Italian Roma and Sinti, tending to refer to all Roma and Sinti generically as 'nomads' or 'gypsies' (*zingari* in Italian), implicitly foreigners;[5] secondly, given the demography and distribution of the population, it is important to look at participation more broadly including also other forms of political and associational mobilization which may involve foreign Roma.[6]

Context

This section provides some baseline information regarding the Roma and Sinti minorities in Italy, in particular in the research locations, and on the local political environments in Bolzano-Bozen, Milan, Mantua and Rome.

Roma and Sinti in Italy and in the localities

In the absence of official statistics on the Roma and Sinti population in Italy, we have to rely on the estimated figures of approximately 130,000–160,000 Roma and Sinti currently living in Italy (Scalia 2006; Sigona 2009), roughly half of whom are Italian citizens. Foreign Roma came to Italy in various migration flows. The most substantial of these date from the 1990s with the dissolution of Yugoslavia, and, more recently, with the arrival of Romanian Roma in correspondence to the easing of visa policy which anticipated the enlargement of the EU (Brunello 1996; ERRC 2000; Piasere 2005; Sigona 2002, 2005). It is difficult to estimate the number of Roma and Sinti living in camps. A study carried out in 2001 (Monasta 2004), shows that there were more that 18,000 foreign Roma living in authorized and unauthorized camps. In 2008, the controversial census carried out by the Ministry of Internal Affairs in Naples, Rome and Milan (Ministero degli Interni 2008) counted 167 encampments, out of which 124 were unauthorized; comprising a population of 12,346, of whom 5436 were minors (under 18).[7]

Rome and Milan have the largest Romani population in Italy. However, while in Milan there is a sizeable presence of Italian Roma and Sinti, in Rome the foreign Roma population is far larger than the indigenous one (Ambrosini and Tosi 2007). In Bolzano and Mantua the Roma and Sinti population is smaller. In Bolzano there are both Italian Sinti and Roma migrants, while in Mantua there are mainly Italian Sinti.

Local political context

Bolzano-Bozen is the main city of the Autonomous Province of Bolzano-Bozen and it is part of the Trentino-Alto Adige region. It has a population of 98,657 inhabitants. The province is officially bilingual, with Italian and German as the official languages. The elections for the Mayor and City Council of Bolzano were held in 2005 – initially on 8 May and again on 6 November. This happened because the centre-right candidate, who prevailed by only seven votes in May, was unable to gain a majority in the City Council and form a government. In November, the centre-left candidate with the support of the main party of the German-speaking population won the election with a large majority. *Rifondazione Comunista* (RC), one of the parties supporting the candidate, presented in its party list for the City Council a member of the local Sinti minority, Radames Gabrielli. The right wing party Unitalia which campaigned openly against Roma and Sinti obtained 3.21% of the votes, resulting in the election of two councillors.

Mantua is a small city in Lombardy with a population of 47,826. The local elections were held on 3–4 April 2005. The candidate of the centre-left coalition was elected with 54% of the votes. *Rifondazione Comunista*, with 8.05% of the votes, managed to get three councillors elected. Yuri Del Bar, member of the Sinti community, was one of them.

Milan is administratively divided into nine boroughs (*zone di decentralizzazione*), each of which elects its local council composed of 41 councillors. At present, the population of Milan is 1,304,263. The local elections were held on 29–29 May 2006. The centre-right candidate, Letizia Moratti, won with 52% of the votes. One of the lists supporting the centre-left candidante, Bruno Ferrante, was led by the Nobel Laureate Dario Fo (*Uniti con Dario Fo per Milano*) and included a Roma candidate, Dijana Pavlovic.

Rome is administratively divided into 20 boroughs (municipi) totalling 2,669,873 inhabitants in 2005. The local elections for the Mayor, the city, and borough councils were held in Rome on the 28–29 May 2006. At the election, there were 12 candidates for the mayoral post and 36 party lists. The two main candidates were Walter Veltroni, incumbent mayor supported by a coalition of centre-left parties, and Gianni Alemanno, prominent member of the right wing party National Alliance and former Minister for Agriculture. Veltroni won the election with 921,491 votes (61.4%). No Roma or Sinti candidate stood for election.

Political parties and electoral platforms on Roma and Sinti

This section briefly examines electoral manifestos and statements of the main political contenders in each location. The research has revealed how the mainstream political discourse tends to exclude actual Roma and Sinti, whose voices are absent from the public debate, and to present them only as 'Gypsies' or 'nomads' who pose a threat to public security, urban decorum and the welfare system. Inevitably, this leads to policy proposals which, rather than being longer term responses to the variety of circumstances and needs of these communities, focuses almost exclusively on control, security and cases of extreme social marginalization but only in terms of 'humanitarian emergency'. For a Milan-based activist, 'In the centre-left coalition there is a tendency to focus exclusively on the latest emergency instead of taking into account the needs, and experiences of settlement, of longer established communities'.[8]

Framing the presence of Roma and Sinti only in terms of 'problem' and 'humanitarian emergency' induces the denial of their political subjectivities by presenting them as either criminals or passive recipients of social assistance; in both cases intrinsically foreigners. This process is exemplified by, and reproduced through the widespread use of the generic label 'nomads' in the political and media discourses (see Sigona 2003, 2005; Piasere 1991; Brunello 1996; Zetter 1991, 2007; ERRC 2000; see also Simhandl's chapter) which, in characterizing the Roma and Sinti as nomads lacking a fixed abode, consolidates their exclusion from the political community and, especially in the right-wing discourse, is used as *a priori* evidence of the impossibility of their social inclusion[9] and to avoid the discussion about the rights of this community to adequate housing.[10] The following quotes from two right-wing politicians, respectively from the *Lega Nord* in Milan and *Unitalia* in Bolzano-Bozen, illustrate how the *nomadic* axiom works:

> Stable settlements must be dismantled. [...] Nomad camps must be only transit areas and not places where people abusively build their houses and villas and where families live for more than 30 years. (Matteo Salvini quoted in *Corriere della Sera*, 19 May 2006)
>
> If the gypsies are nomads, therefore people on the move, why are they asking for council houses? (Donato Seppi quoted in *Alto Adige*, 28 October 2005)

Gianni Alemanno, the centre-right candidate in Rome, uses the term 'nomads' to question the permanence of these communities. The following quotation is a typical example of this approach which is widespread in Italy: 'If they are nomads they should come and go, not stay here for 20 years. [...] And if they want to stay, in that case they must accept the rules for living in Rome' (Gianni Alemanno quoted in *IMG Press*, 19 March 2006).[11] The inclusion of the references to *Italian* Roma and Sinti in the immigration sections of the electoral manifestos, as in the case of Bolzano-Bozen, provides a further evidence of the process of 'othering' of this minority.

In Bolzano-Bozen, only two political parties referred directly to Roma and Sinti in their electoral platforms, namely *Rifondazione Comunista* (RC) and Unitalia, a local Italian nationalist party. The other political parties tend not to take sides on the issue. The following extract from an interview with a senior member of the *Südtiroler Volkspartei*, the main party of the German-speaking population, provides some insight:

> The Südtiroler Volkspartei is the party of the German and Ladino minorities in Sudtirol. It defends their rights and fights for the conservation of their cultural heritage. Because of this, our main interest is to promote the issues of our land and population. That is why our platform deals only with this. (Author's interview)

In Mantua, despite the fact that the population of Italian Sinti is small and long established and there is a low level of social conflict between the Sinti and the majority population, no political parties except *Rifondazione Comunista* included in their electoral platform any positive references to the local Sinti for fear of electoral loss, confirming that in Italy the protection of Roma rights is an issue restricted to one political side, rather than cutting across political affiliations. As a right-wing councillor pointed out, 'A member of the Sinti community could probably be a candidate only for *Rifondazione Comunista*'.[12]

Right-wing parties refer to Roma and Sinti exclusively in negative terms. In Bolzano-Bozen, Unitalia discusses the 'Gypsy and nomad' issue in the platform chapters dedicated to 'Social policies' and 'Security in the city and fight against drugs'. In the first of the seven points programme on social policies, Unitalia promises: 'The interruption of all economic subsidies to the nomads living in Bolzano and the interruption of public funding to existing nomad camps, in order for them to become economically self-sufficient'. In the chapter on 'Security in the city and fight against drugs', there are two points concerning 'the Gypsies': 'Dispersal of the Gypsies living in nomad camps in Bolzano to other camps to be built outside Bolzano by the Provincial authority' and 'firm application of the rules governing the life in the nomad camps with the immediate expulsion of those who commit crimes, infractions of the rules or whoever causes damage to the camp infrastructures'.

The relocation of the Roma and Sinti outside the perimeter of the city is also proposed in Milan and Rome. According to the centre-right then candidate (now Mayor) of Rome, 'Nomads should be allowed to stay only for short periods of time and not for entire generations as it is happening now' (Gianni Alemanno quoted in *Il Messaggero*, 27.05.06). In the centre-left parties the security discourse tends to be counterbalanced by more 'humanitarian' preoccupations. As a centre-left councillor candidate in Milan explained to me, 'We want to experiment with a model of institutional interaction for developing initiatives that ensure legality, avoid any forms of discrimination of the nomads and facilitate their access to social services (author's interview).' However, the distance between the centre-left and the centre-right is often reduced on the issue of Roma and Sinti. According to Daniele, 'The divergence of policies, of initiatives, of attitudes between the opposition and the ruling coalition in Rome gets thinner when Roma are concerned' (2006:1). Although there are minor differences in the public discourse, they seem to converge around two points: increasing state control over the 'nomads' and maintaining their spatial marginalization.

Local press

The analysis of the press in the electoral period has focused on three aspects: the context in which reference to Roma and Sinti were found; the labels employed to refer to these communities; and the space allocated to Roma and Sinti for expressing their opinions. Media coverage of Roma and Sinti appears on average biased, incomplete and lacking any sort of depth, without significant differences among the newspapers reviewed.[13] The main themes of the articles in which 'Roma', 'Sinti', 'nomadi' or 'zingari' are mentioned concern nomad camps and social housing, petty crimes and security, antisocial behaviour, begging and, to a less extent, folklore. Nomad camps are in all localities the main, and most controversial, topic discussed in the articles. The most recurrent subjects of these articles are demonstrations of local residents against existing or planned settlements, sit-ins and political initiatives promoted by right wing organizations against nomad camps, and tragic incidents due to the appalling living conditions in camps.

Even in the few instances in which a more positive image of Romani people is put forward, this goes together with a different process of stereotyping which portrays them as guardians, in a timeless present, of a millenary tradition of nomadic lifestyle, dance and music, as shown in the following extracts.

> They dance as gods [...], they wave, sing and seem happy here in Vasca Navale. Their movements seem to say: there is no time, no hurry, there will be more time later for all the rest. (*Il Messaggero*, 25 May 2006)

> A thousand years of nomadic life has taught these people that an exhausted traveller looks forward to putting down his luggage and sit[ting] down as quickly as possible in a car. (*Il Messaggero*, 9 April 2006)

The topic of the article above is a Romani woman outside a train station in Rome who, for a tip, helps travellers to find a taxi. As an interviewee pointed out, 'Newspapers never report any initiative or event that has been done in the city for or with Roma people unless there is something folkloristic about it'.

What is represented in newspapers seems to be more of a one-sided story where Roma are always *the problem*. Within this framework, by talking about Roma only when an unauthorized camp is dismantled or when somebody denounces the alleged kidnapping of a child by the *'gypsies'*, local newspapers contribute a great deal in creating a negative myth of the Roma. According to a journalist of the daily *Il Manifesto*, 'Mainstream newspapers contribute to the creation of public anxiety towards the Romani population and towards the nomad camps which are seen as *the places* where most horrible things happen with the complicity of the people living there'.[14]

The table below shows the number of articles on Roma and Sinti published in the four cities during the electoral campaign, how Roma and Sinti were referred to, and if they are given space to express their views.

The analysis revealed the absence of the voices and opinions of Roma and Sinti: indeed, in less than 10% of the articles are the viewpoints of the subjects themselves reported. The label 'nomads' is used to refer indistinctly to both Italian Roma and Sinti and foreign Roma confirming a widespread attitude to broad generalization and stereotyping. Italian Roma and Sinti almost do not exist in the public debate and the label 'nomads' tends to capture all those living in camps whatever their origin and legal status.

Finally, it must be noted that in Mantua, where the Sinti candidate was elected as city councillor and Sinti have their own community organization that actively promote a positive image of the local Sinti

Table 13.1   Roma and Sinti in the local press

	Number of articles	Labels			Roma and/or Sinti's voices
		Nomads	Zingari	Roma and/or Sinti	
Rome	25	17	4	9	2
Milan	57	38	15	22	2
Mantua	29	19	8	7	6
Bolzano	34	17	14	16	3
Total	145	91	41	54	13

community, the newspapers give more space to their views. Similarly, a non-Roma activist in Bolzano-Bozen pointed out how a proactive engagement with the public opinion can bring positive change, in her words:

> In the last few months, thanks to the public events, meetings that have been organised and the public interest for the health and safety issues which emerged in connection to the 'campo nomadi' of Castel Firmiano, they seem to understand better the situation. The term 'gypsies' is now less used, the term 'nomads' only appear on some types of articles, and Roma and Sinti is more frequently used.[15]

Political participation of Roma and Sinti

This section focuses on the initiatives and instances of political participation of Roma and Sinti in the four locations. Each case study will be presented separately in order to better render the specificities of each city and the political environment in which the initiatives were grounded.

Bolzano-Bozen

The Sinti living in Bolzano-Bozen are Italian citizens and therefore entitled to participate in the elections; however, as some Sinti interviewees pointed out, they rarely go to vote because of a lack of trust in the impact of their vote. Moreover, most of the political parties, as one of the interviewees noticed, do not even think about them as potential voters. 'There is a lot of confusion [...] Sinti are seen as foreigners so no effort is made to gain their votes'.[16]

In November 2005, for the first time, a local Sinto stood as candidate to the City Council for *Rifondazione Comunista*. Radames Gabrielli's candidature, as a senior member of the party pointed out, wanted to show to the Bolzano population that 'the Sinti are Italian citizens with the same duties and rights' (quoted in *Alto Adige*, 14.10.05: 14). However, Gabrielli did not get enough votes to be elected. 'I believe I didn't speak enough with my fellow Sinti', he explained afterwards, 'I didn't make clear what my candidature represented and why it was important'. But, the responsibility of the failure was to be put also on the party that, according to a senior local councillor, did not support the candidature with 'a specific electoral campaign for him', and added, 'the number of votes he got, 33, is less than what we all expected, especially because half of the votes came from Sinti, half from others'.

But also the local authority has some responsibility according to Gabrielli, who noticed that there has been very little effort and interest from the local administration in the participation of Sinti and Roma in the local polity, even when decisions concern directly the Sinti families had to be taken. In his words:

> Sinti and Roma should, for sure, participate more actively, and this is indeed their responsibility. And it is true that when they are asked to participate, often, they don't. But it is also true that many times, they are not even asked, not even when issues discussed regard their own families.[17]

Instead, among civil servants and local authority representatives, the main reason for the failure is an alleged 'different idea of representation' that Sinti have because of their culture; incidentally, this argument clears them of any responsibility for the lack of engagement of Sinti to local polity.

In contrast, the vast majority of the local Romani population is from Macedonia, and therefore do not have the right to vote. In Bolzano, the position of *consigliere aggiunto* does not exist and the only institutional form of participation for non-EU residents is the *Consulta per l'Immigrazione* (Advisory Committee for Immigration), set up in 2004. The *Consulta* can express opinions and suggestions to the City Council on matters concerning immigration. However, when the first *Consulta* was elected, no Roma stood for a seat.

Mantua

None of the people interviewed for this research could identify any institutional intervention to encourage the participation of Roma and Sinti to local elections, neither as voters nor as candidates. In terms of stimulating the participation of the Sinti community as voters, the Sinti candidate and the Sinti associations supporting him made all the efforts. Local activists anticipated two key problems: the first was that the Sinti were not accustomed to actively participating in elections, mainly due to lack of interest and distrust. The second was illiteracy.

In light of this, the electoral campaign in the Sinti settlement attempted to create confidence in the electoral process and a free transportation service to the election was made available. However, according to the activists, the result showed that more work and more time should have been devoted to giving information on the technical aspects of how to vote as well as on the political aspect of why to vote. Nonetheless, among Sinti interviewees, the fact of having a Sinti candidate was seen as a very positive development.

The idea of a Sinti candidate to be presented in the 2005 campaign had been growing in the Sinti community and associations since 2001. The decision that Del Bar would be the candidate was made later. *Rifondazione Comunista* was the only party to show some attention to this candidature.

In general, the reaction to Del Bar's candidature, as confirmed by a local journalist and a centre-right councillor was neither negative nor positive, with most people external to his entourage feeling a sense of diffidence, tolerating the Sinti 'as long as they stay in their own place'. For the Mantua city councillor for welfare and social policy:

> By presenting himself as an independent in the list of RC, Yuri rightly stressed his role as representative of the interests of the Sinti of Mantua. In general, apart from a few idiots, there was not a great deal of interest, neither positive nor negative, in the city for his candidature. No major contestation or protest marked the fact that he was the first nomadic person participating as a candidate at a local election.[18]

Del Bar was the third elected in the lists of *Rifondazione* with 64 individual preferences, half of which came from members of the Sinti community.

Milan

Dijana Pavlovic is a Serbian Romani woman with Italian passport, an actress and a cross cultural mediator. She stood for a city councillor seat at the election, and her list was led by the Nobel laureate Dario Fo and affiliated with the centre-left mayoral candidate.

> I've never been actively involved with politics before this. I stood for the election because it was important to show a positive

imagine of Roma, to say 'we are here'. In Milan the situation is really critical for the Roma. And there is no way of solving it because there is no political will, because for the rightwing parties in government it is useful this way.[19]

To confirm this point, it can be said that all main centre-right parties (*Forza Italia, Alleanza Nazionale and Lega Nord*) – which have been leading the local government for the last decades – campaigned against 'nomad camps' during the election period.

Pavlovic was not elected but her presence contributed to raising the profile of the debate on Roma and Sinti and for the first time, a Romani person was allowed to contribute to this debate. This point is confirmed by an Italian Romani activist, who argues that Pavlovic's candidature was very useful especially for the quality of the public debate: 'When she was participating at public meetings and political debates on television, the Roma and Sinti issue got surely a better and a more respectful treatment.'

The failure of Pavlovic's candidature can be attributed to two main reasons: the Roma and Sinti's lack of understanding of and faith in the voting system, and the failure of the voluntary sector to help. As the candidate put it: 'I don't think Italian Roma really understood the importance of voting. This was our main mistake: not being able to communicate effectively with them. Moreover, there was the problem of illiteracy and of the voting system that is very bureaucratic.'

One Romani activist suggests that in order to promote Roma political participation,[20] 'You can't just rely on the voluntary sector [...] more time was needed. Her campaign didn't manage to change Roma and Sinti's attitude towards voting'. The inhibiting role of the voluntary sector is stressed also by the candidate. She argues that 'there is a need for an approach that goes beyond charity'. Pavlovic explains this point more in detail saying:

Some associations seem too much inclined to mediation with local politicians because of funding dependency. The situation in camps is dramatic and there is a need for courageous initiatives. Romani voices are always mediated by associations. If there is a violation of human rights you can't simply ignore it or negotiate with the perpetrators.

While the lack of initiatives to promote participation by local authorities, and to some extent, local NGOs, is an important aspect to consider when discussing the causes of Roma and Sinti poor involvement at political level, it is also crucial to take into account, as some interviewees suggested, the frustration, disillusionment and lack of trust felt by the Italian Roma and Sinti, who have experienced years of unfulfilled promises by mainstream politicians, and no significant improvement in the quality of life of Italian Roma and Sinti. The following words from a Romani interviewee give an example of the treatment that the Roma and Sinti experience at the hands of local politicians:

> They used to come here with vans full of pasta and tomato juice. They came this time as well. They promised that ten days after the election the road work we have been long waiting for will finally start. The ten days have passed and I haven't seen anyone working in the camp.[21]

Rome

Moving the 'nomads' out of town and making their presence less visible in the capital were at the top of the agenda of the main mayoral candidates. As one non-Roma activist pointed out,

> The only difference is that the current centre-left led administration uses a different language which justifies the relocation of Romani settlements outside the city as a solution for the overcrowding of the old camps and an opportunity for the creation of 'better' living spaces. But by adopting this kind of discourse they hide the fact that pushing Roma into the outskirts of [...] Rome means also isolating them, making them even more marginal and breaking their social networks.[22]

In 2002, during the previous Veltroni administration, the City Councillor for Social Policies approved an 'Action Plan for the Integration of the Roma and Sinti' as part of the overall Social Plan of Rome. The Action Plan was thought to be a move forward from a mere assistance-based approach towards a more integrated one which views Roma as actors in the integration process in a more dialogical and less top-down way. One of the aims of the plan was to facilitate the participation of Roma through the creation of community leaders and organizations. But Roma immigrants did not participate in the election of the community representatives as advisors at the City and Municipality Councils (*consiglieri aggiunti*). According to an interviewee from the NGO sector, the cause is mainly the lack of a Roma leadership able to represent the community in the outside world, 'their lack of maturity', as he put it.[23] Nonetheless, it must be pointed out also that no effort was made to make the process more accessible to the Roma. Moreover, the main NGOs working on Romani-related issues tend to take upon themselves the responsibility to represent the interests of Roma with the local and municipal authorities, leaving a very limited and ultimately irrelevant space for the Roma for contributing to the policy making process, thereby engendering tokenism and further disengagement vis-à-vis the Romani communities.

Conclusions

This chapter has shown how the 'Gypsy problem' played a major role in 2006 local elections, well before the issue became a national 'emergency' in November 2007. It demonstrates how many of the features we can currently observe at the national level had already manifested themselves at the local level. What motivated the change of scale is still matter of discussion. However, it is interesting to point out that with Walter Veltroni resigning as mayor of Rome to become the national leader of the Democratic Party, we saw a transplant of 'local' issues into the national arena. His 'successful' track record as mayor of Rome – which included also moving out thousands of Roma from the more central area of Rome to more remote areas outside the ring road of Rome – was at the centre of his electoral campaign, setting a precedent for the 'security-concerned' right wing parties to campaign heavily against the Roma and Sinti. In May 2008 the right wing party *Partito del Popolo della Libertà* and its ally *Lega Nord* won the election, establishing Berlusconi as the Italian Prime Minister. In the run up to the election, *Lega Nord*, which has its foothold in the northern regions, made the fight against 'illegal immigrants and nomads' one of its top priorities. This party is now playing a crucial role in the national government, in particular through the appointment of Roberto Maroni to the role of Minister of Internal Affairs.

This chapter has also shown how mainstream political parties (of which *Rifondazione Communista* is not one) represent the Roma and Sinti exclusively as 'gypsies/nomads' who pose a 'threat' to society, dehumanising them and denying them as political subjects. No concrete effort is made to promote the participation of Roma and Sinti in the political process, either as voters or candidates (for Italian Roma and Sinti) or in consultative bodies (for non-Italian Roma).

Media coverage of Roma and Sinti appears on average biased, incomplete and lacking any sort of depth, without significant differences among the newspapers reviewed. The main themes of the articles in which 'Roma', 'Sinti', 'nomads', or 'Gypsies' are mentioned concern nomad camps and social housing, petty crimes and security, antisocial behaviour, begging and, to a lesser extent, folklore.

The widespread use of the term 'nomads' as an ethno-denomination to refer indistinctly to both Italian Roma and Sinti and foreign Roma testifies this attitude towards broad generalisation and stereotyping. Italian Roma and Sinti almost do not exist in the public debate and the label 'nomads' tends to capture all those living in camps whatever their origin and legal status.

The participation of Roma and Sinti, both as voters and as candidates, in the last local elections in Italy was extremely limited; nevertheless there were some positive signs of political engagement in the electoral process. This happened despite the absence of institutional initiatives aimed at facilitating and promoting the political participation of these communities to local polity. On the contrary, local authorities (see for example the resettlement of Roma in rural areas in Rome) often implement policies that, directly or indirectly, discourage and obstruct Roma and Sinti participation.

In the four case studies, three members of the Roma and Sinti communities stood for a seat of city councillor, although only in Mantua did the Sinti candidate manage to be elected. Despite being mostly unsuccessful, those candidatures proved to be extremely important for mainstreaming of Romani issues, promoting a less biased political debate and setting up a precedent and a reference for Roma and Sinti in other parts of Italy.

Moreover, not participating in the elections is in itself a political statement and is a response to the existing situation of social marginalisation and widespread racism; however, given the demographic characteristics of the Italian Roma and Sinti population, there may be other more effective ways to promote the interest of the community, for example through the creation of a network of community organisations and the lobbying of politicians at local and national level.

Notes

1. I wish to thank Julia Bell for her precious help in the preparation of the final manuscript and Will Guy and Nidhi Trehan for their valuable comments on an earlier draft.
2. See European Parliament Resolution on the census of the Roma on the basis of ethnicity in Italy, P6_TA(2008)0361.
3. See OSCE field report on Italy: http://www.osce.org/documents/odihr/2009/03/36620_en.pdf.
4. This chapter is based on field work carried out in four Italian cities at the time of the local elections between 2005 and 2006 by a research team (Lorenzo Monasta, Eva Rizzin, Francesca Saudino and Andreea R. Torre) coordinated by the author (Sigona 2006). It was commissioned by OSCE/ODIHR Contact Point for Roma and Sinti Issues, the full report is available at: http://www.osservazione.org/documenti/osce_italy.pdf
5. This mirrors the results of a recent survey commissioned by the Italian Ministry of Internal Affairs which shows that 62% of the Italians believe that only less of 20% of the Roma and Sinti currently living in Italy are Italian citizens (ISPO 2008). See Simhandl's chapter for a discussion of the 'discursive expatriation' of indigenous Romani-ethnic citizens in Western Europe.
6. EU citizens residing in Italy have the right to vote and to stand as candidates at municipal elections, under the same conditions as Italian nationals. Foreign Roma coming from non-EU member states do not have the right to vote in Italy. However, immigrants can join bodies representing their interests such as trade unions and trade associations, or establish their own NGOs or community organizations. At local level, some interesting experiences have been implemented to enhance immigrants' active participation in local polities (Zincone and Caponio 2005; Caponio 2006; Koff 2003). Three initiatives are particularly relevant here: the introduction, in some municipalities, of *consiglieri aggiunti* (additional councillors). Elected by immigrants in their municipality of residence, they have a consultative and mainly symbolic role and no right to vote in the City Council; the creation of consultative committees on migration issues to which migrants themselves are invited to contribute; finally, there are ongoing initiatives at local, regional and national level, for the introduction of the right to vote for immigrants in local elections.
7. Commenting on the results of the census, the Minister of Internal Affairs stated, in what resembles a self-fulfilling prophecy, 'at least as many nomads as those counted in the census, circa 12,000, have left the camps

since last June' (namely, when the Berlusconi government began to show its 'tough touch'). See press statement at http://www.interno. it/mininterno/export/sites/default/it/sezioni/sala_stampa/speciali/ censimento_nomadi/.

8. The interview was conducted in Milan in June 2006.

9. Gianfranco Fini, one of the leaders of the centre-right and current Speaker of the Italian Chamber of Deputies, in an interview to the *Corriere della Sera* (4 November 2007) stated: 'to talk of integration with people with a "culture" of that sort is pointless'.

10. See the decision of the European Committee on Social Rights concerning the violation by Italy of the Article 31 of the Revised Social Charter on the right to adequate housing: http://www.osservazione.org/documenti/ ResChS_2006_4E.pdf.

11. *Il Foglio* elettronico, 19.03.06 http://www.imgpress.it/stampanotizia. asp?idnotizia=17944.

12. Interview carried out in Mantua in June 2006.

13. In Bolzano-Bozen, we analysed the coverage of Roma and Sinti issues in two local newspapers: one is published in Italian (*Alto Adige*) and, the other (*Dolomiten*), is in German, each reflecting their different readerships. In Mantua, we reviewed *La Gazzetta di Mantova* and *La Voce di Mantova*. *La Voce di Mantova* is considered more right-wing, and in February 2006, its director, Davide Martellini, had to resign as he was accused of publishing anti-Semitic articles in the paper. In Milan, *Corriere della Sera* and *La Repubblica*, respectively the two most read national broadsheets in Italy and locally in Milan, where they publish a significant local section daily, were selected. In Rome, the review was conducted on two newspapers with a large circulation: *Il Messaggero* and *Leggo*. The former is a daily national broadsheet with a large section dedicated to the Italian capital. It was established in 1878 and 300,000 copies are distributed daily. The latter is a free newspaper with a daily circulation of about 1 million copies in key Italian cities. It publishes a Rome edition with 220,000 copies distributed daily. It reaches a significant and variegated proportion of the population and focuses on events in Rome. Both newspapers can be located within the centre of the Italian political spectrum.

14. Interview carried out in Rome in June 2006.

15. Interview carried out in Bolzano in June 2006.

16. Interview carried out in Bolzano in July 2006.

17. Interview carried out in Bolzano in June 2006.

18. Interview carried out in Cecina Mare in July 2006.

19. Interview carried out in Milan in July 2006.

20. Interview carried out in Milan in July 2006.

21. Interview carried out in a nomad camp for Italian Roma in Milan in July 2006.

22. Interview carried out in Rome in July 2006.

23. Interview carried out in Rome in July 2006.

References

Ambrosini, M. and Tosi, A. (2007) (eds) *Vivere ai margini. Un'indagine sugli insediamenti rom e sinti in Lombardia*, Milan: ISMU.

Arrigoni, P. and Vitale, T. (2008) 'Quale legalità? Rom e gagi a confronto', *Aggiornamenti Sociali*, 3: 183–194.

Brunello, P. (1996) (ed.) *L'urbanistica del disprezzo*, Rome: Manifestolibri.

Caponio, T. (2006), *Città italiane e immigrazione. Discorso pubblico e politiche a Milano, Bologna e Napoli*, Bologna: Il Mulino.

CERD (1999) *Concluding Observations of the Committee on the Elimination of Racial Discrimination: Italy 7 April 1999 (CERD/C/304/Add.68)*, Geneva: United Nations.

Colacicchi, P. (2008) 'Ethnic profiling and discrimination against Roma in Italy: new developments in a deep-rooted tradition', *Roma Rights*, 2: 35–44.

Daniele, U. (2006), 'Spostati/sgomberati. Discriminazioni, vecchie politiche e nuove retoriche', *Osservatorio Sul Razzismo e le Diversità "M. G. Favara"*, http://host.uniroma3.it/laboratori/osservatoriorazzismo/note.php?subaction= showfull&id=1149008848&archive=&start_from=&ucat=4&

ECRI (2002) *2nd Report on Italy Adopted 22 June 2001*, Strasbourg: ECRI.

ECRI (2006) *3rd Report on Italy Adopted on 16 December 2005*, Strasburg: ECRI.

ERRC (2000) *Campland. Racial Segregation of Roma in Italy*, Budapest: ERRC.

ISPO (2008) 'Italiani, rom e sinti a confronto. Una ricerca quali-quantitativa'. Paper presented at the *European Conference on Romani Population*, Rome, 22–23 January 2008, Rome: Ministero degli Interni.

Koff, H. (2003) 'L'architettura dell'integrazione: metodo comparato e studi sull'immigrazione' in A. Baldissera (ed.) *Gli usi delle comparazione*, Milan: Franco Angeli.

Mai, N. (2009 forthcoming) 'The politicisation of migrant minors: Italo-Romanian geopolitics and EU integration: in whose (best) interest?', article submitted to the journal *AREA*.

Ministero degli Interni (2008) *Censimento dei campi nomadi. Scheda editoriale*, Rome: Ministero degli Interni, http://www.interno.it/mininterno/export/ sites/default/it/sezioni/sala_stampa/speciali/censimento_nomadi/

Monasta, L. (2004) 'Note sulla mappatura degli insediamenti rom stranieri presenti in Italia' in Saletti Salza, C. and Piasere, L. (2004) (eds) *Italia Romaní 4. La diaspora rom dalla ex Jugoslavia. Roma*, Rome: CISU.

Piasere, L. (1991) *Popoli delle discariche*, Rome: CISU.

Piasere, L. (2005) 'Qu'est-ce qu'un campo nomadi?', paper presented at the international conference *Les Tsiganes en Europe: questions sur la représentation et action politque*, the British Academy/CNRS, Paris, 24–25 October 2005.

Scalia, M. (2006) *Le comunità sprovviste di territorio, i Rom, i Sinti e i Caminanti in Italia*, Rome: Dipartimento delle Libertà Civili e l'Immigrazione, Ministero degli Interni.

Sigona, N. (2002) *Figli del Ghetto. Gli italiani, i Campi Nomadi e l'Invenzione degli Zingari*, Civezzano: Nonluoghi.

Sigona, N. (2003) 'How can a "nomad" be a "refugee"? Kosovo Roma and labelling policy in Italy', *Sociology*, 37(1): 69–79.

Sigona, N. (2005) 'Locating the 'Gypsy problem'. The Roma in Italy: stereotyping, labelling and nomad camps', *Journal of Ethnic and Migration Studies*, 31(4): 741–756.

Sigona, N. (2008) 'Sono il nemico pubblico n.1?', *Reset*, 107: 87–88.

Sigona, N. (2009) ' "Via gli zingari dall'Italia!" ("Gypsies out of Italy!"): social exclusion and racial discrimination of Roma and Sinti in Italy' in Mammone, A. and Veltri, G. (eds), *Contemporary Italy: The Sick Man of Europe*, London and New York: Routledge.

Sigona, N. and Monasta, L. (2006) *Cittadinanze imperfette. Rapporto sulla discriminazione razziale di rom e sinti in Italia*, Santa Maria Vetere: Edizioni Spartaco.

Simoni, A. (2008) 'I decreti "emergenza nomadi": il nuovo volto di un vecchio problema', *Diritto, Immigrazione e Cittadinanza*, 10(3–4): 44–56.

Zetter, R. (1991) 'Labelling refugees: forming and transforming a bureaucratic identity', *Journal of Refugee Studies*, 4(1): 39–61.

Zetter, R. (2007) 'More labels, fewer refugees: remaking the refugee label in an era of globalization', *Journal of Refugee Studies*, 20(2): 172–192.

Zincone, G. and Caponio, T. (2005) 'Immigrant and immigration policy-making: the case of Italy', *IMISCOE Working papers*, Turin: FIERI.

Conclusions: A 'People's Europe' for Romani Citizens?

Nando Sigona and Nidhi Trehan

Based on a multidisciplinary approach and a combination of European and national perspectives, one of the key goals of this collection on contemporary Romani politics has been to provide a critical overview on the emergence and consolidation of a pan-European space for Romani political participation and mobilization in the context of broader socio-economic and political trends in Europe. In the Introduction, we unpacked the nature of the relationship between three key phenomena – the rise of neoliberalism, ethnopolitics and growing anti-Gypsyism – which, during the past two decades, have had a profound impact on Romani lifeworlds in Europe. With official rates of Romani unemployment well over 50% (and indeed, over 90% in so-called compact communities of segregated Romani settlements in Eastern Europe), the prospects for the integration of Romani citizens continue to be grim.

How will a democratic Europe or a true 'people's Europe' cope with and respond to the crisis of growing marginalization of its citizens of Romani background? Perhaps the first and most crucial step is to acknowledge the reality of the subaltern position of Romani Europeans today. The history of Europe's Romani communities is punctuated by catastrophic events (violent persecution, slavery and Holocaust) which have left a legacy of betrayal and mistrust, a troubled inheritance which poses real obstacles to Romani social, economic and political integration to this day. As the respected European statesman, and the Council of Europe's current Commissioner for Human Rights, Thomas Hammarberg (2008) emphasized in an aptly subtitled essay 'Making Amends':

> Even after the genocide of Roma by the Nazis there was no genu-
> ine change of attitude among the majority [European] population,
> and it took years before the issue of compensation to surviving
> family members even came up for discussion. The persecution
> did not end with the fall of the Nazi regime. Roma families, not
> welcome anywhere, were chased from place to place in a number
> of European countries many years after World War II. Afterward,
> governments were slow to apologize to the Roma community for
> these human rights violations. It is not surprising that this history
> has created bitterness and a feeling of exclusion and alienation
> among the Roma. All efforts to encourage Roma participation in
> public life must recognize this basic point. (2008)

Secondly, there is a need for policy-makers in European to recognize the contributions (past and present) of its Romani citizenry, in
all of its erstwhile empires and its diversity of contemporary nation-
states. This would, in turn, set the basis for a real dialogue between
(predominantly silent) Romani interlocutors today and their other
European counterparts. It would also encourage European citizenry
to begin to understand that their fellow Romani citizens are part
of a common future, a collaborative future. This dialogue therefore
must move beyond the confines of liberal discursive platitudes about
equality of Roma, and must enter the realm of co-existence of lifeworlds where shared schools, workplaces and neighbourhoods once
again become a reality for Roma who had begun to taste this in, for
example, the former Yugoslavia. It is a need, nay a requirement, for
a new and expanded Europe, where one currently can witness (or
encounter) the paradox of unprecedented levels of human rights protections alongside conditions of extreme marginality amongst the
majority of its Romani citizenry.

The collapse of the Soviet Union and its satellite regimes, along with
the rise of the neoliberal order in the enlarged European political space,
lays the groundwork for this collection, which has explored the arenas
of political participation of European Romani citizens within contemporary European polities. One result of this political mapping exercise
has been to confront the exclusions and limitations of both formal and
informal civic spaces as applied to Romani political participation.

The multiple dimensions and articulations of the Romani political sphere (EU, state, regional, local and self-organization) permeate this collection which has brought to the fore contributions by Romani and non-Romani activists and scholars, and offered a critical analysis of the EU's involvement with the Romani minority and the emergence of a pan-European Romani political movement since the early 1990s. As several chapters posit, this movement appears many times to be fragile and fraught with contention, both as a result of external influences upon it (ideological, financial and political), and internal dynamics and constraints resulting from a crisis in leadership and a paucity of strategic approaches.

Attention has been paid to the crucial issue of leadership and representativeness both in European institutions, where, for example, Nirenberg's piece offered a poignant critique of the European Roma and Travellers Forum, and at the national level, where important contributions from Slovakia, Romania and Italy were made. The socio-economic and cultural distance between the tiny Romani elite (the vast majority of whom work in urban capitals across Europe) and the grassroots level (Roma mainly concentrated in villages and smaller towns) is a central topic which also highlights the embedded limitations of ethnopolitical mobilization. This distance also affects the capacity of Romani elites to put forward a political agenda capable of mobilizing grassroots communities.

This collection has documented the consolidation of the Roma issue in the European political agenda and discussed the affirmation of minority and human rights frameworks and discourses (at times exclusive) as responses to Romani marginalization and social exclusion. It has also raised key limitations of this approach for example, questioning the influence of the 'NGOization of human rights' and investigating how this development impacts policy agendas and claims-making within the Romani movement, producing the marginalization of subaltern Romani voices. Moreover, the focus on the role of gender as conceptualized within liberal rights-based discourses has enabled us to examine how legal discourses deployed by human rights advocates have in fact been rendered powerless in post-socialist Europe, powerless to fundamentally challenge and alter the position of embedded social, economic, and political deprivation of 'second-class' Romani citizens.

The *othering* of Romani populations, as well as their discursive and physical exclusion is another recurring theme in the book. In the case of Italy, Sigona has shown how mainstream political parties represent the Roma and Sinti exclusively as 'gypsies/nomads' who pose a 'threat' to society, hence dehumanizing them and denying them their role as political subjects. Similarly, Richardson and Ryder have stressed how in England the *othering* of Gypsies and Travellers results in a negative cycle of control and conflict which is a mutually reinforcing problem.

The limitations of the neoliberal 'human/minority rights' agenda, exported by key European institutions and INGOs, are most visible in Europe's newest nation-state of Kosovo, where local Romani activists struggle to mediate between grassroots communities and the diktat and requirements of the international community. As illustrated in the following extract from Gazmen Salijevic's interview:

When the internationals came here in 1999 and they started to talk about human rights, we were like in the jungle, we had never heard about them but they were shiny [objects] and we said 'Ok, we like them' [...]. I like the Socialist era because it was a time when everyone was equal and had equal rights and you didn't think much about differences. Personally, I think the human rights approach is responsible for the fragmentation and loss of our identity. I feel we are playing with fire. Here we heard about human rights in 1999, but human rights began after the Second World War with the Geneva Conventions and the creation of the European institutions. For us they are something new, and if you have lived in the jungle for 40 years, and now you wear a suit and a tie and fly to New York, you can't survive there because you don't know the rules of the game. There are many Roma activists who are not professionals, who don't know the law and are not educated enough. We just attend some training and that's it. We don't really know how to fight using this tool!

The control and surveillance of Romani mobility in Europe has been an important factor behind the EU and the Member States' agenda on the Roma issue since the early 1990s, and the recent violent episodes in Western Member States have brought the issue back to the centre of political debate, this time embedded in a radically different political framework, as the enlargement process has rendered the vast majority of Roma citizens of the EU. The anti-Romani mobilization is a key asset for extreme right groups all over Europe and the recent attempt to develop a pan-European extreme right political agenda constitutes a frightening development which EU institutions and civil society seems unable to combat adequately with its current tools and approaches (Waterfield 2009). The European-wide mobilization over this issue has also seen the emergence of European Romani advocacy at the EU level through the active intervention of NGOs. Much less effort has been undertaken to build bridges with local grassroots NGOs, thereby reproducing once again the distance highlighted above. Finally, the case of Slovakia, where relatively powerless Romani communities mobilized en masse against the neo-liberal reform of the welfare state, has offered an example of an alternative way of doing 'ethnopolitics'.

Whither Romani politics?

In this collection of essays, we have raised key themes – both empirical and theoretical – on how political structures and polities in Europe interact with citizens of Romani origin. There are also key areas for future development which need to be addressed, for example, the gap between the reality on the ground within diverse Romani communities and the trans-European discourse on Roma, which many times reduces the complexity of both Romani co-existence and integration amongst local communities. In this regard, key hegemonic discourses on Roma – often diffused through the NGO vehicle – have also been highlighted, along with possible challenges to them by organic intellectuals who would act as new interlocutors within European civil society.

Furthermore, a more nuanced understanding of the various dimensions of ethnopolitics vis-à-vis Romani mobilization, as well as the impact on Romani populations (through resurgent violence) is critical. The different traditions of Romani political mobilization in both the eastern and western halves of Europe (but also within regions, for example, between Central European states and those of former Yugoslavia) need to be taken into consideration. The attempts at harmonizing these various mobilizations will need to take into account the recognition of the different contexts and histories of past attempts at Romani organizing.

As raised in this volume, the dominant role played by human rights NGOs also requires further examination, particularly their connection to various ideological projects, and this in turn highlights the need for further independent analysis and critical (and applied) research. Another area connected to this, often overlooked apart from a few scholars (cf. Acton 1997; Gay y Blasco 2002; see also Laparra and Macías, chapter 11) is that of the role of faith-based or religious groups in the political mobilization of Roma. Various faiths, from the Pentecostal movement to Jehovah's Witnesses are now sources for the emerging mobilization of Romani communities; to what extent these will take on particular political or ideological contours and how this will translate into the struggle for accessing better education, jobs, and healthcare within European polities remains to be seen. Certainly, the role of the church within the African-American civil rights struggle was critical to the mass mobilization and the eventual gains achieved by an earlier generation of activists and organizers.

Finally, an analysis of the settlement of 'new' Romani communities as a result of westward migrations and its recent impact on political participation and identity politics at the national and EU levels in the medium-term is another area for future research development.

Theories divorced from the empirical realities in the lifeworlds of European Roma will prove inadequate in illuminating the contemporary necessities stemming from the crisis of marginalization. Currently, research on Roma is dominated by particular funders and sponsors, and this too poses an obstacle to the reframing of the discourse and shifting the dominant paradigm. The question of who devises policies on Roma also requires further investigation, as do questions of ownership of political institutions, strategic agendas and additional questions of input into policy design and implementation. The ultimate European democratic project of achieving active citizenship for all of Europe's citizens – and the devising of pathways for the most voiceless amongst them – must envision the meaningful participation and full political subjectivity of its millions of Roma.

References

Acton, T. (1997) 'Mediterranean religions and Romani people', *Journal of Mediterranean Studies*, 7(1): 37–51.

Gay y Blasco, P. (2002) 'Gypsy/Roma diasporas. A comparative perspective', *Social Anthropology*, 10(2): 173–188.
Hammarberg, T. (2008) 'Europe's Roma: Making Amends', *Transitions Online*, 2 September 2008.
Waterfield, B. (2009) 'BNP could be at heart of far-right EU group', *Telegraph*, 15 May 2009. Available at: http://www.telegraph.co.uk/news/worldnews/europe/eu/5329638/BNP-could-be-at-heart-of-far-right-EU-group.html

Index